Graham Coxon is an English musician, singer-songwriter, multi-instrumentalist and visual artist. Though best known as being a founding member of Blur, he has released eight solo albums and frequently composes for film. One of the most innovative guitarists of his generation, in 2010 the BBC named him the fifteenth greatest guitarist of the last thirty years. He lives in London.

Further praise for *Verse, Chorus, Monster!*:

'[A] very rare thing: a memoir by a rock star who doesn't have too much of an ego.'
THE TIMES

'Covers a huge amount of ground – everything from [Coxon's] early years as a kid growing up in army barracks to his current musical incarnation, the Waeve . . . Compelling.'
INDEPENDENT

'[Coxon] tells his self-aware, self-analytical tale with a disarming, unfiltered honesty . . . A bizarrely engaging read.'
CLASSIC ROCK MAGAZINE

'Paints a picture – specifically, a self-portrait – of the tortured artist perpetually at odds with his bandmates, the escalating demands of success and the abject horror of being shackled to the runaway train that was Britpop.'
I NEWSPAPER

'[Coxon's] an intriguing, endearing character who vividly conveys the misery of anxiety.'
DAILY MIRROR

VERSE, CHORUS, MONSTER!

GRAHAM COXON

WITH ROB YOUNG

faber

First published in the UK and USA in 2022
by Faber & Faber Ltd
The Bindery, 51 Hatton Garden
London EC1N 8HN

This paperback edition first published in 2023

Typeset by Ian Bahrami
Printed and bound by CPI Group (UK) Ltd, Croydon, CR0 4YY

'R U Lonely': words and music by Graham Leslie Coxon © 1998, reproduced by
permission of Sony/ATV Music Publishing, London W1T 3LP
'Latte': words and music by Graham Leslie Coxon © 2002, reproduced by
permission of Sony/ATV Music Publishing, London W1T 3LP
'You & I': words and music by Graham Leslie Coxon © 2005, reproduced by
permission of Sony/ATV Music Publishing, London W1T 3LP

The right of Graham Coxon to be identified as author of this
work has been asserted in accordance with Section 77 of
the Copyright, Designs and Patents Act 1988

A CIP record for this book
is available from the British Library

ISBN 978–0–571–37431–1

Printed and bound in the UK on FSC® certified paper in line with our continuing
commitment to ethical business practices, sustainability and the environment.
For further information see faber.co.uk/environmental-policy

2 4 6 8 10 9 7 5 3 1

This book is dedicated to

PAULINE COXON
1943–2021

and

ANDY ROSS
1956–2022

With love to my two daughters,

PEPPER and **DORELIA**

CONTENTS

CONTENTS

PLATES

PHOTO SECTION

ART SECTION

PLATES

All images are courtesy of the author unless otherwise specified.

ODYSSEY
OF
AN
EARWORM

An earworm popped into my head a few days ago, and it's been wriggling around in there ever since. It arrived, like so much music, as if from another dimension entirely. It was out there travelling the spaceways on some inaudible frequency, trying to locate a portal to break through into our world, where it could finally take on an identity and be heard. The odyssey of this song, its journey from there to here, began somewhere dark and invisible. Then one morning I woke up, still groggy, and a couple of parts – ideas for a verse or a chorus – arrived in my mental inbox. Still half asleep, and dangling out of the bed, I grabbed my phone and hummed them into the microphone.

I dream of songs, or they slip into the world while I am dreaming. Most of my waking hours, I have a chord sequence or hook running through my head. Unconsciously, my brain tries to find a melody line or solo that fits. I dream many elements of a song, whether it's rhythm, guitar lines, vibraphone part or doo-wop backing vocals.

Songs like these, when they come – and they come surprisingly often – feel like strange gifts. It's like the fairy tale of 'The Elves and the Shoemaker'. In the morning you discover someone has spun you a little golden chord sequence and a silvery melody or lyric to go with it. The first time it occurred, it was the 'Oh, my baby' refrain in Blur's song 'Tender'. That phrase found me one morning, bleary-eyed and before my first cup of tea, and embarked on a magical journey: born inside my head, captured on a crappy

Dictaphone, then sung back to me a few years later by thousands and thousands of strangers who had packed out Glastonbury or a stadium on the other side of the world.

I don't think this is anything to do with 'genius', as some people say when they're trying to be nice. I think it's more to do with obsession. Musicians harbour these earworms to such an extreme degree that it can end up driving them nuts. Music, and the life that music can lead you into, can be as seductive as a siren. On the other hand, these noisy temptresses, on their charmed isle, can turn out to be monsters. A modern rock band's tour is something like the ten-year voyage home that Homer's legendary hero Odysseus made from Troy: journeying from unknown place to unknown place; never knowing who or what you are about to encounter every time you pitch up at a new island or city; being feasted, seduced and/or attacked in any number of places; never knowing if you're eventually going to make it back in one piece. All the time, the love of your life, waiting for you at home, is being courted by various unwanted suitors.

All we have left of Odysseus' story is the legend, full of drama, heroism, romance and magic. What's missed out are the mundane details, the squabbles, power games, minor irritations and nervous breakdowns that must have occurred on that ship – the same kind of stuff that also besets your average band on the tour bus or aeroplane while on their quest to break America.

My own story so far contains a bit of both. I have gone where music has taken me and tried to channel it the best way I can. Throughout it all, my love of art, which started at an early age, has kept my hands and head busy, and the sketchbooks that I have filled over the years are mainly pages and pages animated with strange and grotesque monsters. These creatures have lived in my dreams since I was little. And they started to arrive at pretty much the same time as I first clapped eyes on a guitar.

GUITAR
ON
THE
STAIRS

On 12 March 1969, Bob Coxon gripped the wheel of his Mini Traveller and fought his way up a mountain in West Germany. Skidding uphill through two feet of snow, he arrived at the British Army hospital in Rinteln (near Hamelin, of Pied Piper fame) just in time for my mum, Pauline, to give birth to their son, Graham Leslie Coxon: me.

I was born in an army hospital because Dad was a bandsman with the Sherwood Foresters regiment, stationed in an area just to the west of Berlin called Kladow, near Potsdam. When I was a toddler, we moved from Germany to Warminster in Wiltshire. Warminster was an attractive, well-preserved market town on the edge of Salisbury Plain that dated back to the Saxon era. It was attractive to UFO spotters, following the sighting of the notorious 'Thing' and other mysterious lights and flying objects in the 1960s. It's also the site of one of my earliest memories, around the age of three or four, and which is of a distinctly more earthly nature.

It is a couple of days after Christmas, and my parents have tucked me up and said goodnight, but I don't go straight to sleep. Instead, I creep downstairs, on a mission to sneak out of the house. I pitter-patter up the street and invade the front garden of one of the neighbours – the Chadwicks. Geoff and Hazel Chadwick are close friends of my parents. Geoff is a clarinet player like my dad – he calls it the 'gloom tube' or 'liquorice stick' – and they have a son called Mark, who will one day play in a band called the Levellers.

That night I sit in their front garden, in the dark, and eat handfuls of soil. I was also known to consume the contents of ashtrays. My mum was great at cooking balanced meals, but I must have been lacking something because I kept on stuffing earth and ash into my mouth. Apparently there's a lot of B12 in soil, and that's why eating grubby potatoes and unwashed carrots is good for vegetarians and vegans – but it's also a treatment for anxiety.

Eventually my mum comes looking for me, wipes the earth off my mouth and escorts me back home. As I am shooed up to my bedroom, I notice two toy guitars propped halfway up the staircase. They are Christmas presents that were given to me and Hayley, my big sister, miniature acoustic guitars with cowboy decorations and sunburst paintwork, plastic tuning pegs and fishing-line strings. Hayley's guitar is still in pristine condition. Mine, however, is already smashed up and unplayable. The body is cracked and all the strings are snapped. A feeling floods over me: why do *my* toys constantly break but my sister's always remain intact and beautiful?

On some primal level, this early memory linked the guitar with overwhelmingly melancholic emotions for me. The poor thing was lying there with the bridge dangling forlornly down, as if Pete Townshend had just had a bash on it. I had treated it the way any kid of three of four might – clumsily smacking and wrenching the strings around, with zero respect for the instrument.

Not long after my first encounter with a guitar, we left Warminster and returned to Germany, living in West Berlin until 1974. Our home was typical of the British overseas forces accommodation set up after the Second World War. Long residential buildings with tall sloping roofs formed a square around a central landscaped area – the perfect playground for army offspring. At mealtimes my dad used to stick his head out of our kitchen window to call me in. Once, he forgot that the window was shut and smashed his head through the glass pane, but still manged to shout, 'Dinner's ready, Graham!' while sticking his neck through the jagged shards.

Apparently the bandsmen were looked down on by the regular soldiers and their families. I wasn't really aware of this, but the pecking order must have filtered down to the army kids. Aged four, I was forced to take my first drag on a cigarette by Ian Appleyard, the local bully. I didn't know what it was. He just said, 'Take a long suck on that,' so I breathed it in and then coughed all the way home. He also used to stuff rotten, brown, wasp-infested apples into my mouth and chuck stones at me.

I was perpetually embarrassed and anxious, and my Britishness often made me feel separate and strange. By contrast, Mum and Dad were very sociable and had plenty of friends, both in the army and in the local German population. There were a lot of cool and risqué things for them to see and do in West Berlin, with no shortage of rude bars to visit. They would often go out on the razzle with friends to what my mum cryptically referred to as 'grot bars', but also to concerts by visiting jazz bands, such as the Count Basie Orchestra. My dad even used to throw *Abbey Road* parties, where people came round to drink, dance and listen to that one album, played over and over again. He also loved 'All Around My Hat' by Steeleye Span, a recognisable folk song with a distinctive, heavy, English pub-rock shuffle.

I loved rifling through my mum and dad's collection of 45s – an activity that turned me into a fount of essential knowledge. If you ever need to know the title of the B-side of Hot Butter's 'Popcorn', don't be afraid to ask. I listened to 'Popcorn' a lot, as well as assorted singles by the Kinks, Adam Faith and Tommy Roe's 'Dizzy'. There was a good deal of 1960s music, but at the centre of it all, assuming biblical importance, were the Beatles' albums. Nothing else came near, until I discovered Blondie and the Buzzcocks. I also listened to plenty of classical music. There was an album called *Symphonies for the Seventies*, on which the arranger and conductor Waldo de los Rios cut many well-known classical pieces – from the *New World Symphony* by Dvořák to Haydn's *Toy Symphony* – into smaller chunks and rocked them up with bass, drums and Latin percussion.

Around this time I loved to bang away on a set of toy drums I had been given, although I ended up sticking my foot through all of them, like a junior Keith Moon. I was dimly aware that my parents were living a full, sociable life; meanwhile, I was usually content with my ration of sweets from the NAAFI, the army shop. They did take me, aged four, to see the Osmonds in concert when their tour rolled into Berlin. I loved the show and came home triumphantly brandishing an Osmonds hat and a toy trumpet.

We were a mixed and fairly rough, at times almost feral bunch of kids, thrown together by the circumstance of our parents being billeted at this particular military base. Some families lived a truly hard-knock life. Ian Appleyard's father, for instance, was a pugnacious sort who was occasionally locked up for his own protection. The gang of scruffs that Hayley and I ran around with spent most of the time playing outdoors in the army compound, swinging on the swings, wobbling around on our first bikes, scuffling in the sandpit that we had been warned to keep away from because it always had dogshit in it. Sometimes we played dangerously close to water. There was a lake near Kladow, where Ian got his comeuppance. He fell on a rusty anchor while bunking off school and lay there in agony for quite a while, with the thing sticking through his leg, before anyone found him.

As well as my first drag, I probably tasted my first drink at the age of four too. Capital 'D' Drink, I mean. A Snowball, since you ask, but this *was* the early 1970s, when a slightly merry parent would happily encourage their other half to 'Give the kid a drink if he wants one!' As I chugged it down, I thought this sticky cocktail of advocaat and lemonade was pretty disgusting, like drinking a gloopy, eggy, vaguely fizzy blancmange. Gross, but it did make me feel quite nice. I remember enjoying the sensation of the confused, anxious tug of war in my head slowing down a bit – rope slackening, knots coming untied. That, right there, was probably early-stage alcoholism.

In 1974, when I was five, my dad got a posting to join the forces in Northern Ireland. Instead of all of us moving there with him, the rest of the family settled in Spondon, Derbyshire, where my mother's father, Percy Samways, lived next to the flyover that links Derby and Nottingham and is now called Brian Clough Way. Dad wasn't around much for the next two years, so me, Mum and Hayley lived with Grandad Percy, while Dad played music for the squaddies patrolling the Falls Road in Belfast. (Once, he went on a tour to Belize, from where he brought us back a football and a ceremonial machete.) Mum had various PA and secretarial jobs, including in the accounts departments of Nestlé and British Gas. Since me and my sister often got home before she did, I became fairly self-sufficient. By the age of six I was walking to school, and often went back to my friends' homes afterwards to play and get fed.

There were plenty of disused junkyards in Spondon, and my chums and I built primitive fairgrounds out of old corrugated iron.

We were quite wild as kids, permitted to do whatever we liked as long as we were 'outside'. We were playing with debris that could easily have cut our arms off or given us lockjaw if we made a mistake with it, but that's how kids were expected to play in those days. You went out after breakfast in a pair of shorts and came back covered in stinging-nettle rashes, dirty and bleeding from all manner of cuts and other injuries.

I was used to army kids being around, but some of them were pretty bloody rough. A neighbouring family in Spondon was attached to the Black Watch, the Scottish battalion, and their son was a maniac. He lived two doors away, and we used to throw rocks at each other across the garden separating us. Our neighbour's garden became a no-man's-land, bombarded by the stones we launched from behind our own lines. I'll never forget watching my well-aimed pebble bouncing off the top of the boy's head and his astonished reaction, glowering at me like an enraged Tasmanian devil. I kept my head down and beat a hasty retreat before he could get his revenge.

My main channel of expression at the time was through drawing. I had to invent a sort of art therapy for myself. As a small boy I drew war scenes and robot battles. 'This one's firing,' I would say, adding the appropriate explosive sound effects to my bellicose robots as I scribbled away on the paper. I filled envelopes with these drawings and sent them to my dad in Northern Ireland. 'Not too many,' my mum would caution. 'They'll think it's a letter bomb.' (The idea of a bomb in the post was the weirdest thing. I knew what a bomb looked like: a bulging steel rugby ball with spiky fins on the back. You couldn't hide one in an envelope.)

As well as violent robots, dinosaurs held great appeal for my young self. I used to run through the names of all the 'sauruses' in my head on the long walk to and from St Werburgh's primary school in Spondon. I had my own set of toy plastic dinosaurs, which I used to play with, along with my miniature cars, at Grandad Percy's house while he lit up the coal fire and his pipe. The house still had an outside khazi, crawling with spiders. Grandad Percy was good to hang out with. I was disappointed, though, when he explained how big – or, rather, how small – real dinosaurs actually were. I had imagined their feet being taller than Grandad's house, so I was crestfallen when he told me a triceratops was probably closer in size to an elephant.

Around the age of six, dark thoughts began to barge their way into my life, uninvited. I was obsessed and disturbed by a children's book that included images inspired by a painting by Goya of Jupiter devouring his own offspring. There was a boy, a beast, a demon and a magic jug from which water never stopped flowing. I don't know what the book was called, where it came from or what became of it. Even my parents don't know what it was.

Another disturbing memory was waking in the middle of a summer's night, having fallen asleep with the light on and the windows open, and seeing the wall covered with a thick layer of insects and creepy-crawlies that had been attracted indoors by the shining light bulb. I've never managed to shake that phantasmagoric scene out of my brain, never quite sure if I dreamt it or it really happened.

Monsters were a big deal at that age, a huge presence in my imaginative landscape thanks to books, TV, films, even movie posters. Perhaps unsurprisingly, given how I had discovered art as a way to express myself, I started to draw them a lot, and even in my twenties and thirties was still filling sketchbooks with them, although by that time they were more like demons of my own making. As a child I was allowed to watch a lot of things on TV and in the cinema that I shouldn't have been exposed to at such a young age. Disney's *Snow White and the Seven Dwarfs* scared the pants off me. A couple of those scenes are pretty psychedelic – the wicked queen morphing into a decrepit hag; the poisoned red apple. I'm not sure I'd let a small child of mine watch that. Throughout the 1970s the TV schedules were full of horror films and monster movies – *Salem's Lot*, silly old Frankenstein and Dracula movies, werewolves, ghosts, witches and zombies – and on Friday nights there were triple bills of horror movies. Me and my sister used to stay up and watch those, but I really shouldn't have – they filled my head with far too much scary stuff. Then there were the dramas about real-life horrors, such as *Holocaust* and *Roots*.

Both my parents worked, so for much of the time I was left alone to explore things that interested me. That partly explains why I went off the mainstream as a kid. TV at that time would reveal weird and wonderful visions, like *Marc*, the show hosted by Marc Bolan of T. Rex. It was sometimes on right after I arrived back from school, and he used to freak me out – he was quite an eyeful. There was another very uncanny series called *Sky*, which featured a mysterious boy who lived underneath a pile of leaves, and also the fantasy drama *Children of the Stones*. Kids' TV in that period conjured up extremely psychedelic, weird stuff on the cheap, and it was great. I was never a big *Doctor Who* fan, though, and ran out of the room whenever *Worzel Gummidge* came on. Those two shows were always scheduled at teatime, and they put me right off my cheese and pickle sandwiches.

———

In 1976 Dad was posted to the Colchester Garrison in Essex. My family moved to the St Michaels army estate three miles outside Colchester, and we settled in the area – for good, as it turned out, because a few years later my dad finally left the army and was hired as the conductor of the Essex Constabulary Police Band. I don't remember much about Colchester itself at that time, as my immediate environment was the rural suburbs around the garrison, where my long-haired self would explore the fields opposite where we lived. There was an ancient Roman pit called Devil's Dyke, where we would pretend to fly while taking a running jump off the edge, and an old castle where archaeological digs were under way, and from which I collected a bag of pig bones that I was convinced actually belonged to dinosaurs. Although I had friends, I also spent a good deal of time on my own, exploring the local area, which contained enough for all sorts of mini-adventures. Near our house was a path that meandered alongside some open fields and farms; I would wander past them, through a small coppice and on to even more farms. There was rarely anybody about, and I could liberally help myself to some of the raw potatoes growing in the fields, eating them straight out of the ground. I was partial to a bit of raw spud (perhaps with lumps of earth still attached?), and whenever my mum was making chips I always begged for a couple before they were consigned to the deep-fat fryer.

1976, with its scorching summer of drought, proved to be tumultuous and significant in all sorts of ways for a young man turning seven. For one thing, I started to become aware of the Top Ten. 'If You Leave Me Now' by Chicago was in the charts. At the same time – although I didn't discover it for another two or three years – punk rock and the Sex Pistols had grabbed pop music by the throat and were shaking its glossy teeth out. I was also beginning to realise that I wasn't the centre of the universe, and that there were these big things affecting people called life, love and death. This awareness came as a result of small incidents that occurred during my regular rambles.

Once, I found something that looked like an old, stiff, woolly mat. I picked it up with a stick and realised, horrified, that it was the corpse of a dead cat, wriggling with maggots. The stench, combined with the smell of drying hay in the surrounding fields, sent me scarpering back home. Another time, I stuck my hand into an opening between the roots of a tree I was sitting under. I groped around and eventually pulled out a small brown stoneware vase. I instantly believed that a genie must have once inhabited it, and since there was no stopper, it must still be at large. I have kept the vase to this day, and as far as I'm concerned, that genie is out there somewhere.

Pillboxes dating from the Second World War were dotted all over the landscape, and occasionally you would find smutty magazines abandoned inside them. I found a lovely bit of quartz in one, which I treasured, until my neighbour – a girl in a blue anorak whose name I have forgotten – stole it off me. I noticed it in her pocket, swiped it and started running, but she was faster than me, tripped me up and grabbed it back. Further up the track was the military assault course, which I frequently put to the test. There were water-logged trenches, a huge climbing wall, nets and various leaps and beams, all built with six-foot soldiers in mind, which meant I never quite managed to finish the whole course. From time to time I came across the odd live round, which I would chuck against a wall to see if it would go bang.

Away from the assault course, my outdoor life mostly consisted of dashing around on go-karts, attending Cub Scout meetings and playing football. I went to judo club once a week in the barracks, run by a bloke who taught us to lie on our backs and lift our heads, then nod them without touching the ground. He made us do this over and over again, while repeating 'Noddy, Noddy, Noddy, Noddy' like a mantra. We all used to laugh at that, while nodding our heads and 'feeling the burn'. It was there that I met this lovely girl with blue eyes and short black hair called Lucy. She became my first proper (in the sense of voluntary) girlfriend. Sometimes as a toddler I had found myself pushed on playdates with other girls, and the adults would make comments about how cute it was that I had 'a little girlfriend'. Even at the time I was aware that the poor mites were just other female toddlers I was being forced to spend time with. But Judo Lucy was my first real girlfriend. However, it was a doomed romance because she lost interest in me the moment I stopped going to judo class.

During my brief stint as a Cub Scout, I took part in the end-of-year Gang Show at a local theatre. One scene featured me and some friends dressed up in red-coated fox-hunting outfits, singing 'A-Hunting We Will Go' in our high-pitched voices. The director of the show seemed to be particularly worried about his young charges getting nervous while on stage, and his advice to us was to wear swimming trunks under our costumes in case we couldn't hold our wee. I stayed dry that night, but the excessive focus on the potential problem added to my nervousness. It was my first experience of stage fright.

On another sweltering day in that incident-rich year, I was inno-cently strolling past the entrance to an alleyway that ran behind a row of houses when a dog jumped out of nowhere and bit me in the face. It was a vicious-looking, SS guard-type hound that used to protect the back gate of one of the houses, and it had positioned itself in such a way that it was hard to give it any kind of berth as I passed by. It was a nasty lunge that left tooth marks on the edge of my eye socket; a couple of millimetres higher and I could have lost my sight on that side. Thankfully a neighbour who witnessed the attack got me out of there and led me, in shock and tears, home to safety. My mum went round to the owners' house to have a word, and I could only look on from the back window of the car as they opened the front door and this dog – which seemed more like a gigantic wolf – barked its head off. She came back rather annoyed that they didn't seem to care much that their beast had torn a chunk out of my face. I still have the scar, but fortunately the incident didn't leave me with a lasting fear of dogs.

My mouth bears scars too, thanks to an attempt, also in 1976, to take a short cut during a run around the block. My sister Hayley saw what I was up to and tripped me up. I was asking for it, I suppose, but one of my brand-new front teeth was smashed. From then on, right up until I moved to London, that left front tooth took up an inordinately large amount of time and energy: having fillings attached, then the fillings coming off, followed by the hell of major root canal work. Eventually the whole thing was hauled out and replaced by a false one. It's still installed to this day, although not so long ago, thanks to me fooling around in a Chinese restaurant and chomping on some wooden chopsticks to entertain my daughter, I managed to chip it in exactly the same place.

Nineteen seventy-six wasn't all maggot-riddled death, unrequited love, neck- and toothache, set to an incongruous soundtrack of the Carpenters and Leo Sayer, however. We got a colour TV for the first time that year, so I saw *The Muppet Show* in its full glory and also discovered *The Ipcress File*. I wore my wellington boots out in all weathers because the sound they made on the pavement resembled Michael Caine's clicking leather soles. I loved spy films – everyone looked incredibly cool. I fancied myself as a spy – or, at least, as someone who could *act* as a spy.

Spy games, play battles and 'Tommies versus Jerries' were popular pastimes in the school playground, at least among the boys. We often played war games at school, making machine-gun sounds with our mouths. Everyone had their own signature machine-gun sound, including me. I thought mine was the best. I was intrigued by the way you could make this 'da-da-da-da' sound and someone would 'drop dead', as if the noise itself was killing them. In my bedroom, I would replay my favourite Second World War skirmishes with plastic toy soldiers, mowing down the bad guys with a spud gun. I used to stick felt-tip pen lids in the barrel and shoot it at pretty high velocity. Once, I tried to shoot the cigarette out of my dad's mouth but accidentally hit him in the eye. That earned me a kick up the bum.

When I was around eight years old, I arrived home from school one day to find Dad putting his coat on. 'Come on, Graham, we're going to the cinema,' he announced, and we drove to the Colchester Odeon to watch *A Bridge Too Far*, Richard Attenborough's epic about the Battle of Arnhem. I've always loved that film, maybe because it reminds me what a treat it was to spend quality time alone with my dad. It felt kind of romantic – we were watching a war film, and with his involvement in the army, it seemed like a real bonding experience. The Second World War loomed large in the conversations of my older relatives, and to this day I have retained a weird obsession with it. I was fascinated to note the differences between the more casual American uniforms and the smarter British ones, and to see the gleaming black insignia of the German Panzer divisions. I've been obsessed with military uniforms ever since.

In junior school, me and my friend Mark were acknowledged to be the best at drawing. We were absolutely crazy about *Star Wars*, closely followed by *Close Encounters of the Third Kind*. I liked the total escapism of *Star Wars* – it was set in a galaxy far, far away and had nothing to do with Earth at all. Mark preferred *Close Encounters*, although I was a bit disappointed that it was set among a suburban human family in Middle America. 'Where are the stormtrooper suits and laser guns? This is crap . . .' I didn't get how cool and weird it was because I preferred films and TV shows that were full of criss-crossing laser beams or ricocheting bullets, such as *Blake's 7* and *Space: 1999*.

For me and my sister, listening to the weekly Top Forty rundown on the radio became a ritual. By the time I reached nine or ten, I was very aware that the charts were filling up with great stuff: the Jam, David Bowie, the Buzzcocks, Chic, Rainbow . . . so many different types of music. There was something for absolutely everybody. I remember buying singles like 'Roxanne' by the Police and 'The Clog Dance' by Violinski, who was a member of the Electric Light Orchestra and appeared on *Top of the Pops* sawing away on a violin painted an electric shade of blue. I liked this weird, classical folk rock with its heavy stomping beat. In those days there was a special phone number you could dial to hear a different, random chart single every night down the line (I'm sure it doubled my parents' phone bill). Me and Hayley made it into a game, in which one of us listened in and had to mime the song to the other, who had to guess what it was. One night, when it was Hayley's turn, she wrapped the cord in a noose round her neck and pretended to garrotte herself. Of course: 'Hanging on the Telephone' by Blondie. Classic! When Blondie performed 'Denis' on *Top of the Pops*, I mimed being Clem Burke, the drummer, and Hayley was Debbie Harry. We were really into the music, but it was Hayley who bought most of the records. My pocket money didn't stretch that far.

My family, like most army families, was pretty conservative and patriotic. My dad was in Princess Anne's regiment, and once I ate some of her wedding cake – everyone in the regiment had been given a slice. It was generally assumed that you supported England in everything it did. At the age of ten, I blurted out that I wanted Jim Callaghan to win the election in 1979 – the year Margaret Thatcher's Conservative Party swept to power – and various adults around me said I didn't know what I was talking about. I did, though: even as a ten-year-old I could sense that Jim had a nicer vibe. I didn't know much about politics, but when the Falklands War broke out in 1982, I took a fairly pompous but principled stand against it. Mostly I found the dehumanising of the 'Argies' and their supposedly ramshackle military in the British media hugely distasteful. (Eventually I toured in Argentina and found them to be the most lovely, passionate, brilliant people.) The general consensus both at home and in the media seemed to be patriotic support for the British task force that steamed into the South Atlantic, and admittedly I was excited by the news footage of Harrier fighter planes taking off vertically, but at school I was becoming aware of other viewpoints coming from the small anti-war faction, who sported CND (Campaign for Nuclear Disarmament) badges on their lapels.

I'm sure this consciousness came directly out of pop culture. The kind of bands I liked – the Jam, the Specials and others – supported Rock Against Racism and openly espoused political causes in interviews. When I flipped through copies of *Smash Hits* or the *NME*, artists like the Clash would be giving the finger to 'Nazi punks' or Tory ministers. The nouveau mod movement of the late 1970s and early '80s brought up memories of clashes between Teddy boys and mods, punks and skins, some of whom were into dub, reggae and other forms of black music. Even films like *Breaking Glass* were dealing with stuff like that. Wearing brothel creepers, or the colour of the laces on your Doc Martens, was a political issue.

Music and the vibrant culture associated with it gave me a massive energy surge. It was how I informed myself about what it was like to be a human being. I discovered rhythm and blues and grew to love music that was rhythmically choppy, percussive and snappy. I liked the drums in soul music, with the snare on every beat of the bar. It was danceable and it was emotional; it told a story, about joy or heartache, and was extremely cool, and the people that played it looked cool too.

I didn't get much emotional guidance while I was growing up, but music helped to explain why I felt certain ways. Even more than science fiction, songs evoked pictures in my mind. When I listened to the Beatles' 'Tomorrow Never Knows', I imagined the Fab Four dressed as cowboys on a raft, racing down some rapids, dodging the arrows bombarding them from the riverbank. Later, I started listening to things like prog rock and Adam and the Ants. But when

I discovered the Jam with their single 'Start!' in 1980, that was it – I was obsessed, and I spooned them up. They somehow made me feel like I was better than I was: more intelligent, cooler, better dressed. I felt different from all the casuals at school in their Pumas or Adidas Trimm Trabs, Kappa jackets and long, permed, wet-look hair. Our school also had its share of skinhead boys and goth/alternative girls in ra-ra skirts. I was a mod, although a furtive one, because I knew they had a reputation for scrapping on beaches, and I didn't want to scare my mum and dad. So I was kind of mod-*ish*: I had a parka, desert boots, stripy boating blazer and a couple of ties, but I didn't go totally crazy. The challenge was to mod the school uniform up as much as the regulations allowed: red or white socks under the black trousers and a Fred Perry jumper. By ironing a new crease in the lapels of my school blazer and with a bit of sewing, I pimped my two-button jacket with an extra button. I modelled my look on the Who film *Quadrophenia*, which my sister saw at the cinema when it was released in 1979. I watched it for the first time a few years later on a rented VHS tape with my parents (who were a bit huffy about the bad language) and immediately fell in love with it. I would wear narrow trousers called Ziggys, Union Jack socks and black bowling shoes from Mintz & Davis in Colchester, which was the go-to boutique for mod accoutrements. A shop called Trading Post had a marvellous selection of stripy T-shirts imported from France; I bought the first of many over their long wooden counter, plus an accompanying pair of green corduroy trousers. And, of course, there was the haircut: short back and sides, with a Paul Weller fringe.

My dad taught saxophone to a young guy who was a mod. He would arrive on his Lambretta, which had mirrors and lights all over it, wearing a big parka and carrying his alto sax. I would go out and talk to him about the Jam. I thought he was coolness incarnate but I probably got on his nerves, and he would push his scooter up the street while I pestered him with questions, until the motor sparked into throbbing life and he leapt onto the saddle and rode off, horn beeping, into his exciting mod life.

Around the age of thirteen, when I was attending Stanway Comprehensive in Colchester, I started to take a fresh interest in playing the guitar and began trying to work out songs on Hayley's acoustic, which she had been given as a replacement for another instrument that had been stolen. The impetus was a visit from my nan – my dad's mum. I wanted nothing more than to sere-nade her like some kind of lute-playing minstrel, so I thought I'd learn a couple of chords. But that got me hooked. It was mostly fairly simple three-chord wonders and Jam B-sides – 'Liza Radley' (the flipside of 'Start!') or 'Aunties and Uncles' (c/w 'News of the World'). Then there was the Beatles, which was a bit harder. 'Love Me Do' was the easiest one to get the old fingers around.

Hayley was getting more into mainstream 1980s chart and pop music, while I was beginning to investigate more alternative direc-tions. By 1982 her guitar had been consigned, unused, to the attic. I took it down into my room and found that the case was filled with little cards with chord patterns drawn on them, so I laid them on the floor and started playing along to records. And that was it. I didn't take lessons, I just taught myself. I was already taking saxo-phone lessons with Sid Cooper, a teacher at Stanway, so I knew how to read music. We didn't have YouTube in those days, of course, but you could send off for a Who songbook, for example, which had the sheet music for the best of the band's songs, including the chord shapes. I remember getting the books for the Jam's *All Mod*

Cons and *The Gift*. You'd send off your postal order and spend three weeks waiting for the bugger to arrive just so you could learn the chord changes in 'Going Underground'. A couple of years later, I got a Kay Les Paul copy and a little Kay ten-watt amplifier from my schoolfriend James Hibbins, which I destroyed very quickly by playing along to records with the volume on full. I felt like, if not a rock god exactly, then certainly an apprentice deity.

Playing the guitar was life-changing. My school was only about a five- or ten-minute walk away, so I usually arrived home at a quarter to four. That gave me a good hour and a half to make a big old noise on my guitar before my parents got back. I used to like playing along to live recordings, because then you'd have a ready-made enthusiastic audience to cheer you at the end. This was how I paid my dues. I did the Who's set from Live Aid, and then a Billy Bragg gig. I started practising finger-picking on a cheap acoustic guitar, which left my fingertips in tatters for a while. My mum would shout, 'All I'm hearing is fret noise down here.' I played my guitar every day for years and years; I discovered it was kind of therapeutic, and I still experience that today. I can pick the instrument up whenever I'm feeling anxious, and no matter what other stressful things are going on around me, it smooths everything out a bit. When I got home from school and played along to Jam and Who records on my ten-watt amp, it had the same effect. It blasted a hole through my feelings; it was empowering and made me forget any problems I was having. I was cocooned in a zone of pure sound where nothing else existed.

There was such an incredible amount of diverse, culturally awesome stuff going on in the mid-1980s. By around 1983–4 I was buying all sorts of music. There were odd singles like 'Sergeant

Rock' and 'Making Plans for Nigel' by the English band XTC, which was almost like country bumpkin music that was trying to pass itself off as coming from the city. Then there was a mod revival thing with 'Time for Action' by Secret Affair and 'Poison Ivy' by the Lambrettas. There was a disco at the local youth club on Fridays, and there was quite a lot going on tribally, what with the mods, casuals, soul boys, Level 42s, psychobillies, breakdancers and alternative goth types who were into the Smiths and the Cure. If you were DJing, that meant you had to fit in some Soft Cell, Lambrettas and Spandau Ballet, but then the psychobillies would demand 'I'm in Pittsburgh (And It's Rainin')' by the Vibes to pogo to. At some point the flattened cardboard boxes would be brought out and a few people would start body-popping and breakdancing. It was fun to be a music fan: you could be really proud of the music you were into, the bands you liked and the camaraderie you had with other people. It does seem to be missing a bit now, that real tribalism.

———

Despite my growing interest, I wasn't *all* about the music in those days. I was also getting involved in drama at school. That's how I ended up on the kids' TV show *Blue Peter*. It was our legendary music teacher at Stanway, Nigel Hildreth, who got us on the programme, performing an extract from the school musical which he had directed, *The Bartered Bride*. We did a little pub-brawl routine, which featured me doing some tumbling. I was really into acting and the musicals, even at junior school in Colchester. I felt comfortable with the idea of acting some other part, of being someone else. Experimenting with clothing enabled me to go out each day looking and acting like a completely different type of person if I fancied it. When I was acting, I could inhabit somebody else's personality, so my own failings were put to one side. It's like when people with a stammer sing or put on an accent as a strategy to help them stop stuttering. I began to become aware of the existence of an inner world, a world that could be opened up and accessed via acting or films or songs or art, one which was generally preferable to my reality, which always seemed so boring.

I played the part of John Styx once, in a school production of Offenbach's *Orpheus and the Underworld*. He leads Eurydice, Orpheus' wife, into the underworld and puts her in Pluto's jail, where he guards her. I had to perform a song solo, which was somewhat scary. I wasn't comfortable doing it, but something about the feeling it gave me made it worth it. It was a kind of affirmation: I might have felt awkward up there, but at least the audience were neither interrupting me nor laughing at my efforts. For a few moments I had a little bit of power and . . . I existed.

From my teenage years until well into adulthood I didn't allow myself to exist quite as much as other people around me did. I didn't grant myself permission to do certain things or try on certain types of persona. Other people seemed able to do that naturally. People like the boy in the year above me whom I saw on stage singing 'Gee, Officer Krupke' from *West Side Story* at a school assembly. I just could not get over the confidence of the bloke – it was unbelievable. His name was Damon Albarn, and his coolness, coupled with his brilliance as an actor and performer, blew me away.

A
DODGY
PAIR
OF
BROGUES

The first time Damon spoke to me was to point out the crapness of my shoes. The most sought-after footwear at the time was a pair of black, leather-soled brogues like the ska boys wore. Ideally you wore your trouser hem quite high, with white socks and black brogues visible underneath. I aspired to that look, plus my parka on top, and asked for some brogues for my birthday. We weren't a very well-off or fashion-conscious family, so what I received was a pair of oil-resistant, industrial black clogs with a rubbery plastic insole. Shoes tended to be purchased right after the Family Allowance came in, and we couldn't afford the top-notch sixty-quid jobs. These were barely passable.

This outrageously confident thirteen-year-old whom I had seen singing songs from *West Side Story*, and whom I thought was the epitome of hipness, approached me unprompted and made a snide comment about my ugly shoes. Then he flounced off, adjusting his hair and leaving me feeling humiliated, which was certainly a familiar sensation by then. Damon, on the other hand, possessed a really nice pair of brogues, which he wore with a black raincoat ensemble and his bleached blond hair. My footwear might not have passed muster, but when he found out I was the only boy at school who could play sax, he came looking for me.

'You play sax, right?'

'Yeah.'

'Well, I need a solo on this song I've written. We're going to record it round Michael Morris's house – he's got a four-track. Bring your sax.'

Michael Morris was a mutual schoolfriend who played bass and lived in a cool, modern 1970s house on a groovy estate in Stanway Green. He was also a bit of a hard nut who once gave me a nosebleed during one of our many mock fights. Michael's front room was all set up with microphones and – praise be! – a portastudio, and it was there we recorded Damon's song 'Beautiful Lady'. It was a mid-tempo, piano-driven ballad, with a drum machine providing the rhythm. I blew a little sax solo on it, to which Michael added a weird phaser or flanger effect. Damon was delighted with the results, and we would be friends for ever after. The name of the band at that time was Real Lives. As well as the sax, I also sometimes played the drums. Having graduated from my junior Keith Moon impersonation, I now scraped together enough money to buy a simple Maxwin kit, and played it pretty intuitively. On other songs we recorded, I would lay down a drum line on track one of the cassette, then play it back over Michael's trebly speakers while adding a saxophone part. It was primitive, but to me the process of capturing each element of a song on multiple tracks was absolutely miraculous. People who heard it seemed to dig what we were doing, including my parents and sister.

Damon was very different to me, a cocky Londoner who didn't give a shit what people thought of him. He was a hugely compelling personality, an arrogant oddment who was extremely good-looking and not only knew it, but knew what to do with it. For that reason, people at our school didn't take kindly to him at all. A lot of the fourth- and fifth-year lads were predatory skinheads, and you had to watch yourself. They used to hide behind one of the Portakabins and round us up like border collies herding sheep. They would make us run round one side of the Portakabin, where these two other skinheads were waiting to kick our legs out from under us as we scurried past. Damon frequently got chased into the loos, where he was booted up the arse and had '666' scrawled on his forehead.

Luckily – and mysteriously – I didn't really have much of a problem with bullying. I spent most of my time out of harm's way in the ivory towers of the school's art and music blocks. I tended to keep my head down, move forward and try to stay invisible. Damon, by contrast, deliberately dressed in a way that got him noticed and was constantly messing around with his hair. By the time I was fourteen and had reached the second or third year, being a skinhead was less of a fashion statement – that gang had left school and the atmosphere had eased. Damon and I were now free to sit in the Portakabins, which were near the music block, and listen to music and mess about on guitars. By this time I was reasonably competent on the instrument, so I strummed away while Damon played the piano.

That earliest band, Real Lives, was a ballady mixture of Heaven 17, King Crimson and Lionel Richie – a very 1980s concoction, in other words. Damon eventually bought a portastudio of his own, and I got into a routine of dropping round on Friday nights so that the two of us could concentrate on writing new material. Real Lives eventually played a few gigs at assemblies in the school hall, charity shows and other small local events.

At the time, Damon was into chart material by Elton John, Madness and Heaven 17, but together we took a slightly deeper dive into more unfamiliar musical waters. We got into Talk Talk, who were having hits with singles like 'Life's What You Make It' and 'Living in Another World' but seemed uncomfortable in the role of new romantic pop heroes and would gradually head off in more experimental directions. I had a twelve-inch of 'Stephen' by Gene Loves Jezebel, and I loved that. James Hibbins was really into Marillion. He was a fan of progressive rock, and it was around then that I started listening to King Crimson, led by the extraordinary guitarist Robert Fripp. Crimson's 'Ladies of the Road' was the weirdest thing I'd ever heard. It disguised itself as a traditional song, but it concealed some wigged-out guitar and sax solos. There was an album Fripp and Andy Summers (of the Police) made together called *Bewitched*, which I thought was fantastic, especially a track called 'What Kind of Man Reads Playboy?' It features a drum machine, with Summers and Fripp going berserk on their guitars and a guy called Chris Winter going nuts on a saxophone. Despite still loving the mod sounds, I had no trouble getting into the more proggy stuff, like Matching Mole, Robert Wyatt, Gong, Caravan, Van der Graaf Generator and Soft Machine, which was the scene Damon's dad had been involved in (he briefly managed Soft Machine in the late 1960s). I was being hit on all sides by so many eclectic sounds and inspiring ideas of what music could be.

———

I generally enjoyed my time at school – at least, I wasn't one of the ones trying to bunk off and was reasonably well liked by my fellow pupils. I was good at English, occasionally startling my English teacher, Miss Wraite, with the range of my vocabulary. She was impressed, for instance, that I knew what 'surmise' meant. She was less impressed when I brought in Paolo Hewitt's *The Jam: A Beat*

Concerto, after she encouraged us to analyse a text of our choice. It described the inspiration behind Paul Weller's song 'Down in the Tube Station at Midnight' and included the word 'neurosis', which I speculated came from the narrator's own fear of getting beaten up in the Underground. She pulled a face at that one, mainly because she didn't consider a book about pop suitable for an English Literature class.

I'm not entirely sure where my appreciation of words came from, as I didn't read a huge number of books in my teens, apart from Hermann Hesse's *Narcissus and Goldmund* and the uncanny fiction of Alan Garner. I was struck by a piece of dialogue between a boy and a girl at the start of the latter's novel *Red Shift*, which, in its mixture of the tragic and the romantic – the incredible odds against meeting a soulmate, given the size of the universe, and the inevitability of being torn apart by circumstances – pretty much crystallised the shape of most of my future relationships. Otherwise, as often as not I would daydream my way through school lessons, only half engaged in what was going on in the classroom. I didn't make much of an effort, to be honest, but I kept myself interested enough to get four O-levels: English, Art, Music and Human Biology.

I also searched out other creative avenues. I began to get seriously interested in art during Mick Knight's art classes at Stanway Comprehensive. I went into the art room one day, and there on the wall was a poster for an exhibition at the Royal Academy by Marc Chagall, a French artist born in pre-Soviet Russia who did amazing work in parallel to the cubists and expressionists. The poster featured one of his lovely series of paintings of him and his wife hovering in mid-air. He's wearing brown trousers and a green jumper, his wife is in a black dress with a white collar, they're both floating upwards off the floor of their kitchen, and he's bending around in front of her face to give her a kiss. The sheer romanticism of this image bowled me over. I'd never heard of Chagall before, but that was it. It made total sense – drawing is not always about reproducing an apple accurately. It was similar to some of my own pictures, but now I realised it was actually possible to get this kind of work exhibited in public.

This encouraged me to look into the artistic scene of early-1900s Paris, around the Latin Quarter and Montparnasse districts – the messy painters like Chaïm Soutine and Modigliani. I loved them – and Picasso, of course. They made me feel better about my own stuff. I wasn't bad at conventional drawing, but to know that you were allowed to be more expressive and not really care about proportion or realism was incredibly liberating. You could have a woman flying around a room if you wanted. It was a cool idea, but apart from my teachers, I was mostly alone on this particular journey. I spent much time in my own inner world, where all this art was being soaked up. My other friends were dismissive when I tried to explain my excitement about Picasso's cubist paintings or Modigliani's nudes. Even Damon was more preoccupied with music, despite him coming from a cultured family – his sister Jessica was already well on the way to becoming an artist herself.

I started to spend all my pocket money on art books. My bedroom became a kind of cultural research centre. I spent hours in there listening to music and leafing through my purchases. I copied Edvard Munch's drawings and Modigliani's nudes, especially his portraits of his girlfriend, Jeanne Hébuterne. They blew my mind, they were so beautiful.

The art I was getting into at around sixteen years of age was referred to as 'modern', even though it was already eighty-five years old – but it made a huge impression on me, and I was determined to get into art school and learn how to make sculptures. I was certainly interested in the expressionists and the New York School – Willem de Kooning and Franz Kline and all the other, more abstract artists – but I generally got the most enjoyment out of work that was representational and figurative.

I began making mental connections between art and music. Listening to composers like Chopin or Debussy, you realised they had their contemporary visual equivalents in the post-impressionist paintings of Bonnard or Degas; likewise, the links between the free jazz of Ornette Coleman and the abstract expressionism of de Kooning. Inspired by my school saxophone lessons, I had started getting into my dad's jazz LP collection. I was particularly struck by Paul Gonsalves's legendary sax solo on 'Blow by Blow' on 1956's *Ellington at Newport* album. I'd never heard anything like it. He was landing on notes that were often totally unexpected, but it launched Duke Ellington's music into some fantastical anti-gravity space, just like Chagall's flying wife.

I also got into Kurt Weill's *Threepenny Opera*, and one day some amazing orchestral music popped up on the TV. It was a bit too modern for my dad, who was really into his Beethoven, but as I watched Shostakovich's Fifth Symphony being performed I thought that this must be the height of art. There are no lyrics to tell you what it means, just musical instrumentation, and yet it communicates so much. It was a formative time in my life, all about soaking things up. Everything seemed to be connected in this big web in my internal world, and it was an amazing, mind-blowing experience.

When my final school exams approached, I wanted to choose Music and Art as my extra subjects, but you weren't allowed to do both together for some reason. I went for Music, but I still carried on doing my art with Mick. At some point around that time I decided that art school was where I wanted to go. Damon's mum and dad were very involved in the arts, and I was a frequent visitor to their house, which was a former bakery. When I wasn't listening to music or writing songs with Damon, I was browsing their well-stocked library of books on painters and prehistoric and non-Western art. Hazel, his mother, sold her paintings out of her shop Dragonfly Designs, which was attached to the Albarn residence. I used to cycle the four or five miles to their house to help her strip and prepare old canvases for repainting in her studio. Once, she asked me if I had any thoughts on a future career. I told her that I had vaguely discussed with my dad the possibility of joining the police force. Like the good, liberal, anti-authoritarian free spirit she was, Hazel appeared horrified. 'You're an aesthete,' she said. Both she and Keith, Damon's dad, were very encouraging about my artwork.

Keith was running the North Essex School of Art in Colchester, so I started to build up a good portfolio of work in order to get a place there. Keith and Hazel would set me up with some paper and leave me alone for a couple of hours, drawing away. I made a big breakthrough with two drawings of a satchel, one in pencil and the other in watercolour. I really understood why it would be dark behind this buckle and why that buckle would stand out, and where to put the shadows and the highlights. The penny had dropped. I don't know what happened to those drawings, but they were my artistic breakthrough – my *Demoiselles d'Avignon*. With dedication, I built up a strong portfolio and got an A-level in Art, which I didn't find very difficult. With that, I was eligible for the two-year Art and Design foundation course at North Essex School of Art.

With everything I've turned my hand to, I've never been into running before I can walk. Art, for me, was never really about trying to provoke or shock people. That was for poseurs. To make a decent abstract picture you've got to be able to draw an apple first. In terms of my technique, I was very concerned about paying the correct dues. I once showed some of my fellow sixth-formers Picasso's little line drawings of women, in which the hair would be in one place and the eyes would be on the same side of the face. They were perfect, but my friends would say, 'Oh, I could do that.' And I'd think, 'Well, you *didn't* do that, did you?'

When I eventually started at art school, I was definitely one of the more serious-minded students. This general Art and Design course attracted the full spectrum: people who wanted to be graphic designers, people who wanted to do commercial art, people who wanted to make models. Of course, the few of us who were fine artists thought we were the best – because we were fine artists.

I was quite romantic as a young man, and when I got into my first relationships I sought out books with the most tragic love stories: Turgenev, D. H. Lawrence and *Thérèse Raquin* by Émile Zola – a heavy library of pain, sorrow and thwarted romance. But I was never exhausted by it as a teenager. I would put down a book and immediately pick up a pencil and make some drawings. Every second was taken up with cramming knowledge into my head and searching for some mode of expression.

In my late teens I had a couple of girlfriends who were a lot older than me. I'm not sure what they saw in me, as I hadn't had any sexual experience. The relationship dynamic seemed to shift towards them 'mothering' a younger, vulnerable man. Around the age of seventeen I met Julia. She was my first love, really, and it was a serious relationship. I learnt a lot from her. Julia had loads of good records: she pretty much got me into Van der Graaf Generator; she certainly got me into Patti Smith. We used to listen to the Pink Floyd LP *Relics* all the time, and she had albums by the Doors and the Velvet Underground. She was cool, and I fell for her rather hard. She was beautiful, with big blue eyes, psychedelic dresses and long hair. The relationship lasted for two years, and there were a lot of firsts for me during the course of it, including my first sexual experience. It came while we were on a ten-day holiday in St Malo, France. Julia was a vegetarian, and as a devotee of both her and the meat-hating Morrissey, I had become one too. In France, we survived mainly on cheese, cheap red wine and Gitanes. Unfortunately my new diet left me with an extremely low haemoglobin count. On the cross-Channel ferry back home, after a sleepless night spent either under a table or smoking cigarettes on deck, I fainted in the breakfast queue. I became very anaemic and had to go to hospital for a while, where I was diagnosed with a peptic ulcer.

––––––

When my two years at North Essex School of Art came to an end, the only way forward for me was to go to London. By that time, Damon had already moved there, attending a drama school in the East End, and I had to be where Damon was because we were now more serious than ever about making music together – that much was signed in blood. During band rehearsals at some point before he left, we had made a pact, or at least a loose arrangement, with each other: 'If you do it before me, you invite me along.' So I was overjoyed when – against all expectations – I got a place to study art at Goldsmiths College in south-east London. I enrolled in the autumn of 1988, and Damon started a part-time music course there as well so we could be closer together.

Nevertheless, when I moved to London, I was suddenly an aimless minnow again in a big pond. After enjoying supreme focus in Colchester, suddenly I didn't know what the hell I was doing any more. I was also set adrift romantically. Julia had ended our relationship just before I was due to start college as she didn't want to be involved in a long-distance student affair. I cried about the break-up at the time, but looking back, it was probably for the best.

At Goldsmiths, it took quite a while to find out who I was. The social aspect of student life became more important, and I spent many lunchtimes eating pizza and drinking Newcastle Brown Ale. There was a huge drinking culture, and a friend of mine held the 'Gallon Club' record for necking eight pints in under an hour without a toilet break. I also felt the urge to be entertaining. A misguided quest for popularity too often drove me the extra mile into stupid or excessive behaviour. In my first week at Goldsmiths, for example, I managed to get myself slung into a police cell. I had been egged on, in the student bar, to try a devastating 'cocktail' known as a Traffic Light: a fiver would get you three pints of snakebite – Special Brew mixed with Merrydown Cider – each with its own chaser of Pernod and black (red), vodka and orange (amber) or blue Bols (green). You put a straw in each glass and sucked them down at the same time. There should have been a red light in front of that right from the beginning, because it sent me spinning out of control. That night there was a band playing at the college, and with the

Traffic Light rampaging around my system I invaded the stage, no longer knowing where I was. Next I was standing at a bus stop, with no memory of having been thrown out. I went back and tried to regain entry by smashing a window, and suddenly I was in the back of a police van. I ended up in a cell in Brixton, which I thought was a trifle messy, so I very helpfully tidied the place up, folding the blanket and putting it on the bed, before going to sleep on the floor. They threw me out at 6.30 a.m., with no charges pressed.

Life at Goldsmiths was confusing and overwhelming. Socially, it felt a bit like having the contents of a butcher's shop hooked on my belt and then being chucked over a precipice into a ravine full of starving wild dogs. My social skills were terrible, so I drank more to counteract all the anxiety. My wide-eyed self felt inferior to everybody else, as well as hopelessly uninformed. One day in painting class we were asked to prepare a canvas in 'rabbit-skin size', an expression utterly unfamiliar to me. I asked a girl near me what it meant, and she said, 'I don't use that, I'm a vegan.' I didn't even know what a vegan was at that stage, and I was too scared to ask any of these way too cool art students what rabbit-skin size meant. ('Size' is an artist's word for adhesive, and rabbit-skin size is a glue made from boiled-down rabbit skin that is used in preparing a canvas. Not very vegan-friendly, in other words.) I looked around surreptitiously at what other people were doing and realised it seemed to be OK to prepare the canvas with a simple layer of emulsion; using the somewhat old-fashioned rabbit size wasn't strictly necessary for the task. It had been a reasonable query to make, but the reaction I got made me more timid about asking questions later on.

It took me a while to settle in. There was a lot of conceptual art around and plenty of discussion in the study groups about advertising. Gallaher had just begun a very minimalist advertising campaign for Silk Cut cigarettes featuring a piece of purple silk with a slit cut through it, which provoked plenty of lively discussion. I thought deconstructing advertising was a complete waste of time and had nothing to do with what I considered art. To my romantic way of thinking, art was still about penniless painters burning their last chair legs to warm up their Parisian garrets at the turn of the century. There I was doing my messy pictures and dabbling with sculpture, but I never really got going. There was a very nice tutor, a Texan called Ferris Newton, who liked my stuff, which at the time was inspired by abstract expressionism. My previous figurative stuff hadn't gone down so well, so I was now working more in the abstract realm, using ripped posters, PVA glue, sand and dripped paint. The sand is crumbling off and the staples are getting rusty, but I still have these works stored somewhere.

Despite my social insecurities, I was rarely lonely, and I made friends fairly easily. My fellow students were serious about their future careers as artists, and I happened to have landed among many of the people who would go on to redefine modern British art: Damien Hirst, Sam Taylor-Wood, Abigail Lane and Michael Landy, the guy who eventually deliberately destroyed all his belongings in a great big crusher as an art project. He and Abigail were going out, and we used to zoom around London in his Volkswagen Beetle.

My residence, Stannard Hall, was in Camberwell, quite some distance from the main campus in New Cross. It stood next to Myatt's Fields, a Victorian park with a bandstand and a disused chapel, St Gabriel's. It was now a church of art, where we art students practised our craft. Living in the halls on the level beneath me was a good-looking French-language student with a lampshade hairstyle called Alex James. He played bass and guitar, so we hit it off. Our music tastes were a little bit different – he was into New Order, whom I hadn't followed so closely – but we ended up bonding over Joy Division's live album *Still*. With his spliffs and his penchant for discussing André Gide, Alex was cool in a detached way, and if he had any trace of hedonism in him at that point, he kept it fairly close to his chest. My room was equipped with an anglepoise lamp with an unfeasibly long cord, and if I dangled it out of my window, I could wake Alex up by hitting his window with the plug. For some reason the catch on his door didn't work properly, and I would often push it open to find him naked and asleep inside. There were definitely a few girls in his year who would have loved to have taken advantage of that, if only they had known about the faulty lock.

We began hanging out regularly, strumming guitars and vaguely trying to write songs together. I was pretty heavily into noisy guitar rock, like Dinosaur Jr and My Bloody Valentine. It was 1988, the year the latter's album *Isn't Anything* came out, which was a massive deal.

I began to notice another resident of Stannard Hall, a textiles student called Jane Oliver, and after asking her out on a date, we became an item. She had a strong interest in music and would later help her friends Donna Matthews and Justine Frischmann to name their new band Elastica (she acted as a kind of non-instrument-playing consultant to the band when they were just getting off the ground). Afterwards she worked for John Best and Phill Savidge at the PR company Savage & Best. A friend of hers from art college in Worthing, Jamie Hewlett, was hanging around at the time too. He had moved up to London in order to get involved in the comic-strip/graphic-novel scene, and his *Tank Girl* strip, created with writer Alan Martin, would first appear in 1988. I became friends with this little comic coterie, which also included artists Philip Bond and Glyn Dillon and congregated around the newly launched magazine *Deadline*. Eventually Jamie would come to play a part in the Blur story.

THE
KIDS
ARE
SORT
OF
ALL
RIGHT

spent my first year in the comparative luxury of Stannard Hall, after which students were expected to move out and find their own accommodation. I was late in getting it together to find a house-share for myself, but Alex James told me there was a flat available in the same building where he was currently renting an apartment with his girlfriend, Justine.

The empty flat was above a health-food shop in New Cross called Cross Currants. Me and my friends Kate Russell and Adam Peacock – whom I had followed to Goldsmiths from Colchester – obtained the keys from the people who were moving out and decided we weren't going to pay any rent. How could we? We had no money to speak of. I had long since burnt through my meagre student loan, and twenty quid was all my mum and dad could afford to dole out to me to cover the long summer holiday. So there we were: squatters.

For a while, our main meal typically consisted of Jacob's cream crackers and brown sauce, and I have to admit a significant portion of my pitiful allowance was spent on tins of beer. But that's how it was. There was an atmosphere of general mischief in the squat. I was never a big drug-taker – beer was my intoxicant of choice – and I found narcotics unfamiliar and frightening. But, of course, we all dabble at that stage of life, so we would get mildly stoned on hash cigarettes, and (faithful acolyte of 1960s counterculture that I was) I would use this for creative purposes, or for talking or thinking or general giggling. On a very few occasions, I took LSD. Once, we discovered two tabs with cartoon characters printed on them that had been left on our mantelpiece. I happened to be in a really good mood, having just returned to London after a visit to my family in Colchester, and I was glad to be back, so I thought, 'What the hell!' I didn't know what to expect, but I took Batman, while Adam necked the Joker, and then me, Adam and another friend, Christine, went straight down to the Dewdrop Inn (which was near a big club called the Venue, which I would play later on with the likes of Lush; I also saw Teenage Fanclub there).

The Dewdrop was a raw, violent old pub next to a big recreation ground. We arrived in an altered state. People were leaving acid echo-trails when they moved, and everything seemed to ring with some strange significance. I went to buy a few pints of Newcastle Brown Ale, but while I was standing at the bar, a fight started up around me. A woman was screaming at a man who must have wronged her in some way, and then she started beating him up. The whole thing rapidly escalated into a Dickensian scene straight out of *Oliver Twist* – and, of course, on acid its intensity was even more exaggerated. At that moment everything turned to sepia and people appeared to be wearing frock coats and battered top hats and brandishing canes, which they were crashing down on this man's head.

I went back to tell everybody what was going on, only to find Christine reading out some haikus she had written. I had never heard of them, and to me she seemed to be talking in utter riddles, while Adam was just giggling away. As I repeatedly asked her what on earth she was talking about, she looked back at me as though my words were piercing her heart.

Suddenly I felt seriously unwell, and as we scampered outside the pub and lay down on the ground, my stomach started to contort and I was sick. As I was puking, with Christine wondering if I was OK, I noticed Adam regarding me, his eyes poking out of his head and then drifting upwards towards the night sky. I realised that the vomit streaming out of me wasn't even hitting the ground, but ascending, turning into stars and forming the Milky Way. We were both seeing exactly the same vision: the puke leaving my mouth, taking a quick detour just before it hit the grass and then spreading across the sky.

Christine didn't share this vision, however, so there was much confusion. Back to the flat we wandered, where I spent the rest of the night listening to Pink Floyd and filling an entire sketchbook with drawings of tanks. (They had a song called 'Tanks', so there was a connection.) I wish I still had that one. When there was no more room in the sketchbook, I went back into our little living room to find that Adam had slathered his face with a bright green face pack, which gradually cracked and fell off over the course of the rest of the night, making him look unnervingly bizarre.

————

Once, on a trip to Blackburn, my flatmates and I hit upon a seam of magic mushrooms in a field and harvested enough to fill a whole sleeping bag. Back in New Cross, we emptied them out, creating a foot-thick layer of fungus on the dining-room table. We had people coming round to sample our special tea for quite a while afterwards. Once, I glugged down two cups of mushroom tea in one go. We were watching the Barbra Streisand movie *Funny Girl*, which as I recall includes a scene where a man talks utter nonsense in a German accent. His babble confused me to the point where I lost consciousness and retreated into the inner workings of my brain. After perceiving the interweaving and overlapping sense of myself, I watched my ego crumble before my eyes. Whenever I briefly surfaced from this hallucination, the music in the film disagreed with me and pushed me back into this strange internal world where my whole life appeared as a series of mistakes and humiliations. The only thing that brought me out of it was having a conversation with my flatmate Kate about John Lennon's top lip.

————

In the middle of 1988 I was invited to play guitar and saxophone in Circus, a new band Damon was putting together. He had been working at the Beat Factory studio in Euston, where resident producer Graeme Holdaway and his partner Marijke Bergkamp were trying to help him shape his songwriting, with the aim of getting a record deal. Circus included Eddie Deedigan and Dave Brolan, a couple of old friends from Damon's drama school, but it didn't take long for the band to fall apart, as everyone was too involved with other projects. (Brolan went on to become a successful rock photographer.)

Even though the curtain had come down on Circus, Damon and I were no less ambitious to keep some kind of band alive. Around the end of 1988 I brought in Dave Rowntree, a guy about five years older than me who had played drums in several of my previous bands in Colchester. Now all we needed was a bass player. At Goldsmiths, Alex James, myself and another friend called Paul Hodgson had been working on an arty pop project called Nichtkunst. It was more of a social gathering than a band or art collective: we would have some drinks, make drawings together and joke around while proposing manifestos and concepts for performance-art pieces. One of our more outlandish suggestions was to build towers of scaffolding connected by a bridge across a stage and then drop metal poles from the top to make an almighty clang. Needless to say, it remained, like all the other ideas we had, a beer-sodden fantasy. Still, Alex seemed like the kind of guy it would be good to have on the team, and it felt only polite to invite him to join me, Damon and Dave in this new musical venture. I was really into J. D. Salinger, so we named ourselves after Seymour Glass, from his book *Seymour: An Introduction*. Seymour it was.

I was beginning to harbour the feeling that I wasn't really going to go anywhere with my official studies, that art was always going to be more of a private, personal journey for me. It was never going to lead to a career of exhibiting work in galleries. It got to an exhausting point where I was attending college all day and sitting in rehearsals all night, which proved unsustainable. The contrary, discordant-sounding music Seymour was starting to make was taking up too much of my mental space and pushed us into a more angular and unpredictable mode. We were coming up with songs involving spiky new-wave chords and tempo shifts, like 'Dizzy', 'Shimmer' and 'Fool'. Not long afterwards we slowed things down a little and created a swirling, psychedelic tune around the repeated line 'She's so high'.

The director of the art school was very understanding about my shift towards music. 'Look, Graham,' he told me, 'I've seen it happen with Malcolm McLaren and Kate Bush and everyone. Just go, see if it works. If it doesn't, come back.' 'Fair enough,' I said, and took that as permission to put aside my art ambitions, go off and concentrate on music full-time.

This leap from art to music was probably the most momentous and decisive choice I have ever made, and it defined everything for me from that point on. I knew I would never forgive myself if I didn't give it a go, and I have never regretted it for one moment since. I had lived for this ever since I started windmilling my arms like Pete Townshend in front of my bedroom mirror. I loved painting, and I knew I would never stop sketching my inner visions and demonic thoughts as a way of ejecting them from my head. But I was never going to make it as a professional painter. I had a sonic paintbrush instead, and I was gonna use it.

Being in London, the epicentre of the music business, rather than in an overlooked satellite town in Essex, we felt pressure to actually try to become a real pop group. Our second-ever gig was at the Goldsmiths degree show of spring 1989, which featured work by the likes of Damien Hirst, Sarah Lucas and Michael Landy. That was a fun night. I used to make silly little posters and flyers, and from the middle of 1989 we began to elbow ourselves onto live bills, including at Dingwalls, the venue in Camden Town. We used to just turn up and insist on opening for whichever artist was headlining that night. It was Damon's amazing confidence that swung it for us, no question. He had already gabbed his way into a job assisting at a recording studio and was also working as a bartender, serving the rich and glamorous denizens of Notting Hill. His charm and powers of persuasion came in very handy when advancing Seymour's interests.

At our earliest shows I was quite shy and didn't do an awful lot of histrionics. But as time went on we increasingly presented ourselves as fairly unhinged. There was a lot of jumping about, puking, dangerous falling over and spinning of guitars in the air. The bar we set for ourselves just kept on being raised. We hardly ever reached our last number without Damon was being sick or the amps keeling over and smashing. Those gigs were quite crazy. I always wanted to get the gig over with, but Damon enjoyed going mental. We used to drink a fair amount before we played, which didn't help, but quite often he would throw up behind my amp, then jump on Alex's back mid-song. They'd wobble like an unsteady tower, and then Damon would collapse on my effects pedals and mess up all my delicate settings. I was usually a bit peeved, because I enjoyed playing, even though it made me incredibly nervous.

Thanks to these chaotic early shows, we quickly picked up a bit of a following. Our antics forced people to keep watching us, just to see if we were going to make it to the end of the set. Luckily we didn't have many songs at that point, so our gigs were relatively short.

When we started, Seymour sounded very different from what we later produced with Blur. In London, we acquired a following from the art school on Holloway Road. A bunch of fans from there used to come along and do this crazy, arty dance to our stuff. Gradually, as we became better known, we emerged into the era of 'baggy' – that period when indie music was infiltrated by laidback dance rhythms – and became associated with that sound and style. Baggy was mostly coming out of northern England, and Seymour was quite heavily influenced by the album *Stutter* by the Manchester band James. Released in 1986, it was a lot more experimental than our stuff. When we began getting gigs further afield, up in Birmingham or Walsall Junction 10 or Dudley JB's, you'd come on stage and think, 'Jeez, this place is absolutely rammed with people with mad medieval haircuts shaking maracas.' It was baggy. We'd walk out of there with a hundred quid. 'Now we can afford a pair of jeans. This is insane!'

There's a half-hour video online of an early Seymour gig, filmed at the Harlow Square on 18 December 1989, that gives a vivid impression of what we were like at the time. As usual, we'd driven up from art school in Dave's Ford estate, and I was still wearing the clothes I'd had on all day. We could just about fit our equipment into his car, and we'd drive to the gig lying flat on top of the amplifiers, our noses touching the roof of the car.

BOWLING
WITH
THE
POPSCENE

S tuff they never tell you before you're famous, part one: if you are serious about signing away your soul in blood, you need to train yourself to become hyper-vigilant about people. Watch them like a hawk for certain behaviours or red flags. Work out if they're on the side of good or evil, as far as your interests are concerned. When you become successful with a band, no one from a record label or management company sits you down and has a knowing word in your ear along the lines of: 'Right, this is probably going to be fun, but you're going to have to get out there and play shows, travel round the world, and it's gonna exhaust you. You're going to get free booze, but don't drink too much. You'll be offered drugs, but don't overdo it. Girls will want to get close to you, but for some of them you might be just a temporary upgrade.'

Amid all the tired old legends of TVs out the window and Rolls-Royces in swimming pools, no one gives you advance warning about all the opportunities for self-abuse or the dodgy characters who circle like vultures – the lotus-eaters and Cyclopes and witch-goddesses who will try to lure you from the path. Danger: clashing rocks ahead.

But as we started to break through as a band, we got lucky in terms of the people who saw something in us. It was at a Seymour show in a pub called the Cricketers, near the Oval in south London, that we first got noticed by Andy Ross. Andy was the A&R man for an independent record label called Food Records, which had been set up in 1984 by David Balfe. Andy had joined Balfe – who came out of Liverpool's 1980s new-wave scene and had played keyboards in the Teardrop Explodes with Julian Cope – as a partner in Food, and they had signed a number of alternative late-1980s acts, such as Zodiac Mindwarp, Voice of the Beehive and Jesus Jones. While quirky in their own distinctive ways, these acts actually managed to have hits.

Andy had quite eclectic tastes. He was a huge music fan: anything from the Wipers to Ann Peebles and everything in between. He was just about the only person I've ever met in the music industry – including the American music industry – who knew who the Wipers were and was actually a fan of them rather than simply having heard their name. He understood so many aspects of the industry, having spent time working in music shops and doing all sorts. He was a bright, funny bloke, never judgemental, and an excellent companion in a quiz or a game of Boggle. I loved him dearly and feel especially sad not to have had the chance to say farewell before he died of cancer in January 2022.

In Seymour, I guess he saw a rough-and-ready motor that badly needed some moulding and a respray. A song me and Damon wrote as a duo called 'Love Madly', with just a drum machine and guitar, changed everything for us: we finally gave ourselves permission to be less elaborate and strip things down to a two-chord, Velvet Underground-type approach. Our early set lists had some strong material, such as 'Repetition' and 'She's So High', and in 1989 we shopped our demos round to a few hot indie labels. The A&R person at Creation Records told Damon to leave when he showed up with a tape. Andy, on the other hand, must have thought, 'These maniacs can write a decent tune.' We met up with him a few times and eventually signed a deal with Food.

Since the late 1980s Food Records had been a subsidiary of the Parlophone division of EMI, one of the massive conglomerates. You know those stock photos of groups like the Beatles sitting at corporate desks and signing contracts, with cigars and champagne at the ready? Doing the Food deal was just like that. We turned up at the offices of a music lawyer, Alasdair George, whom Andy set us up with, and there were the documents, all laid out, with people standing around in suits and ties. By today's standards we probably didn't get an enormous amount of money, but it was enough for me to be able to afford a new Gibson Les Paul guitar. And anyway, the smaller your advance, the quicker you'll recoup the money and earn royalties.

'Well, boys, sign your life away . . .'

We all signed our names. 'Fuck it, yes, we've signed a deal!'

And that was it. Handshakes all round, and the best part was going to the EMI building in Manchester Square and having ourselves photographed in the same stairwell where the Beatles had that famous picture taken of them gazing down from a balcony. Afterwards, we got taken out to lunch, and then we went on to the Ladbroke Hotel for some celebratory drinks, where we got predictably slaughtered. On my way home I had some sort of blackout as I was crossing a road and got hit by a car. I ended up in hospital and had to phone Jane, who answered the payphone at our hall of residence. I had a few scratches and was a bit concussed, but otherwise was miraculously OK.

The contract stipulated that we had to change the band's name, and from a long list of suggestions they offered us we rejected all the vaguely fascistic and terror-organisation soundalike options and settled on Blur. After that, we would often drop in to hear our new masters' voices at Manchester Square. It was extremely exciting. EMI was still full of music-biz veterans, like Malcolm Hill, who would tell us stories about the parties he'd been to with artists like Queen. He always had a couple of bottles of nice ale hidden behind his desk, and we'd sit in his office and suck on a beer. And there were plenty of smiling, friendly young women working there who would bring you a cup of tea and give you a little wink or ruffle your hair. You felt like a special new pet.

Our publishing deal was with Mike Smith at MCA, and after we'd signed that – using his heavy, expensive fountain pen – I think he took us out for snails. I say that because my memories of the eating bit are vague. There would have been a few glasses of *vino* involved, but I'm pretty sure we had snails.

The starting gun on our career had been well and truly fired, and we were off. Just after we officially signed to Food, the newly renamed Blur was offered a significant support slot on 27 February 1990 at the Brixton Academy. Andy Ross pulled a favour and we were squeezed onto the bottom of a bill with Mega City Four and the Cramps. A very big, tough tour manager warned us not to go anywhere near the Cramps' dressing room, but we saw the unmistakable figure of Lux Interior creeping down the corridor between the dressing rooms in winklepickers, looking like a spider drawn by Odilon Redon. Like the characters in a Scooby-Doo cartoon, we backed against the wall as he passed, regarding him with fear and wonder. On stage, his band's gothy girl fans smiled at us and didn't give us as much gyp as we'd expected.

In those early days we sometimes went clothes shopping together, but we never worked with stylists, apart from Alex occasionally. Dave had zero idea about clothing and took no interest in that side of things. For photo shoots we'd throw on a pair of DMs and jeans and grab a T-shirt and jacket. One day I came home from an expedition to the Lonsdale shop, just off Carnaby Street, with an extremely expensive orange T-shirt. I got a telling-off from Jane about that, because now I'd squandered most of our money on one garment, we had nothing left to pay the rent.

We got enthusiastically involved in every part of the process, from making demos to designing T-shirts (as well as the more obvious stuff like recording music). Frankly, I was most excited by things like climbing into the tour bus one morning to find a just-delivered, unopened box full of freshly manufactured Blur T-shirts – all purples and pinks, based on the rings of Saturn, drawn and lettered by us together with the designers at Stylorouge.

Touring itself was incredibly cool at first, racing up and down the M1 in a van. It kicked off in March 1990, and one of the first dates happened to fall on my twenty-first birthday, at the Marquee in London. My parents came along to see me perform at this legend-ary venue, the scene of barnstorming appearances by the Who, Jimi Hendrix and a whole generation of my 1960s heroes. This gave my mum and dad an opportunity to meet the people, such as Andy Ross, who were currently holding the keys to their son's career. After the gig I went with my family for a Chinese meal in Charing Cross. They didn't have strong opinions about Blur's music, but with all credit to them, they never nagged me to 'get a proper job' and could see that Andy was a legitimate operator, not a shark.

At that point, I thought I had found the perfect balance on stage between self-control and abandonment. Just before our show at the Lady Owen Arms, a pub venue in Islington, north London, I drank two-thirds of a bottle of wine and then placed it under the chair that my amp was balanced on. We played a great ten-song set, and I grabbed the bottle as I walked off and polished off the remainder at the side of the stage. If there exists a perfect equilibrium between intoxication and artistic performance, I think that night I hit the sweet spot.

Writing songs with Blur was never as fraught as some have implied. If a song wasn't really working, we just put it aside – there were always more where that one came from. Damon was writing tons of songs, and in the early days we would go to a rehearsal space called the Premises in Hackney Road, east London. Jane and I were living in a basement flat in Lewisham at that point, so I had to take the bus into Hackney to get there. It was a cheap and hence popular studio for alternative artists to rehearse in and store their equipment – Lloyd Cole and the Commotions' flight cases seemed to be permanently stashed there – and we usually booked the smaller of its two rooms. Damon sometimes brought along a cassette containing some new song idea, such as 'Come Together', which he would play for us through the crackly PA; or if we had a gig that night, we'd knock our current set list into shape so it was fit for playing out on the road, before hopping into a van driven by Jason, our new roadie.

When we came to record our first album, *Leisure*, all the songs were fully formed. We'd been listening to so much music that we knew how songs worked structurally, what sort of shape they should be in. That was when I'd get excited. 'How does this song start? What happens after the second chorus? Are there any instrumental sections, does it change key, does it go back into another little half-verse after that instrumental or middle eight? And then how many choruses? Are there going to be some fun, unexpected bits? How do we end it?'

I loved all that sort of thing.

When we latched onto the chords and started jamming it about, we used to tweak each other – 'Play a bit faster, Dave.' Eventually we'd end up with a song we were able to play.

I'm the first to admit that our debut album was a somewhat baggy affair. Well, not quite all of it: 'She's So High' was on there, and there were other tunes that were more like thrashed-up Beatles or Pink Floyd. After all, we were from London, so we weren't so 'loose fit' as the Manchester mob. We were more estuary-ish, more Grantchester Meadows than Trafford Park. Our outlook was a little more bucolic and melancholic (with emphasis on the colic). That's just how we were as people. It was partly an expression of the loneliness of growing up on windswept army estates, or of me and Damon hanging out by the river at the back of his house in the wilds of Essex. A lot of that English local colour flavoured the music, right from the start.

We had no shortage of songs, but 'There's No Other Way' was an obvious single. It had a catchy little chorus and was propelled along by Dave's drums laid on top of a Madchester-ish drum loop. From the label's perspective, David Balfe commented that he liked it but wanted to hear more oomph from the intro. When Damon added his two-note organ line over the intro, Balfe said, 'Yes, that's a hit,' and that was settled. That one detail tipped it over the line, transforming it from merely a good song into a hit. Balfe's trick was to be able to recognise and exploit those tiny details.

That said, when Balfe got angry, he really exploded. He would confront us across his desk like a scary headmaster, his face reddening, eyes bulging and froth appearing at the corners of his mouth. 'David Balfe from Teardrop Explodes is shouting at us,' we'd think.

'What have we done now?' He could get exercised by anything from a bad gig to our supposed unprofessionalism and lack of a long-term career vision. He wanted us to be racking up hit singles like REM and U2, not spaffing out this arty nonsense with over-fussy basslines. I often felt afraid of him and usually took his criticisms personally. He didn't always shout; in fact, he could be quite nice on occasion.

He worked closely with us and even directed the video for 'She's So High', which featured giant rings of coiled neon wobbling like jellyfish. It was probably really expensive and didn't add an awful lot more than a few lights could have done. When he directed the video to 'There's No Other Way', he was getting into David Lynch and wanted it to have a *Blue Velvet* feel, with an ear covered in ants. It's kind of Lynch with Inspiral Carpets haircuts (not that I knew it was an Inspirals hairstyle – it was always a Beatles haircut to me).

The first album was produced by Steve Power and Steve Lovell, who were the producers of the double A-side 'I Know'/'She's So High'. Mike Thorne, who had worked with the Sex Pistols, also produced a few tunes – 'Fool', 'Wear Me Down' and 'Birthday'). We were impressed with Mike because he had produced the early post-punk albums by Wire. We were still feeling our way towards what our sound should be, but Mike definitely helped us get closer to it. And it was great to be able to record the music properly, because our demos usually missed the mark. We were generally overwhelmed, when we got into a studio, by just how real and crucial this was. It's been that way ever since, especially when it comes to the mixing stage. I find this part of the process, when you are battling to get all the instruments and vocals balanced correctly against each other, extremely stressful. William Orbit calls it 'the agony and the ecstasy'.

There we all were, yammering away in the control room and demanding to be turned up in the mix. I confess there are a few places where the guitars ended up a bit too loud, and that's my fault. Stephen Street, who ended up producing nearly half the songs on *Leisure*, was pretty good at talking us into a compromise. 'If I turn you up and then I turn the drums up again, then we'll have to turn the bass up, so I'm going to have to turn everything down again.' He reminded me that the fader doesn't go on for ever.

For me there was always a magic about the studio. We used to record our B-sides with John Smith in Matrix Studios, in Coptic Street, near the British Museum. It was a small studio, and John was the only engineer present, so the mixing desk and all the rest of it became our territory.

All these experiences gradually taught us a little bit more about the music we wanted to make. A lot of early-1990s music came out of the rave scene or was related to Madchester, the Haçienda and Ecstasy, but that was never really my cup of tea. I was much more interested in hearing real drums, and for them to be a little more expressive than robotic drum machines. That looseness has gone now, to a certain extent; it's very rigid and to-tempo because more and more people are using digital audio workstations. Blur managed to get a few really good albums in, on which there were some loose, interesting, weird, terrific little songs. I'm especially proud of 'Country Sad Ballad Man' because the guitar is out of tune, but it works; it's got this woozy atmosphere, and I was able to squeeze in a bit of noise guitar at the end.

Even in the early days I discovered that something magical happened when you plugged your guitar into a distortion unit and strummed it through a flipping great Marshall amp. At that volume it was quite intoxicating. I wanted to reproduce the sound of the guitars on *Abbey Road* – that thick, bluesy sound – and the Marshall seemed to do it for me. This desire comes from my dark side. I was on the way to becoming 'the noisy person' in Blur, which was a little reductive, because as I've already pointed out, I liked a lot more than just noisy music.

———

Meanwhile, Young British Art was enjoying a big surge in media attention and popularity – not to mention commercially. It was a new sort of art that was about punchlines, humour and absurdity – not to mention dosh. In that way, it was pretty similar to the music industry, and I realised I would have felt just as fraudulent as an artist in that milieu. At least I could see a clear road ahead of me with the guitar, though not necessarily with painting. That was something I did purely for my own enjoyment.

The world of visual art and Goldsmiths was veering further away from me now, on a different forking path. Music and art had been equally important to me for so long, and I hung on to both of them for as long as I could, but I knew that with Blur I had chosen the right road. Either music or art was always going to be the thing that propelled me forward, with the other one taking a back seat. Still, I continued to make visual art and drawings for myself. I've just never been able to picture my stuff hanging on gallery walls. It's always been a little more private, a bit like how I listen to music. I don't listen to music in a very sociable way. I don't particularly enjoy doing it with other people. It's a very private thing for me. I couldn't sit and listen to Kate Bush's *The Kick Inside* with somebody else. It's the same as my drawing: it's very personal, depicting very specific moments of introspection that are perhaps only really meaningful to me.

Towards the end of 1990 we had to admit to ourselves that if this show was going to stay on the road, we were going to need a manager. At that point it was a toss-up between the rather old-school Chris Morrison and Mike Collins, who had previously managed one of my favourite British post-punk bands, Wire. We settled on Mike, for the sole reason that he took us out for a meal at Fred's, which was a small private members' bar in Soho, whereas Chris didn't take us anywhere and we didn't like the décor in his office. When we went to see Chris, he was giving someone a terrible hiding over the telephone – 'Get it fucking *done*!' – before slamming the receiver down, all smiles, when we came in. 'Oh, hello, boys . . .' We didn't think it was very nice, slamming phones, but what we should have been thinking was: 'This is the man for us.' But what did we know? We went with the guy who bought us bangers and mash at Fred's.

We got into trouble with the image we appropriated for the cover of our debut single, 'She's So High', released in the autumn of 1990 (the track also opened *Leisure*). It's a pop art painting from 1967 by Mel Ramos of a naked, raunchy young woman, based on Ursula Andress, lying on top of a hippopotamus. The posters got ripped down in a couple of student unions by feminists, which is fair enough. I didn't really know much about all that: I'd had my time at art school, trying to get my head round feminism and veganism and things like that, but I still wasn't very well equipped or prepared to deal with that kind of stuff. I was confused by it. I'd never come up against anything particularly political, but that was one of those things I would have to learn about very fast, through experience. Frankly, at the time I was just ecstatic to be able to walk around London holding hands with Jane and see the poster hovering above me on advertising hoardings.

'She's So High' only nibbled at the outer edges of the Top Forty. However, our follow-up, 'There's No Other Way', produced by the legendary Stephen Street, was a different story. Stephen's artistry punched some extra weight into the song's flickering dance beat, and after its release in April 1991 it soared all the way up to number eight. It didn't hurt that Kurt Cobain, one of the most visible rock stars on the planet at that moment, named it as his favourite track of the year in an interview with the *NME*. Thanks to these lucky breaks, the second half of 1991 saw Blur becoming an increasingly well-known name, and we found ourselves embarking on all sorts of promotional tours. The sole purpose of these jaunts was to do interviews around *Leisure*, and we were treated really well, with free food and first-class flights. I lost count of the weekends that were like a flip book of rides in private jets and expensive cars, posh food, then coming back to London and cadging drinks down the pub from Andy Ross, scraping together money from the back of the sofa for some chips and not really being able to afford to live. There was never any question of being paid a retainer. At that level of the pop music world, being a big name doesn't automatically translate into having a big bank account.

I did a few drawings for the band's cover art in the beginning, but they were sort of pooh-poohed by David Balfe and the rest of the team working with us. I could understand why: I was a draughts-man and painter, not a graphic designer. Damon and I were pretty arty buggers, and we had a strongly aesthetic attitude to the logos for Seymour and Blur. That rounded Blur typeface, with the 'r' that bleeds off the edge of the sleeve (which appeared for the first time in that form on the sleeve of 'There's No Other Way'), was how we originally conceived it.

———

In the late autumn of this momentous year we flew out over the Atlantic for our first tour of North America. Our debut on that continent was in Toronto, just before Halloween, followed by a couple of dates in New England, before our trial by fire in New York City. The New York show took place at the Marquee, in the city's Chelsea district. It was pretty good, even though we were a bit tanked-up before we went on. We knew it was an important show – representatives from our record company were sitting at a table in their posh suits. 1991 was a strange time to be an ultra-English band in North America. As they regarded us warily from their carefully positioned vantage point, we realised that, culturally, they just didn't get it – and that feeling was reciprocated from our side. English record labels were very down to earth, but the American ones reeked of business – money-lovers, not music-lovers. We were pretty pie-eyed when we got on stage, and we went totally nuts. It must have been a great show to watch, I imagine, and we played well. I'd been to a thrift store that day and had bought loads of toy soldiers, which I stood on my amplifier. There were so many cool things to buy in America, and I used to enjoy littering the stage with all the stuff I'd bought. Damon was up to his old tricks, swinging on the lighting rig, and he fell straight down onto the record execs' table, smashing all the glasses and bottles and a vase of flowers. They were horrified.

It was our first time in America, and it was hard. We were all petrified and insecure, and we hadn't been living away from home for very long. It was hard to be suddenly in this new world, facing an audience of Americans who, despite the common language, were massively different from us. We thought it would be fun, and it was – probably too much. But there was an awful lot of boredom too: long bus rides that stretched over nights and days, from East Coast to West, with us nursing hangovers and only each other for company. It wore us down. We didn't know how exhausting so many late nights and so much partying could get. I got very homesick and missed Jane an awful lot.

When I arrived back home, the fainting fits from my teenage vegetarian phase returned. A doctor ran some tests to see if my peptic ulcer had come back, but luckily it wasn't as drastic as that. Jane, however, was merciless. Every time I complained about my legs feeling wobbly, she asked, 'Do you need a doctor to put a finger up your bum again?'

———

Even though 1992 kicked off with some dates around Europe and our first trip to Japan, the multi-band Rollercoaster tour of the UK in March–April 1992 was by far and away the most rock 'n' roll adventure we had experienced up to that point. Blur was part of a package of co-headliners featuring some of my favourite 'alternative' bands: the Jesus and Mary Chain, My Bloody Valentine and Dinosaur Jr. It was the initiative of the Mary Chain's Jim Reid, who wanted to create a British equivalent of the Lollapalooza events in the US. Most of my memories of those eleven dates around the UK, culminating in three nights at the Brixton Academy in London, are somewhat blurry. The most abiding image is a hazy vision of a bowling alley somewhere in England where we all stopped for some rest and recreation. Picture the scene: three parallel bowling lanes, each occupied by one of the hottest indie acts in the world at the time. There's Jim Reid, a bottle of vodka in one hand and a heavy bowling ball in the other, which he proceeds to loft as high as he can into the air, cackling with glee as it slams down on the wooden flooring with an almighty bang. Next to him, Bilinda Butcher from My Bloody Valentine rolls her ball elegantly, oh so elegantly, so that it practically floats towards the waiting pins. In a third lane, the mighty yet quintessentially slack guitarist J Mascis from Dinosaur Jr is keeping score. He rouses himself from his customary torpor and knocks the pins flat with one shot. 'Are you guys havin' fun yet?' yells William Reid from under his straggly mop of black hair.

I find myself chatting with MBV's Kevin Shields. He hands me a joint, which I toke on, not wanting to seem uncool in front of one of my all-time guitar heroes. As the marijuana takes effect, I am massively overwhelmed by the moment: here I am, hanging out with Kevin Shields and Bilinda! The piercing reality of it freaks me out so much that I have to remove myself for a while. 'You'll have to give me a minute . . .' I say, as I back away in the direction of the toilets. Kevin just sits there like a Buddha in a pot cloud, beaming his beatific smile at me as balls roll and skittles tumble around him.

Considering this was an indie tour (rather than an orgiastic odyssey by one of the more famously decadent 1970s bands), things got pretty dangerous at times. The trio who made up Dinosaur Jr acted in a particularly off-the-chain fashion, largely because in the States – as we ourselves would discover all too soon – bands were held on a tight leash by their record labels and management teams that feared for their reputations. On their own, cast into the maelstrom of a British tour, they let their hair down, resulting in scenes like Dinosaur Jr's bass player Mike Johnson lobbing a beer glass across a bar at Damon while he was vamping on a hotel's grand piano, showering him in diamond-like shards and causing expensive damage to the instrument. On the tour's opening night in Brixton, Damon decided to 'do a Jim Morrison' – in other words, he pulled down his trousers and underpants and ran around the stage displaying his undercarriage, to be admired by all and sundry. (Well, My Bloody Valentine were a hard act to follow in those days.) Next day, after our soundcheck, J Mascis slouched into the dining room, sidled up to Damon and said, in his deadpan way, 'You gonna whip it out tonight?'

———

Our 'Popscene' single, which came out in March 1992, is often described as the exemplary proto-Britpop track. For us, it was just a little punk-rock number, whipped up like a pizza. We already had our basic margherita; we just grabbed whatever toppings and garnishes we liked and sprinkled them on top – the Beatles, Pink Floyd, the Kinks, the Who. Wire was the pepperoni, David Bowie the olives . . .

I got a bit grumpy about including the brass section on 'Popscene'. I thought of us as a guitar-driven indie band; anything else was a dilution. When the brass players from the Kick Horns started turning up at Matrix Studios, I was afraid the track would get a whole lot lighter. I preferred it when Damon wrote in a more introspective vein.

Although our manager Mike Collins was a lovely bloke, he didn't do a great job. In fact, we had to replace him, because it emerged that there had been some kind of screw-up with the accounts, which meant that tens of thousands of pounds disappeared, and as 1992 got under way we were abruptly informed that we were £60,000 in debt. I wasn't aware of any of this. I think Dave Rowntree probably understood it best, as he was the only one who was good with figures and paying attention during our long, tedious accountancy meetings, while I munched through an entire packet of biscuits (my only meal of the day). Suddenly we needed to do a lot more touring. The answer would be a hastily arranged, forty-four date trip around North America, from mid-April to the end of May, at the peak of the grunge era.

A mere seven days after the Rollercoaster tour had come to a standstill after three nights in London, and now under the new management of Chris Morrison (the Jesus and Mary Chain's manager), we were back on a plane to begin our make-or-break, last-chance-saloon American tour, with the sole purpose of recouping our calamitous debts. One of the earliest dates was a return to the Marquee in New York, a city whose music scene we now felt we comfortably fitted into. That was the first time we met Daniel Glass and Charles Koppelman, the owners of our American label. SBK Records, like Food in the UK, was affiliated to the giant EMI, and they projected a corporate, business-like attitude that we never got from Andy Ross back home.

These were first and foremost executives and industry men, who dressed like lawyers in expensively tailored, pinstriped suits. Blur was now a business asset. This was all about revenue, and it was made clear to us that everything we did as a band was ultimately a tributary to their wider income stream. They were upset to discover we weren't that kind of professional. 'Don't fuck up,' they warned us. We had formed a band believing our job was all about causing chaos. The way we saw it, SBK was pulling up the roots of rock 'n' roll and leaving them exposed to wither and die.

Their idea was that an artist could *hint* at a kind of vague freakishness, but they demanded professionalism above all else. Meetings with SBK were full of motivational management speak: 'This is your chance to reach for the golden ring.' To us it was just marketing bullshit from suits with big fat cigars. In the course of one meeting, their expectations became significantly diminished, and the ring was quickly downgraded from gold to brass. It all confused us, and we repeated phrases from these futile meetings in a spirit of mockery. But they were giving us deadly serious ultimatums.

This emphasis on not offending anybody was something we only really encountered in the US. Nevertheless, SBK was quite happy to put a promo sticker calling us 'The most shaggable band of the year' on our albums. Throughout the tour, local radio hosts asked us to explain what 'shaggable' meant.

The irony was that audiences – or customers, from SBK's perspective – weren't having any of that enforced professionalism. They wanted mayhem, a crazy night out with blood, sweat and rock 'n' roll. (In Japan, by contrast, audiences would sit still and respectful. I learnt to let my feedback resound for ages, because I knew they wouldn't start to applaud until the song had completely died away.) At dates around the Midwest, or in little college towns like Ithaca and Providence, in difficult venues like Club Babyhead, which were real toilets, we'd just get drunk, play loud and go nuts, then carry on partying until we could party no longer. That's how we got through the homesickness and the freakiness of it. We didn't really know how to do it any other way.

While we were touring America, I took a photocopied picture of Audrey Hepburn everywhere we went. I had been in love with Audrey ever since me and my sister watched her in *Two for the Road*, a film with Albert Finney. We loved her purely for her sunglasses and outfits. The picture was a lovely portrait that reminded me of Jane. Wherever I went, I Blu-tacked this thing up: in the tour bus, on my headboard, on a wall in my hotel room. She was very beautiful but also sweet and kind of awkward. She suited the person I thought I was at the time.

But my thoughts about women like Audrey Hepburn remained in the realm of aesthetics, even sculpture. When I think about the female form, it's something other than sexual attraction. For me, it's about observing proportions, shape and how the face is put together. In the history of art there have been thousands of sculptures inspired by particular areas of the female body – the lower back or the spot where the hip begins to extend from the waist. That's why many artists, such as Degas and Picasso, were obsessed with ballet and dance. So my relationship with Audrey was purely aesthetic. That said, it hit me very hard when she died in early 1993.

That US tour of 1992 lasted two months, and it was even more gruelling because we were with the Senseless Things, who were smashing company but liked to live in the fast lane. I'd never had that amount of freedom before, and it was the first time I've ever pushed things to the limit. There were no adults in charge, and tour managers were quite bad influences in those days. One of them was the legendary Gimpo, an associate of the KLF and Zodiac Mindwarp, who was deaf in one ear after serving in the Falklands

War. He was a total lunatic. His party trick, which he used to perform on board our very long coaches, was to crouch at the rear
end of the aisle and instruct the driver to slam the brakes on at the
next red light. When the coach screeched to a stop, he would be
propelled from where he was sitting like a frog and fly the entire
length of the vehicle, slamming into the dashboard and crumpling
onto the floor. When it came to our per diems, or daily spending
money, he would ask if we wanted to be paid in cash or acid. 'If it's
acid you want, it's in the fridge.' We just wanted fag money. Lovely
bloke, but mad as a hatter.

Since we couldn't afford to fly everywhere, we'd be on a tour bus,
travelling through the night. Alex loved the glamour of it – this was
what he had signed up for. Dave did his job without much fuss,
and Damon gave the impression of coping well as the frontman.
If anyone in the band was finding it problematic, they kept it to
themselves. I found the whole stint very difficult over the long haul.
At times I felt like Odysseus carving his way slowly home across
the wide Mediterranean. Back home in London, Jane seemed to
have several suitors. Meanwhile, I was being driven mad because I
could never seem to get the American phones to work. I couldn't
understand how to call an outside line from my hotel. Sometimes
I'd chance on a phone in the kitchen of some grotty venue, dial her
number and get through, exchanging a few words with her in the
middle of the night.

I didn't like being away for that amount of time. I was twenty-
three, and while playing the songs was fun, the sort of life we were
living on the road telescoped down to an ultimately exhausting
cycle of drinking, playing, travelling. One morning we had to leave
particularly early, which irritated me so much I chucked a couple

of things at a mirror on the tour bus. Emotionally immature, I was learning my partying limits the hard way. The tour manager is meant to keep you in some sort of order, but there's not a lot they can do if you're determined to stay up extremely late. In the end the lost sleep catches up with you and leaves you tired, emotional and very grumpy.

I'm not sure the touring really fixed our financial troubles either. If any discussions were taking place about the band being in debt, I was left out of them, thankfully. As far as I was aware, we were in debt because of Mike Collins's incompetence, rather than anything darker. We were still mates out on the road, living in close proximity to one another, mostly remaining professional. We didn't discuss our problems or frustrations, so they came out in short emotional outbursts. My role became defined as the moaner of the band, while the others were more relaxed about living it up. As well as homesickness and missing Jane, there was the culture shock to deal with, day in, day out. The language proved to be pretty different, as did the culture of the record labels.

One evening, en route from Minneapolis to Vancouver across the Dakota Hills, we stopped off in a tumbleweedy town called Miles City in Montana. It boasted a single hotel and a bar/brewery, plus a scattering of shacks, run-down houses and other bits and bobs. On this tour I had become mates with the Senseless Things' drummer, Cass Browne, and he and I conceived this fantastic idea of going to the pub, whose parking lot was crammed with pickup trucks. It was a proper all-American bar, with a billiard table and massive blokes covered in grease, baseball caps and beards. Me and Cass started a game of pool as partners, playing doubles with another couple of guys. Foolishly, we tried to follow the rules that we'd use in the Good Mixer back in Camden. We were playing English pool, and our opponents were absolutely outraged. After we'd had a couple of drinks, Cass shot the break, hitting the balls as hard as he could, putting so much effort into the shot that his feet actually left the ground. As he landed he shouted, 'BANG!' This didn't sit well with our opponents, who started shouting at us, asking what game we thought we were playing. 'We're playing fuckin' billiards here! Fuckin' limeys! Pinheads!' I tried to calm Cass down, but he was totally unaware that these guys weren't the friendly types you get in films. 'Oh, fuck, don't listen to them idiots,' he said. These, however, were the kind of idiots who would happily smash a pool cue over our backs. Even though we were rather light-headed by that point, we came to the mutual understanding that we ought to vacate the place before someone knocked our lights out.

We were sailing close to the wind on stage too. We had gained a certain notoriety because of our health-and-safety-baiting live act, and people came anticipating a spectacle of self-destruction. I thought that's how bands were meant to be. I didn't watch a Mick Jagger documentary as a teenager and decide that being intelligent and prudent with money was the way to be a musician. After all, I grew up watching *The Kids Are Alright*, the Who film. Keith Moon and Pete Townshend were role models, and although we never achieved anything near to what those two got up to, what we did was painful enough. We would play big American dates with the same level of frenzy as a show at the Cricketers in the Oval. I think we did our bit for rock 'n' roll in the US.

A lot of this is visible in the *Starshaped* documentary, which was shot on trips to Sweden and Germany and at various weekend-away festivals around Europe a little later in 1992. Ceri Levy, an old mate, accompanied us and filmed all the mayhem. There was a lot of being sick at airports and increased craziness at gigs. Damon was back to swinging from the lighting rigs or head-butting the speaker stacks – on one date a wobbly pile of speakers rocked and spilled over his feet after he attacked it. There wasn't a single gig that didn't see blood being shed at some point, whether it was coming out of your finger or you'd ripped a bit of your toe off because you'd done something stupid. Once, I broke off the headstock of my guitar because I used to do these backward rolls, but I could never get them quite right – I never practised!

In order to achieve the energy and mental state needed to perform, Damon and I fed off each other. If he took to the air, so did I. Sometimes I would be moody and contrary, or play deliberately badly – usually if I was feeling fatigued or had drunk too much before the show. The audience could also inspire you to certain behaviours. The American males who dominate the mosh pit can be more frattish – 'Blur, you fuckin' rock!' – unlike the sensitive indie types you'd find in the UK. While the girls shot us sweet and endearing looks, I would mock the lads by repeating their ape-like noises back to them. The girls would laugh at that.

Strangely, though, Blur's stage antics didn't feel like we were going bonkers as a team. It was more like four individuals externalising the feelings and frustrations that had been building up all day. All of us were overheated, sweating out the previous day's alcohol intake. Damon was working his arse off, attempting to conduct all his endless jittery energy down towards the earth. Alex was just trying to look sexy. Dave banged away at his drums, head down, drenched in sweat, trying to avoid Damon's occasional assaults on his tom-toms. Me, I was exorcising my general on-stage discomfort and paradoxical need for affirmation. After-show parties provided a necessary oblivion, removing the need to discuss any of this. We probably should have carved out a bit more time for ourselves.

BRIT
EXPLOSION

America cleansed us of any lingering desire to ape the music that was coming out of it. Besides, by the time we returned to Britain, there was a new phenomenon to deal with: the first stirrings of the musical tendencies that would soon be dubbed (or cursed?) with the name 'Britpop'.

Stuff they never tell you before you're famous, part two: the world loves the next big thing. And when you eventually become part of that big thing, a lot of people turn up wanting to play some part in your story. You need to learn who to allow through the security rope – and learn fast. You want to experience everything, and pretty much everything is on offer. You're still going to feel too shy and mistrustful to fully jump into it, and you can't bring yourself to believe that the people who want to get to know you might be beasts who only want to steal something from you. But that's how it is.

For the first year or so, we would all merrily sink as much booze as we wanted before a gig. Soon we realised how unworkable that was going to be and came to mutual agreement: no more than two bottles of beer before we went on stage. That was the rule, and we didn't break it. Post-show was a different story. There was no one around who was going to say, 'Graham, do you really think that's a good idea? Maybe you should have an early night.' It was always, 'Yeah, yeah, come on, Graham,' and then we'd all explode and grab whatever nightlife was going, and before you knew it, two or three weeks later, you'd be sitting in the bath in tears, at eleven in the morning, and be like, 'What's going on? Why can't I stop crying?' That's what touring was, and that was the whole of the 1990s.

The one exception where we broke our own rule – or rather, it was after this that the rule was instigated – was at the Town & Country Club (now the Forum) in London, on 23 July 1992. Blur, Suede, Mega City Four and another band called 3½ Minutes had agreed to play an event called Gimme Shelter, on behalf of the homeless charity Shelter. Suede were third on the bill, and we were headlining, so during the afternoon we found ourselves in the local neighbourhood with time to kill. Dave and Damon both went home to do some laundry, so Alex and I looked at each other and decided to go on a wander around Camden. This was before we knew the area so well, and we got lost and ended up on an impromptu pub crawl, bumping into various characters, including, fatally, the notorious indie scenester Jon 'Fat' Beast. By the time we got back to the Forum, we were a tad the worse for wear. Damon took one look at the state of us, and instead of brewing up some strong black coffee, decided he needed to catch up fast. Dave had also started on the booze, so naturally he joined the party. To be blunt, we went on stage completely off our nuts.

I'll be honest: the show that night was a total embarrassment. But what made it worse – apart from the disrespect to Shelter – was that we were totally outclassed by Suede. They triumphed that night: they did a tight, energetic show, while Blur's set was a kamikaze, drunken, mad thing. It was certainly a legendary night and helped propel Brett Anderson's band into the first division of the new British acts. Ironically, I think more people remember our gig than Suede's, though, just because it marked a make-or-break moment for Blur. Chris Morrison was fuming and gave us a sharp dressing-down in front of everybody at the aftershow. David Balfe threatened to drop us from Food unless we got our shit together within a month.

Musically, Suede were not really my cup of tea, though I didn't have any issues with the individual members. It was all a little too obviously Bowie-influenced for my taste, and I wasn't a big fan of the romantic squalor of Brett's lyrics. There was always bound to be a frisson of rivalry between Suede and Blur, of course, because Damon had stolen Brett's girlfriend, Justine Frischmann, from under his nose.

———

When I returned from that second US tour, Jane and I moved from Lewisham to a new flat in central London. The block in Moxon Street, just off the Marylebone High Street, overlooked Paddington Street Gardens, a small city park, and we could climb out of our kitchen window and sit on the roof, looking over the treetops and beyond to the massive expanse of London. It was a beautiful summer, but the pressure gauge was rising. Blur was already becoming the target of tabloid gossip columnists. In the *Daily Star*, for instance, Linda Duff wrote some fake news about me having an affair with Emma Anderson from Lush. In the second half of 1992 my relationship with Jane broke down. Perhaps the two big absences while I was away in America had holed it below the waterline; more likely it was never going to be sustainable anyway, but it hit me quite hard. Blur demanding more of my time, and her working for Savage & Best – the 'Britpop' PR agency – complicated things.

After we split up, there was a period when we still had to share the same living space in Marylebone, which I found heartbreaking. That was the hardest relationship I have ever had to get over – it took me a couple of years. Sometimes I ran into her at shows, so it was difficult to forget her and move on. With hindsight, it may not have been a particularly healthy relationship, but I certainly felt at home in it at that point in my life.

I was effectively homeless when we eventually left Moxon Street, but Andy Ross came to my rescue by inviting me to live in a flat he owned in Marlborough Road, Archway, in north London. He himself lived near the Good Mixer pub in Camden, with his partner Helen Potter, and he charged me only a peppercorn rent for this ground-floor, two-room flat with a tiny kitchen. I don't know what I would have done otherwise. Andy kept me reasonably buoyant with a couple of pints of lager every so often and made sure I was fed at least once or twice a week, usually at the local Lebanese restaurant in Camden, or with a home-cooked chilli con carne. He was quietly supportive and ensured I stayed fairly grounded. As an example of Andy's limitless patience and tact, one night I discovered I had lost my set of front-door keys after coming back from the pub. He was away, and I had to call him in a state of some distress. Instead of 'fessing up, I concocted some preposterous fiction about having been mugged on my way home by a man who looked like Walter Matthau. I'm sure he didn't believe a word of it, but he didn't make it into a big deal.

In other respects, I didn't have an outlet for confiding my painful thoughts, so I relied a good deal on my sketchbooks. I sort of invented art therapy for myself. My pages from that time veer all over the place, from hilarious caricatures to scribbles so violent they almost tear through the page. My mood swings are pretty apparent in the art. I used to be fond of drawing creatures with the heads of pompous old men and the bodies of gerbils that stood in a glass and said something silly in a speech bubble. In some ways my output was quite similar to the sketches and cartoons John Lennon drew while he was in the Beatles.

———

We never planned the whole Britpop explosion. In the early 1990s British music could have gone in so many directions. There was a band I adored, the House of Love, who were signed to Creation Records and touted as the next big follow-up to U2. But their guitarist, Terry Bickers, flipped out and went on to start another, more psychedelia-influenced band called Levitation. We used to go and see bands together and would end up drinking at the Camden Falcon with Terry's bandmate Bic and the drummer, Dave Francolini. These people were fun but extremely dangerous to hang out with. I was happy with a couple of pints of ale, but those guys used to call themselves space pilots and were into the heaviest of psychedelics. It was a merry band, but not good for my long-term mental health. I have a hazy memory of encountering Shane MacGowan around the same time and trying to have a conversation, but he couldn't speak, so we had to communicate by laughing. The way you laughed communicated a certain idea. You could study his teeth, or lack of them, for however long you wanted, because his mouth was constantly open, laughing.

It was Damon really who made the biggest difference in shaping a distinctively English voice, thanks to his lyrics and the way he sang. My guitar-playing got more sophisticated, less noisy; my admiration for George Harrison, Dave Davies of the Kinks and even Mick Ronson began to come out. People around us were commenting that the songs sounded a bit 'Bowie-ish' or 'Pink Floyd-ish' – in other words, more English. Even the song title 'Ernold Same' sounded like 'Arnold Lane'!

We just allowed the 'Englishness' to happen; we didn't search it out. We didn't have much time to think about it because we got signed very quickly – we'd barely written ten songs together before we got our deal. We didn't quite know who we were yet or where we were headed. If our career was a high-speed train journey, then our second album, *Modern Life Is Rubbish*, was a very important stop on the way to the big city called *Parklife*. It was a transitional album but is still one of my favourites, and it opened the way towards the later ones, on which Damon's lyrics really matured. From D. H. Lawrence to Martin Amis, it all came down to whatever he was reading at the time.

Embarking on the recordings that resulted in *Modern Life Is Rubbish* in the early autumn of 1992, we invited the quintessentially English Andy Partridge to come in as our producer. At Church Studios in Crouch End, he took control of our sound in a way that, to me, sounded really good, only it didn't quite have the edge we were hoping for. If anything, it resembled his own bands – XTC and the more psychedelic Dukes of Stratosphear – a little too much. There's nothing wrong with how these early tracks sounded, but at that particular point in time I don't think it represented us as a band. But he was fantastic to hang out with and he taught me lots of XTC licks. I nearly killed him when I told him about a dinner lady at my junior school who had a distinctive mole with hairs coming out of it, which I always used to think of whenever I saw one of those chips with hairy black bits that used to turn up in school dinners. He found that so hilarious he almost suffocated with laughter. These days I don't think Andy speaks too fondly of us. I believe he thought we were all nuts and that I was drinking too much. To be fair, I probably was.

It took Damon a while to allow himself to write about his personal experiences, or to present them in a way that made it obvious they related to him. It would be 1999 and the album *13* before he did a song like 'No Distance Left to Run', which expresses how cut up he was about him and Justine Frischmann splitting up. As a band, though, we didn't have the kind of relationship where we could truly open up about these things to each other. We were emotionally quite stunted and didn't really get into all that business. In some ways, that made us guilty of exactly the thing we claimed to hate: the classic English stiff upper lip. 'Don't bring that crap in here,' someone once actually said to me when I arrived at the studio. 'Leave that shit at the door, we're here to work.'

Bands can very quickly become a macho realm. Put a bunch of men together in any kind of group, and pretty soon they'll be slotting into their stereotypical roles (in a band it's alphas, betas and drummers). There's always one who's more inclined to throw his weight around – in Oasis it was Liam, in our case Damon. Not that Damon was a conventional alpha male by any means: he may have been an extrovert, but there was also plenty he held back. After all, English blokes are not so upfront about their emotions, and in the 1990s it still felt quite uncomfortable to talk about your feelings. Damon had his own anxieties, for sure, but he dealt with them by keeping more to himself. As the lead singer, he was Blur's most recognisable face; it was him that made the news, got interviewed more often and had to soak up all sorts of criticism and ridicule from the press ('Who is this middle-class person putting on this East End accent?' and all that). It was a huge burden to shoulder, and we mentioned it among ourselves sometimes but tended to laugh it off. 'It's a bummer, innit?' we might say, and clap him on the back. But telling someone, 'Chin up, mate,' is not the same as real, constructive support.

That was just how we dealt with things. You put your lab coat on, went into the studio and you worked. By now we were being let loose in Matrix Studios on our own – no producer, just the in-house engineer, John Smith – and on one particularly success-ful and efficient day we managed to record 'Peach', 'Bone Bag', 'Resigned' and 'Oily Water'. That was our best day of recording ever, resulting in some of my favourite Blur material, and the last two tracks proved to be of good enough quality to be included on *Modern Life Is Rubbish*. Damon had an incredibly strong work ethic and expected everyone to fall into line. I loved that. I had a great time in the studio; there was something for me to do every day. Using a cheap reverb box and a wah-wah pedal rocked back to its least trebly position, I tried to create a spooky, atmospheric guitar sound – like a ghost in an industrial space. I hated sitting around at home, not doing anything. If I ever found myself in that situation, I would just head for the pub.

These days the music industry is much more willing to acknow-ledge the issues around addiction and mental health. That's a good thing, of course, but I sometimes find it's talked about too much. When constantly checking your mental-health status becomes obligatory, that in itself can generate anxiety when there wasn't any beforehand. It creates a kind of hypochondria, leading you to question whether natural, problematic feelings are actually some kind of syndrome.

Dave was the first member of Blur to admit to needing help. As with many bands, there was always plenty of alcohol swilling around us. We were well aware of each other's capacity when we were together. Alex was very much the Sinatra-style drinker, brandishing a champagne bottle or cocktail glass as an accessory, but you never knew whether he was actually drinking any of it. It surprised me to discover that Dave's drinking carried on in his private life, and I began hearing from people I knew that he was out of control. Things happened to him that were borderline dangerous – he fell over, bashed his nose on the road, fell asleep in front of a fire and woke up with his face half cooked. He was older than us and had begun drinking in Colchester, to compensate for his boring job as a computer programmer for the council. He managed to quit just before we made the 'Girls and Boys' video. It's incredible looking back on it, but the rest of us weren't terribly respectful of that decision and gave him rather a hard time for it. Applying peer group pressure – and joshing with anyone who resisted it – just seemed like the natural way to behave in those days.

When we had our studio lab coats on, metaphorically speaking, the recording sessions for those first albums were hard graft. We had to be on our toes. We stopped working material out in advance at rehearsals. Instead, Damon would arrive in the middle of a studio session with a hastily taped demo on a cassette; or he would announce, 'Hey, I've got this song,' and then would play it on an acoustic guitar. I would have a very short amount of time to get to grips with what the song was about, its emotional drive, how personal it was, and then we'd jam around the chord sequence and chip away at what we had until there was some shape to it. Damon's demos are often crackly and inaudible, but it's usually obvious whether he's come up with a song that will work or not. He has a special gift for chord changes, and for singing melody lines that really show those changes off well. His piano songs are more melancholic, more sophisticated, but when he started writing on an acoustic guitar later in the decade, the songs became simpler and more direct in some ways. By the time he got to the chorus, we would know.

A strong bassline, a rhythm that fitted, a good little lick on the guitar, a riff – we just needed to find them, and when we had all that, the rest wrote itself. Once we had got those bits right, and once Damon started to sing his verse-y part, we would very quickly know whether or not it was a good song.

'Let's do it. What are the chords? Write them down. OK, Dave, let's go!'

Some of our odd, very English tunes, like 'Villa Rosie' and 'Clover Over Dover', started like this. After a few run-throughs of a new song, we would reach a point where we felt ready to begin recording it. I'd be trying to make the chords interesting instead of just strumming the rhythm, which wasn't enough for me. That was my job: to add the ear candy with lead-guitar lines, unexpected instruments and backing vocals.

We had to earn our freedom. At first we had to have our demos approved by the label, and they'd go, 'Yeah, you can record these three songs.' After they'd booked us studio time, Damon would bring another demo in, such as 'Girls and Boys', and Stephen Street would say, 'That's good, let's have a go at that.' Then we'd all get told off because the label hadn't given us the go-ahead to do it. In the end they trusted us to come up with the goods. Stephen was the adult in the room whom we badly needed. It all worked best when we had someone like that who could say, 'That's a bit too much,' or, 'I think seventeen hooks in this song is enough. Let's not have any more.' We did some fantastic work with him, and with other producers who were confident enough to give us useful critical feedback. I loved being in the studio. It was magic to me, and it still is. I love the idea of two or three pieces of music which didn't exist that morning existing after a day's work. Plus, you've been creative and you've been hanging out with your mates in an interesting environment. It's my favourite workplace.

Outside the studio, I had fallen in with a new group of friends, mostly from London's small-label punk scene, who hung out at places like the newly opened Blow Up club at the Laurel Tree in Camden Town, which was the prime watering hole for emerging Britpop musicians and scenesters. I had even started a new relationship with Jo Johnson from Huggy Bear, who were becoming the most notorious act of the riot grrrl movement. They supported Blur at a strange little gig at the Hibernian Club in Fulham on 17 December 1992, when we gave out our 'Wassailing Song' seven-inch as a Christmas present to the audience.

I had seen a couple of Huggy Bear gigs at the Camden Underworld and loved all the shouting and chaos and noise and attitude; plus I thought they looked cool. Their bassist, Niki Elliott, and Jo, the guitarist, loved to dance, and they turned up frequently at the Blow Up club. Jo and I got chatting and totally hit it off. I thought she was super-hip, we made each other laugh a lot, and she and her bandmates were into great music. That was enough for me. They got me into artists like Irma Thomas, Maxine Brown, Nation of Ulysses, Pavement, Fugazi, Rites of Spring and Slant 6. That's when I started actively championing girl bands. It became important to me, and I realised there was a whole bunch of female American groups doing much more interesting stuff than the English boys on guitars.

It was an interesting time for me, and for the music scene generally, with a rare openness among my new friends and a feeling of opportunities to be seized. There was an overriding freedom and plenty to absorb musically, but all of it got sucked into the Britpop vortex. I think of all the bands associated with that movement, Blur was the least narrow-minded. We didn't limit our music-listening. We came out of the indie scene, but we were rooted in the 1960s, the 1970s, new wave, disco and Chic, Rainbow, the Buzzcocks, Bowie's 'Ashes to Ashes' and 'Start' by the Jam. I was listening to Duke Ellington, Beethoven, all my dad's records – whatever was lying around. And, of course, you can always learn a lot from the Beatles. There was so much potential that it was almost overwhelming. In contrast, the little planet of indie music was governed by so many petty regulations. You were not supposed to walk or talk like a mainstream, major-label act. If it looked as though you were actively trying to write a hit, you could easily be accused of selling out. Rockist gestures such as guitar solos were constrained too. I wasn't afraid of playing them, but I had to stay away from being particularly cock-rocky, masculine or bluesy. That's why so many of my guitar solos were so awkward, even self-effacing at times.

By the time the 1990s came around, our generation of bands didn't seem to carry a weight equivalent to the big hitters of the 1960s or '70s. Blur wasn't as heavy as Cream or Led Zeppelin; we didn't sell as many records as the Beatles or the Kinks; we weren't as disruptive as the Sex Pistols or the Buzzcocks. Graham Coxon was just the name my parents slapped on me; did it send thrills through people's bodies in the way hearing the name Pete Townshend did to mine?

Perhaps we should have been more obsessed with being cool. We were vulnerable, and I sometimes overcompensated for my reticence by openly confessing how I felt. We had no party line; we were not very professional. All of us are actors to a certain degree, but if you compare people like me and Damon or Jarvis Cocker to somebody like David Bowie, he was an incredible actor and took the idea of playing a character to a whole other level. He never seemed to be out of character and made this entity, 'David Bowie', into an ongoing work of art that kept on evolving right up until his death. It was extremely serious, groundbreaking art, yet it also succeeded in selling tons of units. I was always so impressed with how Bowie gave the impression of having so much time on his hands to achieve everything he did. We in Blur were just too manically busy to dress elegantly. Our haircuts were important, and we dabbled with being reasonably smart, but our work clothes had a Barnardo's charity shop or Velvet Underground via Primal Scream look: narrow jeans, stripy T-shirts, suit jackets and desert boots. That was the aesthetic of the anti-Establishment tribe we felt we belonged to.

As the 1990s scene became marketed and sensationalised, everything seemed to get more commercialised, which wiped out a lot of what had inspired me in the late 1980s. For Blur, the amount of recording we had to do became an exhausting conveyor belt, leaving little time to rest and recuperate. The amount of B-sides we had to write on the hoof was equivalent to an album. Sometimes it came without warning from the label: 'We need a B-side quick. There's a studio round the corner' – and this was while we were in Philadelphia. 'Jesus, quick, we have to record a B-side. Have you got anything?'

It felt like business; it wasn't fun. Perhaps I was being a spoilt brat, but I had a problem with the fact that our band was doing really, really well, yet it wasn't just ours any more. It pained me that we'd become this commercial thing, with people around us using *Spinal Tap* language about 'working this band' and 'breaking America'. I couldn't quite believe that this cute, innocent band we'd started was turning into a business concern for so many people. Ownership seemed to have been handed over to the fans, and to record labels all over the world, and they all had their own idea of what Blur should be and how we should behave, and because of our exuberance we always seemed to mess it up in every territory we went to. My revenge on the suits and breadheads would come at the live shows, where every song would be twice as fast and five times more noisy than on the record. But it was a pretty hollow kind of victory.

———

Every band has its arguments, but I started to bicker with the others over silly things: for example, when Damon got into football and adopted the Britpop uniform of football strip and sportswear. Personally, I didn't think the cultures of soccer and indie music mixed very well (although I wasn't averse to donning a green Nike T-shirt every once in a while), and ever since my school days I'd considered 'casuals' to be the enemy. It was all part of a new emerging lad culture, and it coincided with a time when I was rejecting all that. I was against anything remotely sexist and was championing girl bands and female musicians, and taking it seriously. It was the era of magazines like *Loaded* and *Nuts*, which were mainstream publications promoting unreconstructed sexism under the cover of irony. Damon was our spokesman, even though he often didn't actually say very much at all, while Alex would be slightly rude about the younger audience members. Next to those two good-looking blokes I felt great frustration that I wasn't really heard or taken much notice of. I kept on getting interrupted, and it just seemed like my childhood all over again, so I reacted pretty badly to it.

My escape hatch at the time was my relationship with Jo and her friends in Huggy Bear – Chris, Jon and Niki. They were the total antithesis of *Loaded* culture. From the outside they came across as spiky and confrontational – they famously started a mass brawl on the late-night youth TV show *The Word*, like cowboys smashing up a saloon in a western. But in private they weren't as serious about life as people made out. They had a particular aversion to Linda Duff from the *Daily Star*, who wrote all kinds of negative things about them, implying that they were man-haters. They weren't.

Evenings at the Slampt club at the Laurel Tree and energising gigs by punk groups like Lung Leg, Fugazi and Skinned Teen felt like my community. Nobody in that scene was bothered that I was in a much bigger band. I was a guitar player and had just as much to learn as anybody else, and I picked up an awful lot from Huggy Bear and the other groups I hung out with. Huggy Bear were painted with this big brush of negativity, when actually they remained very positive: they believed in putting your heart and soul into music, and they weren't especially hateful of anybody. They were just honest and not particularly interested in what was happening in the mainstream. That was their only crime.

I've never laughed so much as I did with them; their sense of humour was incredible. I still love them all as people, purely because of what they got me into and how they treated me. They could have been horrible to me. I could have been this misogynistic idiot from a Britpop band, but they actually saw me as I really am, which many others didn't at that time. I was clashing heavily with the Britpop thing and didn't feel the need to refer to women's body parts in a rude way, as the people around me seemed to enjoy doing. I thought it was a backwards move. It's not that I didn't have the odd raunchy thought about a woman; it's just that I didn't feel the need to mouth off loudly and crudely about it.

Blur was never a groupie-ish kind of group. We were a bit too polite and decent for that sort of thing, on the whole. There were plenty of girls around Blur, but it wasn't how I imagine it was in the 1960s and '70s, when seemingly you had only to trip over a pair of shoes and you'd land naked on top of some willing person. Alex went the furthest of all of us in that respect. He was more interested in the idea of glamour, hanging out with models, wearing nice clothes, going to all kinds of clubs, both gay and straight. He was living in Covent Garden and mixing with celebrities, artists like Damien Hirst and chefs at the Groucho Club – all very chic compared with the north London pubs I was haunting. There was a lot of mischievous fun, but to me it felt fairly superficial, without much integrity. But who was I to say?

Alex took to his playboy role with ease. For me, there was effort involved in getting physical with a girl – approaching them, talking to them, and so on – and these were skills I didn't naturally have. I confess that occasionally I would be talking to a girl, and she'd get so frustrated that she'd burst out, 'Just come on, for fuck's sake. Will you stop messing around? Are we going to get on with this or not?'

It was never really at the top of my list of things that I wanted to achieve in an evening. Maybe if I hadn't been drinking so heavily, I'd have had a little more propensity to talk. I always felt there was something hollow and not very pleasant about those experiences. I wouldn't call them groupie encounters, because I was very fond of everybody it happened with. It's fair to say I wasn't very good at one-night stands, however. The guilt and hollowness of them left me feeling pretty grim. Many times I'd be so wrecked that nothing would happen anyway.

More often than not, on a typical night in around 1993–4 I would head home at closing time. I'd buy some chips in pitta bread, get the bus and go home to bed. It wasn't until much later that I realised that stuff actually happens *after* closing time. Then I started going to the Underworld in Camden on Friday nights, and it got that little bit more messy. I had to buy the doormen a drink just so they would be nice to me when they were throwing me out.

I loved dressing up in my parka and desert boots and heading off to dance at Blow Up. A pair of DJs – Andy Lewis, who often played records as a warm-up at Blur shows, and Paul Tunkin – opened Blow Up at the Laurel Tree pub in Camden in late 1993, and their eclectic music tastes helped to define the mod-influenced sound whirl around Britpop in London for most of the 1990s: a colourful, sparkling mix of lounge music, danceable jazz, French pop, psychedelia, cult TV themes, glam rock and new-wave bangers. When I arrived, I would usually buy a lager straight away and then go to the cloakroom to hang up my parka. The attendant would drop a little 'bomb', wrapped in a Rizla, into my pint and that would be it. It was a really nice time: everyone was happy, dancing and looking fantastic. There wasn't much room for dark thoughts at Blow Up.

Things happened on the streets when alcohol made me let my guard down. Once, I was leaving a fashion party that I had grown tired of. I was dressed up in a blue jacket, desert boots and purple cords, with a canvas bag at my waist and a fag between my fingers, standing in front of a row of popping camera flashguns. Blinded, somewhat oiled and desperate to escape, I sprinted across the street and rolled onto the bonnet of a moving car and off the other side. The driver and his girlfriend were petrified. They phoned for an ambulance, but it took so long to arrive that in the end I asked the couple to drive me home themselves. They very kindly did just that, and I was fine. I was lucky that the car had been moving relatively slowly. That situation could have ended up a whole lot worse, even fatal. Nowadays, thanks to my paternal instincts I have become a one-man Tufty Club when it comes to road safety.

———

Incidents like that didn't exactly help my mood. Alcohol gives me such hideously dark thoughts. The monsters were starting to creep back onto the pages of my notebooks whenever I was struck with the urge to do some drawing – sometimes even when I got home after a night out.

My anxiety stems from internalising an awful lot of stuff. Mix together equal parts anger and shame, and you get a nice cocktail of humiliation. All those negative feelings seemed ever-present. I used to call it my 'constant buzz of embarrassment'. Without being fully conscious of it, I was looking for a way to keep that anxiety at bay. When you're young, you don't necessarily know what anxiety is. You don't even know that it exists; you can't give those feelings a name; you don't know if it's unique to you or whether everybody feels it. I thought it was just part of the general sensation of being alive. And that quickly led to me feeling that I didn't particularly like the sensation of being alive. Which, in turn, would often lead me towards other, darker thoughts.

I think my attachment to alcohol began with that desire to chisel the edges off that constant anxiety. At parties I would usually be a little bit more oiled than everybody else, but also funny with it. It wasn't like I would turn nasty, although eventually I would get a bit growly. I think that people tend to believe it's the drink, drink and a chaser of drink that make you an alcoholic, but I reckon it has more to do with your general levels of anxiety – feeling isolated, or not fitting in or being heard. When you're an adult, you discover that all these things, which often start in childhood, can be soothed by alcohol, and then you become reliant on it.

There's nothing more horrible than when your mind is in what I call a 'washing-machine state' – when there are far too many things in there, spinning round and round. A shirt and a pair of jeans would be fine, but everything else seems to have snuck in there; the drum is too full and stuff is banging around. Whenever my stressed mind got like that, as soon as a drop of alcohol touched my tongue that washing machine would slow down and come to a stop. All those dogfighting, buzzing little fighter planes in my mind would coalesce into a single, beautiful silver blimp. You could tap it and it would just float, weightless, and it seemed like peace.

If you talk to people who rely on alcohol to unwind – which is always the first sign of trouble – quite often it's because they don't have peace of mind. The problem with me was that when I became reliant on it, the relief was very short-term, and the anxiety that followed that brief respite was even worse than it was before. It was a pretty nasty little cycle. I wasn't particularly fond of that feeling, although sometimes it felt like a fair trade. If I hadn't drunk for a couple of months and then things started to get on top of me again, I'd think, 'I'm going to feel terrible tomorrow . . . but it's going to be worth it for those few hours of peace of mind.' Afterwards, the hangover would assume dominance, and I'd wonder if it really had been worth it. So I'd drink the hangover away, come to my senses a couple of days later with even higher levels of anxiety, and the whole cycle would have escalated another notch.

All our gigs were either great or terrible because of alcohol. For me, medicating with beer or wine was the only way to have fun on stage or deal with my social awkwardness away from it. There's nothing worse than playing a big show in front of tons of awesome people while feeling like you look idiotic, ugly and awkward. It's not the best sensation, but unfortunately it was one that came over me regularly, especially when we were about to go on stage. Yet if you time it right and bang down a couple of IPAs before you go on, you feel cool as a cucumber! And when you feel cool as a cucumber, you play better, you sing better, you're less nervous, you make fewer mistakes. Given my propensity for stage fright and nerves, I'm not quite sure how I ever managed to do any shows while sober.

Sometimes you go on stage thinking, 'Oh, I'm not going to go too mad tonight,' and then you do, because it's how you get all of that day's energy out. You've spent the day on a bus, travelling what feels like halfway across the world, you've soundchecked, you've sat around, bored out of your head. All that's left is the show you came here to do, which will last around an hour and a half. If you have a crap hour and a half, it's easy to feel you've short-changed yourself, and you've got only yourself to blame.

On a really good night with Blur, if I decided to try something new and one of the other band members realised what I was doing and responded, and we all took it somewhere else in an improvisation, it would break the monotony. It happened surprisingly often with Blur, maybe every two or three shows. If the audience was especially fantastic and supportive, something would spark and off we'd go. Damon's job was to make sure that that was the normal state of affairs. It's quite a heavy thing to keep doing, especially when you're exhausted and jet-lagged. Are you going to have a good time or not? It is entirely up to you. Well, you and the audience. Sometimes I would concentrate on a group of people in front of me, and if I was feeling knackered and not particularly into things, they would usually drag me out of my doldrums. It seemed to trigger some good stuff about myself in my brain, but when I came off stage again, I would relax back into my usual self-loathing state. But for a few minutes out there I'd read the cards they were holding up, saying things like 'I love you', and it would prevent me from feeling like that idiot up there, at least for a bit.

I don't like being on autopilot when I'm playing. Every gig, in its own way, is a mountain to climb – especially when they run to two hours or more, and you've got such a large amount of songs to get through. We would often change our nightly set list, always going through it with Stuart from our road crew, because he was in a position to observe the crowd's reactions to each song the previous night. 'Why don't you put that one in there, chuck that one out, swap those two around?' he would say, tweaking the set throughout the tour.

But there were always favourites. The whole set, like a song, has to have a shape. It has to smack the audience round the face when you first come on, there's a bit of a break before it builds up again, then chuck some punky ones in, and now let's do 'Advert' again. Then, at the end of the set, we'd do 'This Is a Low' to calm it all down. There's a certain cruel art to it – soften them up, bomb them, destroy their will! We'd get to the end, and many would be wondering why we left out such-and-such a track. Then we'd hit them with the encores.

Even after the most high-octane gigs, we still needed ways to pass the time, and a healthier option than just drinking the hours away was our on-the-road art club. It came out of my art-school days, when Alex and I, along with our friend Paul Hodgson, used to sit around inventing concepts for performance-art pieces, making automatic drawings or coming up with obscene, perverse doodles for each other's amusement. Even the studio walls would sometimes get covered with the ridiculous caricatures that I was so fond of drawing – of Damon and the others, or the obscene half-man, half-gerbil mutants standing in little jars, or horses flying over fences with shit streaming out of their arses.

It was puerile stuff, but it used to make me laugh. I am one of those people who follows somebody walking their dog and can't avoid noticing the resemblance of the dog's bumhole to a sausage roll. It's a very English way of expressing oneself – one that turns discomfort or trauma into scatological jokes and sarcastic humour.

I could never approach my hardships like the Mexican artist Frida Kahlo. Obviously, she was in some serious pain and endured experiences that were truly horrendous compared to mine. But in her self-portraits she regards the world with an extraordinary detachment, a deadpan, dispassionate cast across her face, and with a very personal range of symbolic objects. My own approach is more like an exorcism: grotesque distortions and exaggerated, almost cartoon-like figures. It's an externalisation of stuff that's bothering me.

———

Modern Life Is Rubbish was released in May 1993, and with it came another significant bump in the Britpop roller-coaster ride. For the promotional shots to accompany the album, we dressed up in Fred Perry togs, rolled-up denims and Doc Marten shoes and lolled in front of a wall, on which was painted 'British Image No. 1'. The clothes were standard-issue uniform for art students at Goldsmiths. I preferred slovenly sneakers, and wore a pair of rare (at the time) Converse low-tops that day. I liked them not only for the way they looked, but also because they were the only shoes grippy enough to get a purchase on stages slippery with rain, sweat or spilt beer. I was also wearing a favourite cardigan, which I was devastated to have to dispose of after Andy Ross's cat chose to defecate on it.

In the photos, Damon was clutching the leash of a slavering Great Dane, which is hardly the most British of breeds. Still, for Blur at least, Britpop style derived from the idea of a mod revival. It was an antidote to grunge. Although we admired the power of that music – especially from pre-grunge bands like Dinosaur Jr – I wasn't so keen on a lot of its growling rhetoric or its scruffy visual image.

The more home-grown style we adopted looked good with guitars and the other trappings of a pop group. The clothes became part of our toolkit. As we got bigger, there would always be a stack of Fred Perry clothing backstage, and we'd just pull something out for the gig. Afterwards we'd chuck it in a corner. It was a theatrical costume. I wasn't lounging around at home in that get-up; I'd be back in my old stripy T-shirts and crappy jeans. That's not to say I don't admire a nice bit of tailoring. I love tweed jackets, so more often than not I was rocking more of a James Herriot look than a Pete Townshend Union flag jacket. Give me that Merchant–Ivory 1930s thing any day. The heavy, overdriven, bloated sound and a fashion philosophy best described as 'Pigpen gone to the dogs' (shapeless black clothes and unwashed freak-flags) were not for us, and felt like a throwback to the last days of hippiedom, when the psychedelic dream turned sour at the end of the 1960s.

During the period when we were recording *Modern Life Is Rubbish*, we felt free. The looped dance rhythms of 'baggy' had constrained music, rhythmically, and this album allowed us to get back to a more expressive, improvisational set-up – tougher drumming, and lyrics featuring a wide range of characters and situations. Compositionally, we were heading back to the 1960s, but bringing more recent technology and production techniques to bear on the way the tracks were recorded. The technology allowed us to make the transitions in songs more interesting, more dynamic. I wanted the heavy, compressed drum sound of the Beatles and the psychedelic guitar sounds of the 1960s – tremolo, and the kind of effects you would hear on that era's film soundtracks, like the primitive fuzz pedal in *Casino Royale*. Equipment such as the old fifty-six channel SSL mixing desk at Matrix Studios, where we recorded a good deal of that album, helped to make that possible. That desk is legendary, having previously been used by Genesis and Phil Collins in the 1980s (there's a whole underground scene of second-hand desks that have done the rounds from studio to studio), and it was instrumental in getting the sound right on *Modern Life Is Rubbish*.

Left to our own devices at last by our label, we found ourselves coming out with more adventurous music than before. There was the hypnotic outro to 'Oily Water' and the repetitive chord sequence at the end of 'Resigned', my homage to mesmeric, bucolic, contemplative tracks such as Pink Floyd's 'Cirrus Minor' and 'A Saucerful of Secrets', or the mindless repetition of the Velvet Underground's 'What Goes On'. All of Blur were into the shimmering tremolo effect on my guitar, which faded in at the start of 'Resigned'. That song necessarily took a full six minutes to stretch out – it required a certain space and duration in order to envelop you, giving you time to take in the lyrics. Fading out too early, or cutting it dead, would be inappropriately jarring. It applied the sculptor Brancusi's idea of truth to materials to the art of songwriting. It also opened up a quiet space where my anxiety could find peace.

Among our many inspirations, the films of English director Mike Leigh loomed large. 'Sunday Sunday', on *Modern Life Is Rubbish*, is a very Leigh-influenced song. For us, this was comfortable, even safe territory. Damon, being from Leyton originally, was quite happy navigating this urban terrain, despite his arty background. We always had to have a conceptual focus or drive, and we took away an awful lot from Leigh's work, especially *Meantime*, the film he made for Channel 4 in 1983. Damon and I used to watch and rewatch it on a scratchy VHS tape while we were still at school. The downtrodden, working-class Pollock family and the suburban interior and exterior landscapes accurately reflected the small-town England that all of us experienced while growing up. There were a few folks like Coxy – the skinhead played by Gary Oldman – at our secondary school. They were the ones chasing me out of the youth club on Tuesday nights for wearing a parka. There was always a strange subcultural tension in the air when they showed up.

Leigh's films frequently showed characters struggling while doing everything they could to forge an identity and make a difference within their community. This was the mid-1980s, and the dole queue was a great leveller; plenty of characters took solace in opening a few tinnies after signing on for their unemployment benefit. *Meantime* was effective at showing how unemployment could leave people disenfranchised and at a loose end, leading to unpredictable behaviour. Mark Pollock, the family's eldest son, hung out doing idiotic stuff with the loud-mouthed, impetuous Coxy. (Phil Daniels, who played Mark, would soon become a member of Blur's entourage thanks to his vocal contribution to 'Parklife'.)

When it came to the cover for *Modern Life Is Rubbish*, at first we considered a photo of a baby in a bath that we had found on a Turkish postcard. That would have been a continuation of the kitsch pop art imagery that we had already used on our singles. Then we happened to see a birthday card featuring a Ladybird Books-style painting of the classic Mallard locomotive, and it occurred to us that nothing could be further from what most people expected of an alternative rock LP cover. We couldn't get permission to use the original painting, but sleeve designers Stylorouge sourced a stock image painted by Paul Gribble. Recalling my own joy in learning from pop songbooks when I was a kid, I drew out the chord shapes and included them on the lyric sheet on the album's inner sleeve.

———

One of the most important Blur gigs ever was on Saturday 28 August 1993, at the Reading Festival. We were headlining the *Melody Maker* stage, which was in a giant tent, and we absolutely packed it out. It was a joyous show, with the whole crowd behind us, cheering us on. Blur worked well in a big, stripy circus tent. Radiohead had just played below us on the bill, and that night the place was bulging and heaving with bodies, and people were backed up way outside the tent itself, watching us wrestling with our instruments on this little stage, like a flea circus, surrounded by a massive throng who were going berserk. I felt like we could touch every single one of them, even those who were just there for a brief ten-minute gawp.

We'd been rubbing our sticks together for so long, and now finally we'd got a good old flame going. Stephen Street, who was in the crowd, told me that was the moment he looked around and realised Blur was really happening. It was after that gig that people started to become aware that we had a lot to offer as a band, wherever you were coming from. I just wanted arty-farty people to like us, because I thought *we* were arty-farty people. That's why I was uncomfortable when the hooligans and the new-lad brigade caught wind of us – we weren't particularly a lad band, and our audience was pretty much fifty–fifty male and female.

———

Parklife was the second in what is often referred to as our trilogy, coming between *Modern Life Is Rubbish* and *The Great Escape*. There were a few barrel-scraping moments, jokey tracks and throwaway antics – like the silly jazz pastiches on 'Beard' – a result of us being forced to come up with B-sides or extras for the bonus material disc. But that was just us mucking around, and it served its purpose, showing that we didn't mind making idiots of ourselves and that we were mischievous and silly and having fun. There's nothing wrong with that. The Velvet Underground did that, and they were arguably the coolest band that has ever existed; even when they were mucking around and doing something absurd, they created brilliant work.

'Girls and Boys' was the stand-out smash hit from *Parklife*, and it marked a bit of a departure musically as well. I wanted to put some irksomeness into the chord progression. That was my job, to cut across the flow of Alex's Chic-style bassline. He was sort of Sister Sledging out, or John Tayloring out – a mixture of the two – and I was trying to add a Wire-like guitar part, taking the mickey out of the fact that we were practically playing a disco tune. The first chord is disrupted, so it transforms from major to minor. It's a very jarring, contrary part to start with, which shifts to a C major seventh, which is like a jazz chord, and then into an ordinary seventh. What all this adds up to is me trying to awkwardise the song. Without that, it would have just been a flat indie disco song with predictable chords. I was still finding myself as a guitar player and was investing a lot of my sense of humour into the songs. They were reflective of who we were as individuals and our specific roles in the band.

Recording 'Girls and Boys' was very straightforward. I didn't really have much to do. I overdubbed some additional high parts with heavy vibrato, trying to make synth sounds from my guitar, like a kind of disco Robert Fripp. The rhythm had to have the hi-hat open between the kick drum and the snare drum, and a bassline that makes you want to boogie around on the dancefloor; and then along comes my guitar part, the young brat in the group who didn't really want to be in a disco band, who wanted to keep it indie and taint it with a slightly uncomfortable, discordant dimension. Which reflects the words of the song. After all, it's not an anthem to disco glamour like 'He's the Greatest Dancer'. We're not describing someone who's dancing beautifully, who looks amazing and all the rest of it. It's about a load of hooligans who want to go to the seaside, drink gallons and shag everything in sight. So my guitar-playing is more a reflection of that sort of sarcasm. Unfortunately, the borderlines between irony and being taken at face value were about to become confusingly blurred.

MILKMAN
AT
THE
JUNKET

C ulturally, Damon and I certainly didn't feel like part of any mainstream. It wasn't that we felt superior; we just didn't quite understand it. I recently visited YouTube and watched myself and Damon being interviewed by Jools Holland on his music show *Later . . .* It was 1995, and even though we're there to talk up our *third* – and most successful – album, *The Great Escape*, both of us (but me especially) look terribly self-conscious.

By the time we started forming bands at art college, so much of the music history that we loved and admired had already been cemented into the nostalgia industry. The big earthquakes had shaken things up and the debris had been cleared away. The Beatles and the Who, punk, mod and new wave, acid house, even grunge – all the moves had been made and the stories told. It was hard to manoeuvre anywhere within the musical landscape without feeling you were treading in the footsteps of giants. Here we were, doing all the things we dreamt of as teenagers. We were in a band, making records, having hits and going on tour. We were even making money. We should have been revelling in it. So why, when someone stuck a TV camera and a mic in our faces, did we feel so awkward and squeamish?

Damon, me and the rest of the band were very attuned to the absurdity of it all. That's both the curse and the strength of Blur, as we could also adopt the pompous seriousness of 1960s stars like Pete Townshend, who really thought of themselves as artists and had an almost messianic belief in the power of popular music. He once said that Rock – with a capital 'R' – should be capable of societal change; for him it was a matter of life or death. It's complicated. To us it felt more like a matter of art or death. None of us, after all, was fighting poverty or dealing with any sort of brutality. Oasis came from a tougher background than us – they certainly had more to fight for. Whatever Blur did was mostly done on a whim.

Sometimes, for me at least, all of this felt fraudulent in a way. Now we had got there and seen what it was, most of it turned out to be pretty flimsy. A lot of the mystery was being revealed, and it wasn't a shining palace but more of a shed. Even if we couldn't admit it to ourselves, there was certainly a bit of anticlimax and disappointment about it. At the same time, we believed it was up to people like us, Oasis and Pulp to take what we had learnt forward, to put it in our rucksack of music and trudge on into the next decade and try to figure out what to do with it all.

I look at that Jools Holland clip and think, 'That's a creative person, and music is a crucial part of his life, but he can't allow himself to deserve it.' Instead, I relied on Damon, who was this inexhaustible motor on the back of our boat, powering us onward. I didn't feel like I had much of a job to do other than to make the songs better by putting into practice those years of listening to music, along with a natural gift of being able to pick up on the thrust and emotional drive of a song.

I want to tell that kid on the telly in 1995 that he has as much right to take his place in the history of pop music as anybody else.

———

17 June 1995, and it's off to Mile End Stadium in east London for another milestone Blur moment. 27,000 fans have gathered to see us headlining and support bands like the Boo Radleys, Sparks and Dodgy. Never mind the light summer drizzle – Phil Daniels is on board to do his thing in 'Parklife', and Damon is making his entrance wearing a blond wig and a fake pot belly. Above our heads, giant inflatable cheeseburgers are dangling like the fast food of Damocles. It would be a memorable show.

I got embarrassed when Damon pushed his theatrical side, because it made me feel like I was just a workman with a bag of tools. But Damon put a lot of pressure on himself to communicate in that way – it's a big side of his personality. Whether it was coming on stage surrounded by ironing boards and lampshades, with Harry Enfield appearing as a tea lady, or my idea of getting Phil Daniels involved in the first place, it was a big part of that 'British image'. We weren't aiming to be just a big, famous rock band. We were reaching further than that, into the world of film and TV and art and popular culture in all its forms. I don't know why Damon felt it was important to make comments about service stations, mock-Tudor houses and the Americanisation of England. It was easy, but paradoxical, to take the mickey out of Essex boys ordering burgers and fries at American diners in the middle of the countryside. It had shades of the Village Green Preservation Society but also expressed a certain disdain for the mainstream, and for the average bloke in the street – in other words, the kind of people that turned out in their thousands, in the rain, to watch us at Mile End Stadium.

As homecomings go, this extravaganza was a triumph. Blur's sound had thickened up nicely and easily carried across the huge crowd. My guitar on a track like 'Stereotypes', which we unleashed in the first encore, was gleefully distorted, with a very fast echo. It could have gone any number of different ways, and it was possibly too much. But Dave and Alex, the rhythm section, were forced to raise their game in response to the fudgy effects. I was trying to reintroduce the guitar sound I admired in players like J Mascis, of Dinosaur Jr, and Black Francis, of Pixies, into the band's overall sound.

While recording *The Great Escape* during the first half of that year, I had to fight for the guitars to be so extreme. Stephen Street let me browbeat him and the others up to a point, and then I would have to accept his view. If I were a different sort of personality, I'd have told him to piss off and turned myself up a few more notches. But Stephen was reasonable, and I trusted him. He would say things like, 'I think that's as far as we should go with the loudness of that guitar.' It was all about balance and sculpting depth in the songs. Some guitar parts were supposed to be distant, some were supposed to be echoey and send you off into a brief reverie before you're dragged back into the chorus. It was about how you manipulated the listener.

Listening back to the album, I can hear that I was hugely interested in the double-stopping method of guitar soloing that George Harrison made his own. That harks back as far as the 1950s, and I think a lot of what I did was actually aping that era. The Pixies did that too, of course. Alex was a really underrated bass player, and he was constantly coming up with fantastic parts. He was effectively a lead guitarist who happened to be using fatter strings. He was never interested in just staying on the root notes, but sometimes we had to insist he did so that the music didn't get too confusing. On top of all this, Damon had started to add perverse *danse macabre* interludes on the organ. It was a mish-mash of stuff that no one else, it seemed to me, was getting anywhere near.

Songs like 'Dan Abnormal' (from *The Great Escape*) or 'Peter Panic' (from *Parklife*'s bonus material disc) sound way too full of information now – far too rich. Editing yourself is one of the hardest but most important skills you can have as a musician and as a band. Coming up with a definitive guitar part became much more important to me, and I came to appreciate the value of leaving space, even though I still loved the ultra-dense sound of bands like My Bloody Valentine. I always thought 'Best Days' from *The Great Escape* was lovely, with more of a Kinks-like, melancholic quality and a nice double-stopped guitar solo. Most of my favourite Blur tracks are the sad ones, like '1992' and 'Blue Jeans'. I thought we were absolutely at our best when making songs like those, not the old oompah-oompah stomps like 'Country House', 'Parklife' and 'Girls and Boys'. On those tracks it felt like we were trying to be too clever, whereas I thought the ones that actually came from real, universal feelings like grief and loss were our strongest.

We were a very complicated band with too many ideas, most of the time. Damon would stamp his foot to get what we wanted, as a group, from our management, and I would stamp mine because I didn't feel heard or appreciated. That was my problem. But then I wasn't very good at being heard or appreciated. Whenever the spotlight did finally fall on me and the others said, 'Go on then, Gra, let's hear what you have to say,' I would just mumble or be unable to cope with the sudden limelight.

———

Strange things happen out in the country, far from prying eyes. Damon, Alex and Dave are rolling in the hay with a bevy of page-three girls, a snuffling pig is running amok between the cameras and boom mics, bathtubs are overflowing with soap suds. Actor Keith Allen is gurning in a bowler hat and pinstripes. Comedian Matt Lucas is chasing the girls around like a perverted mad scientist. You guys enjoy your Britpop-meets-*Little Britain*-meets-Benny Hill moment. Begging your pardon, squires, but me, I'm just here to deliver the milk.

Welcome to the madhouse. Most of Blur's videos in the 1990s tried to make a statement, to offer a markedly different atmosphere from the majority of promos that were popping up on MTV at the time. There definitely was a conceptual drive to them. 'Country House', the first single from 1995's *The Great Escape*, was the product of an ironic mindset, but already things had changed so much – both within the band and in the wider culture – that it was all too easy to take it at face value.

In our songs we wrote a lot about things we disapproved of. It came out as a criticism of aspects of society that we considered beneath us or of characters that we felt were following the herd. But even within the band we disagreed with each other, and there was one notorious occasion when I took the higher moral ground over the rest of the group. That was when we came to film the video for 'Country House'. It was a very MTV-friendly design: bright colours and goofy grins, a giant rat-race board game, cobwebbed skeletons in a Hammer horror dungeon, the pig, drum majorettes and cheeky models dressed as milkmaids. For me personally, though, it was complicated, because I felt it was demeaning to the girls. The video featured Jo Guest, who was well known as a nude model and page-three pin-up at the time. One bit that I found particularly uncomfortable was a shot of her smiling vacuously at the exact moment Damon sung the words 'wonderfully bland'. I didn't think that was very fair. Occasionally some of our road crew were female, and whenever they got shouted at in a coarse way by groups of lads in the audience, I'd shout 'Shut up, you fucking idiots' over the microphone. Afterwards, the woman who had been heckled would usually tell me she appreciated it, but she didn't need me to look after her. That's why I don't really call myself a feminist: I don't believe feminists need men to call themselves feminists. They're quite capable of doing what they need to do, without men offering their services. Anyway, the 'Country House' video displayed more than a little cognitive dissonance – as did the whole of the 1990s, to be honest.

In the end I said, 'Look, dress me as a milkman and give me a milk float to play with, and I'll do it.' I was in a very bad mood. I mean, filming most videos tended to put me in a bad mood, because they took up my time and they were ridiculously expensive. I had friends, far less high-profile musicians, who were playing great music but didn't have two pennies to rub together. Here we were, blowing anything from fifty to five hundred grand on a film shoot and half a day's work that resulted in a piece of rubbish which got screened only a couple of times on *The Chart Show*. It didn't sit well with me. Why, I wondered, should somebody who stayed in their bedroom from an early age, drawing, writing stories and learning instruments, be expected to flick a switch, throw themselves into this professional mode and sing down the lens of a camera with zero self-consciousness? I'm afraid I had far too many scornful inner voices mocking me to get into that. I'm not saying I was a bad actor, but it requires a different, more cocksure part of yourself to properly let go of the self-consciousness. 'Who do you think you are, Graham?' the voices were saying. Others seemed to be deaf to those voices or knew how to override them, thus enabling them to stare down the lens and dance without feeling like they were about to fall over. I couldn't allow myself to do this stuff.

The video was directed by Damien Hirst, who by then was a massively successful artist. He, of course, connected back to my time at Goldsmiths, when we worked in the same block, but he was now bigger friends with Alex. It was a reminder of the artist's life I could have had. I felt pretty cynical about Damien's involvement. It seemed to confirm what I was afraid of – that 1990s culture had become tacky and cheap. For me, the decade wasn't as golden and beautiful as my idea of what the 1960s were like – which, of course, would have been very different to the reality. I felt let down by what the Young British Artists were doing. Once, in the Colony Rooms, I bumped into Sarah Lucas and had a healthy old discussion with her about all that. We got a lot out of our systems. We didn't necessarily agree with each other, but she explained a few things about her intentions. The way I saw it, her brand of 'provocation' owed so much to what Dada and surrealism had already achieved decades earlier. It seemed like a trade in cheap visual puns, and I couldn't see the point. Her fried-egg breasts and penile sausages were an echo of Picasso's bull sculptures made from bike saddles and handlebars, but with a more trashy tone. OK, so musically we were ripping off the Who and the Beatles, but at least we were upfront about it. Sarah argued her position passionately and reasonably, but ultimately encounters like this reassured me that I had been right to leave the art world behind.

It made me angry because here I was, finally in a band, and the experience seemed to be getting cheapened by page-three-type imagery, a revival of sexism and football hooliganism, and bands wearing windcheaters and trainers. Something about this grated with me. And art – mainly thanks to the college I attended – had become more conceptual, all about punchlines and jokes. Seeing things like Damien's shark in formaldehyde up close in a gallery was undeniably impressive, well-put-together, but there was something disappointing about it too.

————

British pop music became highly competitive in the mid-1990s. It felt like whenever a new English guitar-based band arrived on the scene, the press would pit Blur against them, even when it wasn't really appropriate. First it was Suede, then Oasis. Did they do that in the 1960s and '70s? Did Led Zeppelin and Slade have fights? Did the Hollies and the Animals get into a scrap? Were there fisticuffs between the Who and Jimi Hendrix? There were rivalries – most famously between the Beatles and the Rolling Stones, and even between Ray and Dave Davies, the brothers in the Kinks – but back then any genuine unpleasantness, jealousy or feuding was rarely reported on in the music press and celebrity gossip columns. On top of that, there were no mobile phones to capture any affray in night-clubs such as the Scotch of St James. So whatever went on between these high-flying artists was left to your imagination. In Blur, thirty years later, we saw the effects of band rivalry at first hand.

Any group usually includes at least one competitive personality. Sometimes there's more than one, which can make for some sparky results – look at the Gallagher brothers in Oasis, for example. In a band context I'm generally pretty non-confrontational. I've always wanted everyone to be all right and to act as peace-maker. At the same time, I'm not one for solidarity! If Damon decided to be competitive with somebody – I remember a festival where we had some tense moments with Primal Scream – that wouldn't stop me from having a nice little chat and a drink with them later on.

We released 'Country House' in the summer of 1995, and the media pounced on the idea of a race to the top of the charts between us and Oasis's 'Roll with It'. I would have preferred to have an uncomplicated number one, where it didn't feel like half of the country thought we didn't deserve it. At the time I felt, 'What's the point in manufacturing this rivalry? We're all from England and we've won the war on grunge. Let's just flipping enjoy being British bands who are doing well.' Much of the rivalry was framed in terms of class. Oasis were seen as genuine, rough-diamond examples of the working-class north, while Blur were cast as southern, arty-farty, pretentious gits. Well, Damon and I were arty-farty and pretentious by design, of course, but the description conveniently glossed over several fairly important facts. I was an army kid – not from a rich background, and not middle class by any stretch of the imagination – and was originally from Derbyshire. I had been doing all sorts of jobs since I was at school – from paper rounds onwards – and had to break into the Family Allowance whenever I needed new shoes. I certainly didn't have everything I wanted.

Not all the British bands were my cup of tea, but everyone was trying to make their own *Revolver* or equivalent classic album. All the groups were in different places, though. Pulp I always saw as Tom Courtenay in *Billy Liar*: fantasising about quitting the north and reinventing yourself in the glamorous south, but never quite managing to catch the train. And then there was Oasis.

Noel and Liam, the Gallagher brothers, were tricky personalities. You didn't know which Liam you were going to get on any particular awards night. Was he going to be reasonable and say, 'Yeah, you're the only one I like out of your shit band'? Or was he going to act stand-offish and threatening? Noel was always decent and friendly. But they had a lot to prove. If you throw a bunch of competitive young men into the ring and all they have is music – this is their one chance at a money-making career, the single door that might lead to them becoming rich and famous – then of course they're going to stand their ground, get ratty and act territorially. I wasn't really built that way.

In August 1995 Parlophone threw a party at the members' club Soho House in London to celebrate the release of 'Country House'. The band and many others involved in the business of promoting and marketing Blur all assembled to drink champagne and discover the answer to the great question of the age: whether or not the single had rocketed to number one ahead of Oasis's 'Roll with It'. For my part, after a few glasses of bubbly I decided the whole thing was so unbearable that it was necessary to jump out of a window. In attempting this sensible course of action, I managed to spill a glass of red wine all the way down our agent's white jeans – but he could definitely afford another pair. I wasn't actually going to jump; it just hit me in a rush that the circus that had been created around Blur was taking away my genuine joy of being in the band. Of course, people thought I was really going to do it, but it was just histrionics, and I would have twisted my ankle badly. It was thirty seconds of brattishness. I wasn't getting my own way, and people were getting off on this thing that I thought was cheap and nasty. It was my problem, not theirs. It took me a while to realise that I was ruining it all for myself. It's up to you to make your life decent. Nobody else is going to do it for you. In the end it was 'Country House' that made it to number one, selling 270,000 copies in its first week, while Oasis came in at number two. The track remains our best-selling single.

———

I don't remember too much about the day in September 1995 when we played on the rooftop of the HMV Megastore on Oxford Street, bang in the middle of London. Famously, the Beatles had done something similar, making their final appearance as a live band on top of Apple headquarters in Soho. Blur's show was far from a farewell gig, of course – more of a jolly day out for record-label execs and their mates. I felt like a bit of a performing monkey, because it wasn't exactly the easiest job to set up on a retailer's rooftop and knock out a show. We were in the middle of an exhausting schedule, so it was hard to stop and enjoy the moment.

I would over-romanticise the 1960s and all the larks bands got up to in those days. You hear stories about Dave and Ray Davies of the Kinks pouring a pint of beer over each other's heads backstage at *Top of the Pops*, or Dave and the band's drummer Mick Avory having a proper fist fight. These things happen in groups when you're tired and emotional. At one time members of The Kinks were seen with at least one black eye, as if these injuries were as infectious as cold sores. But in my idealisation of what it should be like in a pop band, I sometimes got stroppy that it wasn't all how I had imagined it would be. We often found ourselves chucked together in a car on the way to some gig or interview, not having had time to unwind since the previous night's show. Four young, homesick, sexually frustrated blokes in that situation are inevitably going to get on each other's nerves at some point. Alex developed a mildly disrespectful way of referring to our female fans, which he exaggerated on purpose because he knew how much it twisted my melon. There was one time he put a stop to my whining with a thump on the nose. I retaliated by saying the word 'arse' every few seconds for the rest of the three-hour drive. It was like a puerile, frustrated monster had resurfaced in retaliation for my distress at being silenced, and it made me come across like a spoilt child.

What did I imagine stardom would be? I guess it was the image presented in videos and documentaries – the dream, and the lie. Beneath that cool, polished facade, what you don't see is the stupendous amount of work, travel, boredom, frustration, hangovers and tiresome little power struggles that go on in the background. Record labels telling you everything you do is shit. Sweating through material in studios with producers, only to find something didn't work, so you have to re-record everything. There's a lot that is tedious, which leaves you too tired and cynical to enjoy the good stuff when it comes along. You become inured to it, and it loses its shine. The first couple of times you get asked to do a photo shoot, you're like, 'Wow, photo shoot tomorrow – nice! Have an early night, everybody!' Three or four years down the line, and it's, 'Oh fuck. I've got a bloody hangover, I look like crap. Do we have to?'

Up on the HMV rooftop, during this oddity in the Blur gigography, Damon was unstoppable. As we launched into 'The Universal', he yelled, 'You'll all be singing this at Christmas!' Down on Oxford Street, there might have been one or two people vaguely aware of some commotion going on somewhere above their heads. Burnt out and disillusioned as I was, from my perspective it was an anticlimax.

———

In part Blur operated by following the model laid down by the pioneering pop groups of the 1960s, even twenty-five years after the fact. Advance, album, promotion, tour. I didn't know there was any other way. That opened up quite a gap between expectation and reality. Whenever we went to New York, I didn't know what to do with myself. The record label would take us out, but then people would wander off to see their friends, leaving me a bit lost. It took me longer than the other Blur members to gather friends in different cities. Each time we went back on tour, I would make more connections in Chicago, Detroit, Washington DC and even Seattle. One time I hung out with Matthew Horovitz – the brother of Adam Horovitz from the Beastie Boys – for a day in New York City and had this exotic meal called 'brunch'. There was also Michael Guarrine and his girlfriend in Chicago – I went on to produce a record by his band, Assembly Line People Program.

Alex was by now living a rock 'n' roll playboy lifestyle, going to parties with models, film directors and producers, swimming in a big pond filled with a lot of pike. My pond was much smaller and less pike-filled, and my friends were very different, mostly coming from the straight-edge riot grrrl or punk side of things. They were people like Allison Wolfe and Erin Smith, from Bratmobile, or Elliott Smith who were totally into music and not interested in what they could get out of you. I normally met up with them in a New York bar – not exactly an outrageous cocktail of drink and drugs till four or five in the morning, more like a few drinks and a chat, get some pizza in and then carry on talking and listening to music. This was my world: friends who were involved in music for what I considered the right reasons and who were willing to share what they knew and loved, with no sense of competitiveness.

Sometimes, though, the nature of touring meant you could find yourself parachuted into all manner of unknown places around America, where you could never be quite sure who the hell you were talking to. Occasionally this could lead to some fairly dicey, almost mythological journeys into the dark side of American gothic. There are creatures of all stripes everywhere, some unambiguously either good or bad, some who merely present themselves as good – or even a very attractive kind of bad. I remember hanging out in Philadelphia with a couple of new friends – one a Californian boy with long blond hair and cowboy boots, the other a black Jewish girl. They had been following Blur on our tour and had come to a few of our previous shows, so I'd got to know them a little bit. Another girl appeared, with blonde hair and dungarees, looking quite cool, and she invited us to her place. 'It's just round the corner.'

We walked up the stairs, and she unlocked the door of her apartment to reveal about five drunk, bare-chested, tattooed skin-heads lolling around. Here I was, accompanied by this long-haired Californian lad and black Jewish girl, who was nudging me to look at the wall, which had a number of Nazi posters and portraits of Adolf Hitler on display.

'Holy shit, what is this?' I said to the dungarees girl.

'Don't worry about the guys,' she replied, 'they're OK.'

'I'm not sure my friend feels entirely comfortable here, and I certainly don't, so I think we're going to leave,' I announced.

Our host didn't appear particularly bothered, and watched as we carefully stepped over the outstretched legs – all tight bleached jeans and chunky bovver boots. The Californian boy gave a parting 'See ya, fellas!' and as we gratefully nipped out of the door, we heard a ragged shout of 'See you in hell!'

That was my run-in with the Cyclops. It's all too easy, like Odysseus's crew in Homer's saga, to get lured by sirens to an island and brainwashed or drugged by witchcraft, unless you learn to be assertive, lay down some boundaries and think less about pleasing other people. You leave yourself vulnerable to a lot of manipulation and abuse if you don't get that shit straight.

Whenever I came back from a tour in America, I'd feel a strange compulsion to plant a kiss on every crooked garden wall in the whole of north London. There's something beautiful about English gardens, with their scents of roses and moss and their musty weirdness. For me, they're an antidote to the coarseness that is also such a strong part of British culture. It makes me wish I could try living around the time of the Second World War, because I have this fantasy that people's vocabulary would have been so much better back then and that men were actually polite and courteous to women. Of course, in reality people were being rude to women then too, and females still had limited rights and freedoms – so 'fantasy' is really the operative word.

I increasingly felt like I was caught in a kind of ethical vice: a key member of a band called Blur, who – if you believed the tabloid columnists – were unapologetically into blondes, boobs and Britpop brawls. We were being lumped in with the overall 1990s upsurge

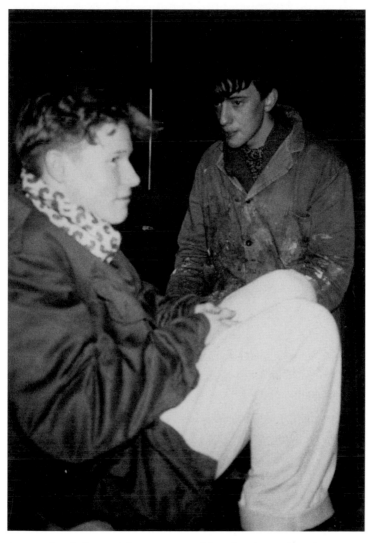
Aged about eighteen, covered in oil paint and turps,
with a good friend, Noah.

Art-school days: with my friend Christine, and a misbuttoned
jacket, in the grounds of Colchester Arts Centre (formerly
St Mary at the Walls church) during the late 1980s.

On the ancient Roman wall, where a cannon known as
'Humpty Dumpty' is supposed to have been placed.
Sketchbook and pencils at the ready.

My first-year student room at Stannard Hall, Goldsmiths, 1988.
Decorated with a rolled-up canvas and some Pixies lyrics.

Self-portraits with my new Praktica camera in
my old bedroom in my parents' house.

Celebrating our diploma show with my gang from Colchester
Art College: Julia, Sharon, me, Amy and Rosalynd.

With Julia, my first serious girlfriend, on
Remembrance Avenue, Colchester.

An end-of-the-pier moment with Blur during a photo shoot for *Modern Life Is Rubbish*, 1993. The cap was chosen so I would look like the chauffeur.

A boozy Blur interview with me and Damon in around 1994.

A new Waeve: me and Rose Elinor Dougall, 2022.

in publications and attitudes that weren't particularly right-on. This gave the impression that, politically, Blur and Huggy Bear were at opposite ends of the political spectrum, which meant Jo's association with me became problematic for Huggy Bear. It placed more strain on our relationship, which was already under pressure with my being away so much. On a personal level we were fine – and ideologically we were on the same page – but the gulf between what each of our bands stood for became increasingly unbridgeable.

Despite Blur's traumatic American jaunt of 1992, there were still things I enjoyed about being on the road. I liked being around people who could be a distraction. I liked going to new cities. I liked being able to lie down and cope with my anxiety on my own. I liked the aftershows and the parties. I enjoyed meeting people – and, occasionally, meeting people who were really lovely and interesting. I still know people now from those sorts of encounters. A fan I might have first spoken to in 1992 can still be a very good mate even thirty years later.

I could probably count the number of parties I've been to on the fingers of at least fifty hands. The ones I remember are usually memorable for all the wrong reasons. I used to get excited about going out, because I knew it meant having a few, and in my nervous excitement I often drank myself close to unconsciousness before many guests had actually arrived.

At the height of Blur's fame, and as millennium fever seized London's nightlife from the mid-1990s, we were spoilt for choice when it came to parties. We had no idea that this would be the last chance to experience what being in a band was like in the 1970s and '80s, when money was still sloshing around the music business and you had to burn it. If more than three people were in a room containing alcohol, that was a party. Album playbacks, for example. Every time we finished a record, we'd get some snackeroonies and drinks in, and A&R people, reps from the label and a few friends would come over to have a good old listen to what we had done, nice and loud. It was an exciting moment, when you still had huge faith in what all your hard work had produced and invited other people into that world for the first time. But I loved big music-industry celebration bashes bubbling with free booze just as much, like the big EMI conventions, which were notoriously naughty and chaotic.

For me, it was party time after every show we played. Occasionally, although I was too wasted to realise it, it was a party of only one. It took me some time to figure out that actually, a lot of people weren't in the same headspace, or altered state, as I was. They just thought I was mad. In reality, I was medicating my anxiety but always managing to overdose, by which I mean overcompensate. I never found the sweet spot between pleasure and excess.

That's what you do in London, or on tour, to avoid boredom: go out for a drink. Whenever I was at a loose end at home, I'd soon get bored. I can really understand why a musician such as the Who's bassist John Entwistle felt like he didn't have much of a purpose when the group weren't touring, and so formed his own band in order that he could go on tour again or generally misbehave. When there was nothing else to distract me, I just went to the pub.

It was better if we were in the middle of recording an album. In the main, we were business-like about the actual recording and worked without any drinks at all. We were efficient too: no sitting around waiting for the vibe to arrive; it was a day at work. We started at around ten or eleven; we'd get into a track or two, maybe have a bit of lunch, and then carry on until eight o'clock, unless we were in the middle of something and felt inspired. Then we would go on a bit longer until the song we were working on was finished enough to be able to put it to bed or know that it was safely stored on tape.

More often than not we had our own private time after working in the studio. I liked being able to go back to Camden and then head out to the pub, have a couple of drinks, go home and zonk out. My anxiety wouldn't be so bad if there was a structure to my week. As long as I was required to be in the studio by ten, it was absolutely fine. It worked.

———

Ever since that US tour when we struggled to recoup our lost finances, we had grafted hard, hoping to get some money together. *Parklife* and *The Great Escape* supplied us all with enough to feel secure and be able to afford somewhere to live. Around March 1996 I suddenly went from cadging pints and borrowing money for chips to putting cash down on a four-storey Victorian house in Rochester Square, Camden, buying some furniture and stocking up my fridge.

It felt brilliant to have a lot of space, although it wasn't like the kind of superstar houses featured on the telly. Once, the Queens of Noize came round and did an *MTV Cribs*-type report on the house. It needed a lot of work doing on it when I first moved in – all the windows on the top floor were falling out because the woodwork was rotten, and there were a number of other issues, including a leaky roof – but it was a big, old London townhouse where I could settle. I lived in it as it was for quite a while, and then hired an architect to make a few adjustments. He made some cool improvements, including building a glass extension on the back, laying new tiles on the floor and installing a kitchen island with a seating area nearby. Upstairs, the living-room floor was covered with a rug woven with my own design.

I loved how it looked, but I got uptight in such a neat, designed environment, constantly on guard in case something got damaged. I like to be able to carry something across the kitchen, drop it and not have to worry that I've taken a chunk out of something. It made me nervous: I didn't want to sit on the nice chair, I didn't want to put my tea on the table. I'd lounge on my favourite sofa, a Danish Poul Kjærholm original sourced by the designer's own son, but it was impossible to let kids loose on that. You're trying to be Harry Palmer in the morning, whipping up an omelette and flicking the switch on the coffee percolator, but then you look across the room and notice the sofa splattered with jam and crayon.

There's a documentary about John Martyn, filmed after he had had his leg amputated and was living in a cottage in Ireland. I was fascinated by his house – a hovel really – with his long-suffering partner cooking up a curry on the wood-burning stove. John was sitting on a knackered old sofa, surrounded by bits of recording equipment shoved into the corners, and with a few musicians knocking about. I think I could live like that (though hopefully without the long-suffering partner).

Despite the material success, in other ways this was a difficult period for me. Touring and all the other demands on my time, energy and creativity were wearing me out. Blur was now a machine running out of control, forced to keep up with the music industry's appetite, trying to milk every release for as much cash as it could. The pressure was huge, and I thought we were short-changing our fans with live versions of the same song on the B-side of a vinyl single, different CD editions, a twelve-inch, a seven-inch and even a cassette, each one with a different B-side. All that meant that every time you released a single, you had to supply ten new tracks, with all the extra logistics and costs that involved, and they were usually needed while you were in the middle of a tour. It brought enormous pressure, and all of us were feeling it.

In Blur's early days we'd go into the dressing room and there'd be this pile of free booze and a promoter urging, 'Drink that, get on stage, do a great show!' 'OK,' we'd reply, and drink up. The next day, slightly bigger dressing room, bigger pile of booze, and another promoter exhorting us to drink deep and play well. It's like the fable of Rumpelstiltskin, where someone is propping up your efforts but at the same time binding you into a pact that you never asked for. This leads to some murky waters.

I was young and I didn't understand what 'having a drink problem' really meant. For me, an alcoholic was the nutter with a sunburnt face shouting at a lamp post in Camden, or Sue Ellen from *Dallas*. I was neither of those, so I had no reference points for what proper alcoholism was. No one talked about it, and no one told me to ease up.

The only one who did mention it was Jo. 'For fuck's sake, Graham,' she said, 'you look like you need to go to Alcoholics Anonymous.' I couldn't believe what I was hearing. It wasn't even denial at that point; the idea was as alien to me as if someone had told me that my skin was bright green. 'What are you talking about? You can't be serious.' 'No, I really think so,' she insisted. Coming from her, I knew it was not to be ignored. But I was scared.

Somewhere in the mid-to-late 1990s I lost my buoyancy and started to feel more depressed. In the back of my head I knew that alcohol was no longer making me feel great. I took Jo's advice and attended an AA meeting in Camden. After that I managed to stay sober for sixteen months in around 1996–7, just before our first tour to Australia, and felt an awful lot better – more rested, settled, less anxious, optimistic. My first gig sober with Blur was at the Doctor Music Festival in Escalarre, up in the Spanish Pyrenees, in July 1996. It was a tricky one, and I burst into tears after coming off stage at the end of the set because the effort had been so big. I'd had loads of coffee, so I hadn't made it very easy for myself. We had been travelling all day without eating much, and coffee kept us going. We had to be in a transit van for two or three hours to get there, which is not a pleasant experience. You arrive, you're stuck in a tent, and there's a distinct lack of facilities. It sounds like excellent fun, but when you're actually there and you're really, really tired, and you have to play your gig without a tummy full of the 'best mate' that usually gets you through all sorts of stuff, then it's a whole lot harder.

When people knock booze on the head, they often say, 'I feel fantastic! I can get up early in the morning and get so much done!' But give it a couple of weeks and they're back on it, feeling awful again. It's a tricky beast.

Sobriety was required during that summer of 1996, because Blur still needed to get its own shit straight and find a new direction for the next LP. We all felt the urge to give the music a jolt in the arm, and I wrote a letter to Damon explaining that more than anything I wanted to work the band harder and aim for music that was so scarily powerful it would give people the shivers again. I was afraid that Blur had become too easy to caricature. With 'Country House' we had ridden the Britpop horse into the dust. It wasn't possible to cram any more hooks into one song. I wanted to give the sound a harder edge, an approach we generally held back for our B-sides. I was thinking about tracks like 'Oily Water', 'Resigned' and 'Bone Bag', from the *Modern Life Is Rubbish* period, which were less identifiably British, less to do with London or England, instead taking on board other influences from American hardcore and the more experimental 'post-rock' movement. I was soaking up a lot of interesting, inventive music from Beck's *One Foot in the Grave*, Pavement's *Slanted and Enchanted* and the first couple of albums by the Chicago band Tortoise, who managed to groove while sounding improvised and free.

And, yes, I did want to scare people. I wrote that letter to Damon at a time when I was feeling pretty exhausted, right after coming off our 1996 tour. I don't know what he thought about what I wrote. It was a conscious effort to reconnect, at a time when none of us were communicating on an emotional level with each other. No one wanted to acknowledge or discuss the fact that Blur increasingly felt like a business venture. Forces outside the band had turned our mutual friendship into a professional relationship. We had been getting increasingly tetchy with one another while on tour, and it was a time of constant small-scale conflicts that ultimately ground you down. We left that stuff outside the studio and didn't talk about it. It was easier to scribble it down and stick a stamp on it.

I brought my Beck, Pavement and Tortoise records into Mayfair Studios when we convened there in June 1996 to begin recording the album that became *Blur*. Everybody was sceptical at first, but some of the things I envisioned ended up on the album. 'Essex Dogs' had elements of that Tortoise vibe, with a lovely loop at the end. Stephen Street was starting to work digitally with a system called Radar. It wasn't as complex as Pro Tools but offered a similar experience to chopping things up on a tape machine. Its controls replicated a standard tape transport, with buttons for record, rewind and fast forward. That made it easy for him to delve deeper into the sonic material and make loops out of what we had already played. It meant that we could capture things live and then loop them and have fun. A good example of Radar in action is 'Country Sad Ballad Man', which ended up with a woozy lilt, slightly out of tune and off the rhythmic grid.

This method promised a whole new way of approaching music. Songs didn't have to be pre-written, sorted out and structured beforehand; we now had more freedom to shift things around later. My shake-up letter, coupled with the examples of more adventurous US musicians, definitely infiltrated the album. Without wanting to sound overblown, it was 'my' Blur album. It had the lovely 'Look Inside America' on it, with swirls of classical harp decorating my masculine, Big Star-ish guitar solo. I found 'Song 2' frustrating because I could never quite reach the disgraceful levels of noise I really wanted with the equipment I had. I probably could now because there are lots of other bits of kit I could try doing it with, but at the time it always sounded underpowered.

Things flared up between me and Damon after some musical disagreement while we were recording 'St Louis', a track intended for a forthcoming B-side. Another time we were on the tour bus and Damon had a bit of a pop at me about something; I didn't accept what he said and shouted at him from the back seats. That's the only time we have had such a big bust-up that we have spent the next day not talking to each other. For my part, I could be really moody, and my type of wit is such that if I am in a dark mood, I can be pretty ungenerous, if not downright nasty. But we were all like that. We were intelligent people who knew how to push each other's buttons.

I used to get stick from the rest of the band about the intense letters I would receive from certain Blur fans. Taking the mickey about the unhinged missives was harmless up to a point, until I started attracting individuals who were in seriously poor mental health. Of all the letters, pictures, intimate clothing and objects posted to the Blur fan club, I definitely ended up with the weirder stuff. I didn't wilfully present myself as the 'lost boy' of the band, but that was how a lot of fans imagined me. Alex was the louche, party-loving lad; Damon was an intense, beautiful artist with a deep voice; Dave was the serious but quietly smouldering drummer. I was harder to fathom, dripping in contradictions and as defensive as a snarling dog.

———

To breathe some fresh air into the group, Damon and Alex flew out to Iceland that summer, hoping to record some parts out there. Personally, I didn't like the idea of recording outside London. I liked turning up at the studio, finishing a day's work there and then enjoying my own time. I liked being at home. But Damon and Alex fell in love with the place and its people, so Dave, Stephen Street and I flew out to Reykjavik to add our parts to some of the tracks. It was more of a hangout than a working trip in the end. I did a bit of work at the studio, but it was more about us lot bonding all over again at our favourite bar, drinking Brennivín and going out for meals. We explored Iceland's stunning apocalyptic landscapes, met wild horses in geyser country and dropped in on the famous hot-water springs at the Blue Lagoon, a salt lake that smells of sulphur. Dipping your hands into the aquamarine waters felt like reaching into blue egg yolk; you'd run your fingernails through the mud at the bottom and bring up all kinds of unidentifiable squishy stuff – a living metaphor for making drawings or writing a song.

At least on this album we managed to leave behind subject matter relating to aspirations, money, big cars and other clichés of success. That was the good thing about Blur: we had the intelligence to be aware of clichés and to use them in fresh ways, if we used them at all. It was closer to quotation than rehash. As a guitarist, I placed elements picked up from, say, Robert Fripp or George Harrison together in the same song. With *Blur*, we achieved a looser, more free-flowing sound, harvested from Pink Floyd's 'Cirrus Minor' and other expansive psychedelic tracks, which worked comfortably here and fed through to the next album, *13*, which was even more improvised. I felt we were growing up as a band.

In some respects, anyway. It would still felt tense whenever someone other than Damon volunteered an idea for a song. When I brought in my screwed-up little song 'You're So Great', the rest of the group said, 'Well, yeah, you can record that if you want. See you later,' and shuffled out, leaving me to my own devices. I still wish I could have added an electric piano to that one, but with its scratchy vinyl noises and tinny vocal effect, it remains a weird, tea-stained piece of paper of a song. My voice was compressed to make it sound like it was coming out of a telephone. If Stephen or anyone else had encouraged me to sing out and make it bigger, I would have done so gladly. As it is, it's a loveable little piece that described exactly what I was like at that point, and in several respects it foreshadowed my earliest solo material.

Within any band, there are always going to be different ideas about what success means and what your goals are. I think Damon always wanted Blur to be massive, while I was happy to achieve a similar sort of indie notoriety to Dinosaur Jr. But if you achieve any level of success, you can't avoid becoming a business, a partnership. Massive amounts of cash are flowing in and going out; you think you've earned a big chunk of money, but you see it only very briefly in your account before it vanishes to pay for something else, and you never quite know where you are. That's why I was never a great fan of bringing things like brass sections into Blur's music. Not only was it very expensive to hire those sorts of musicians, but, as with our earlier 'Popscene', I was on a mission to discover how much a guitar could do, including getting it to do the job of a brass or string section.

———

The *Blur* LP came out in early 1997, heavily trailed by the single 'Song 2', which received a huge amount of airplay. Listening to the radio was never a big part of my musical obsession when I was at school.

Apart from the Top Forty rundown on Sunday evenings on Radio 1 and Annie Nightingale's enjoyable show, which usually followed, in the Coxon bedroom the radio played second fiddle to drawing and sketching, listening to records or watching the telly. John Peel's legendary alternative music show was completely off my radar.

Peel makes a cameo in the Blur documentary *Starshaped*, saying that if we had expunged melody from our songs, he would have had more time for us. Eventually, on 22 April 1997, to celebrate the release of *Blur* he invited us to play a live session from the patio at Peel Acres, his home in rural Suffolk, where he had a home studio set up and an ISDN line linked to the BBC in London. We did that a couple of times, and it was always good fun. We felt honoured, in fact, and he was very friendly to us. Some of his neighbours came over to listen, and his wife Sheila and the kids laid on a nice big buffet. It was an ancient country pile that had been renovated in the late 1960s. The bathroom was massive, with a shagpile carpet and the bathtub peculiarly positioned in the middle of the room. Playing Peel Acres afforded us a nice little trip out into the countryside.

The tensions in my life at the time weren't solely confined within the band. Although I had managed to last more than a year without touching a drink, since the summer of 1996, Jo and I ended up splitting for good. In the end we simply weren't compatible as a couple in the long term. Two years appeared to be my relationship time limit, and things eventually ran their course. It was hard breaking up, though, because I thought she was great. We shared plenty of good times, and I'm grateful to her for those. I'm sure she occasionally had a hard time with my drinking, though.

In August 1997, inspired by our positive experience in Reykjavik the previous summer, Blur decided it would be a jolly idea to go and play some dates in the Faroe Islands, Iceland and Greenland. I was feeling particularly blue at the time – still reeling not only from my split with Jo but also the aftershocks of my break-up with Jane, even though that had come five years earlier. I don't feel like I'm a particularly depressive person, but I can get a little bit lugubrious at times.

I was still sober and was reading *The Bell Jar* by Sylvia Plath and a load of Salinger, so that wasn't helping. But I was finding *The Bell Jar* pretty hilarious. I mean, the first half of it is pretty funny, but then the book suddenly becomes incredibly bleak, yet I hardly noticed the transition. That's what stayed with me about that book: you couldn't quite pinpoint when it all started to go wrong. The same applies to anyone who's had problems with their own mental health. It's usually such a gradual thing.

Those Nordic shows were somewhat odd. Greenland is a quite amazing place, with extraordinary-looking people. We played in Nuuk, the country's only city, and it happened to be on payday. The whole nation gets paid on one particular Friday each month, and everybody from the ages of two to ninety-two heads out to whatever is happening, especially if it's a gig. That show was absolutely insane, and it was a massive event in that part of the world. Everyone in the audience was absolutely blind drunk and loving it.

In the Faroe Islands, we wandered around in a heavy mist. We couldn't see anything in front of us, and occasionally we'd bump into Faroe ponies. They are tiny and unique to the islands, and they're allowed to trot around freely, so you just bump into them when you're trying to find your way through the fog. Our hotel had grass growing on the roof, so it was very hard to see from afar, when we were walking back from a local bar in the twilight. The only thing keeping us going in the right direction was the sound of our feet on the gravel path.

Our Icelandic gigs were always crazy, because the country was like the Wild West. We had some fairly hairy moments. Once we went to a club in the middle of what looked like an industrial estate. There was nobody there. Just as we began to acknowledge that this was awkward, we heard the sound of shouting from an office in the corner and a man emerged, off his head, swinging a gun around and telling everybody to get out, otherwise he was going to shoot them. We bolted down the stairs and got the heck out of there. You never really forget a night out in Iceland, because anything goes. From brawls to hugs, the whole spectrum of human emotion is on display during an evening of havoc.

In October 1997, after a month-long US tour promoting the *Blur* album that culminated in Las Vegas, we crossed the Pacific, stopping off for a single date in South Korea, before hitting Australia for the first time. That tour turned out to be a little chaotic, and I fell off the wagon. At one point I was sitting on a barstool in some hotel, waiting for a car to come and collect me, drinking Baileys. Completely out of the blue, I slid off the stool and collapsed onto the floor. The hotel staff, according to their policy, called an ambulance, and there was a lot of fuss, but I managed to get myself on my feet and told them I had just fainted with exhaustion. I brushed off the incident as a small blip in an otherwise fun and enjoyable tour.

At the end of that year, a friend I had made in Australia unexpectedly got in touch to tell me she was having a family holiday in Fiji. If she were to stay on, would I fancy flying there to meet her? At first it seemed ridiculous. I got the message on New Year's Day; the trip would involve a ten-hour flight to LA, another six hours to

Hawaii, and a further six-hour hop to Fiji itself. I mentioned the scheme to a couple of friends, and they advised me, 'It's better to regret what you did do rather than something you didn't.' I bought the ticket.

We spent most of that holiday lying on the beach. I was reading *Behind Blue Eyes*, Geoffrey Giuliano's biography of Pete Townshend, and managed to relax completely. On the last day I went to the beach-hut bar and ordered a nice big fat going-home drink. 'It's flipping hot today, isn't it?' I said to the barman. 'Yeah,' he replied, 'the sky is too high!' That's a special kind of Fijian genius, and it made perfect sense – at the time anyway. The sky's too high. It's like one of those James Bond film titles, *Tomorrow Never Dies* or *The World Is Not Enough*. As if you're always striving for something that's just out of reach.

TOO

HIGH

THE

SKY

S tuff they never tell you before you're famous, part three: it doesn't matter how big you get as an artist. It makes no difference if you are getting everything the industry wants you to – blanket press coverage, sold-out tours, healthy record sales. No matter how big it all becomes and how much profit people are extracting from your hard work, don't make the cardinal mistake of expecting positive encouragement from those around you.

This is supposed to be the time of your life. But, miraculously, there never seems to be any shortage of people saying things designed to beat down your confidence, as if they don't want you getting too big for your boots. If you're not mentally steeled for it, you'll find yourself trapped in an atmosphere where everyone feels defensive and threatened, backed into a corner with nothing but your own negative thoughts and plummeting self-esteem for company. And in that corner, alone, there's no one to help you challenge any of it, no one to tell you there's a different way to be. All of this is hard enough when you are in a band, which is like a little gang. But it's even tougher if you decide to do things off your own bat – in other words, make a go of going solo.

———

At the beginning of 1998 I was trying my hand at being a one-man band, squirrelled away at home, reaching for the sky. Finally,

I was recording a collection of my own material, from the drums to the vocals and the production. I also had a new girlfriend, Anna Norlander, a photographer from Sweden, who was a huge fan of Smog, Bill Callahan's early band. His dark, introspective music was often swirling around our house, and I liked the way it sounded as if it was recorded in a bathroom, on the loo. He also had this excellent cruel wit. I liked his vibe, as they say, and it made me realise it was possible for music to sound this way – it needn't be a big deal nor sound expensive.

I wasn't even going to release *The Sky Is Too High*; or, if I did, I wasn't planning to put my name on it. I didn't really know what to do with it: it was just a bunch of songs that I'd started to write because a neighbour of mine, Tony, had asked me a favour. He was a bit of a tasty geezer, with some vague connections to Madness and the London underworld. He also happened to be fascinated with boxing history and had written a screenplay about the life of Tom Sayers, a Victorian bare-knuckle fighter who lived in Camden and once owned the Laurel Tree pub. 'Come on, mate,' pleaded my friend, 'you're a musician: write us a couple of songs for the soundtrack.' So I wrote 'Me You, We Two' and 'A Day Is Far Too Long', which was the first time I'd written any songs of my own. I just thought, 'Let's try some simple words of poetry, quite emotional, and simple music, and see how it goes.' Then I went into Matrix Studios with engineer John Smith. There was a great old mixing desk down there, and we recorded the whole thing in a few days. It was like a lovely playground.

Recording each instrumental layer presented a whole new set of challenges, and I loved it. It was still unusual in 1998 to use a computer to record rock instruments, so I did it with an old-fashioned tape machine. There was no click track either; I simply sat there with my guitar, counted myself in and played the part all the way through. Then I got behind my old Slingerland drum kit, turned up the guitar really loud in my headphones and whacked the drums along to it. Bass and vocals followed in the same way, and I even added piano to a few tracks. Because there was no click track, the music sped up and slowed down in a slightly ramshackle way. Some of this was deliberate, I admit – I didn't want it to sound polished and professional. On 'Who the Fuck?', a very petulant punk-noise number, I did the drum track first, just to be extra contrary. There's a ridiculous, scrambled mess of a drum fill at the beginning, then it's *doof-doof-doof* and we're in. I just grabbed a guitar and followed the drums as best I could.

At one point Damon came over and had a listen to some of the songs. I said, 'If you think any of this stuff could be useable with Blur, then just say,' but after he had listened through everything he went, 'Nah, there's nothing there for me.' A few days later, I went over to his studio in west London, and he was singing my little song 'R U Lonely?' 'Oh, that's one of mine,' I mentioned. And he went, 'Yes, it's quite catchy, that one.'

I had written the second verse of 'R U Lonely?' in a hotel in Spain. I was at a festival where the lighting rig nearly fell on a band. It was pretty hairy, but the gig ended up being rained off, so everyone dashed back to the hotel bar. All sorts of people were there, including Dinosaur Jr, Pavement and Teenage Fanclub. I stayed for a bit, but eventually I couldn't handle it – there were too many people I thought were great in the same place. So I went up to my hotel room and wrote that second verse of 'R U Lonely?': 'In the daylight hours, I go out and kill the flowers . . .' Lyrically, it was a bit of a breakthrough – I felt that it really hit the nail on the head in terms of the weird existential angst I was experiencing. There's something quietly angry, lonely and alienated about it, compacted into a few phrases about cutting your own hair out of spite, setting your hands on fire and killing flowers.

'R U Lonely?' is in standard tuning, but elsewhere on that album I consciously tried to get out of the habit of automatically coming back to the same chords and progressions, such as D to G. It was a habit that was hard to break, and I used to annoy myself with it. 'That's All I Wanna Do' is in an open G, and the intro was made up of shapes on the fingerboard that sounded good. I tried to get into writing a song before my brain had properly woken up, before it could impose its habits on me.

Just round the corner from where I lived in Camden were some little brick huts that had been built to conceal an electricity substation. One of them had a strange pink elephant graffitied on the side that looked a bit like a mammoth in a cave painting, and that became the front cover of the album. It had been there ever since I could remember, and I just thought I'd take a snap of it. Not long after that the hut was knocked down, so I'm glad I managed to record it for posterity. It's a funny picture, and a lot of people think I painted it, but I didn't. I put some more enigmatic cave-painting-style graffiti on the back: a skull with the letters 'IT' sprayed across it, superimposed on the words 'Jeanne d'Arc May 1429'. There was no buggering about: I just took a picture of it, banged it on the album artwork, and that was it.

When it came out in August 1998, *The Sky Is Too High* was a respectable three-out-of-five-stars sort of thing. At least none of the reviews were especially bad. Journalists can generally smell a rat

– once they get a whiff of inauthenticity, then you're doomed. But if they think your work comes from a place of authenticity, whether they like it or not, they usually have some respect for it. I think that's what went on there.

At first I was planning to slip the album out into the world apologetically, without really telling anyone. My (and Blur's) new manager, Niamh Byrne, insisted otherwise. 'Just put your name on it – it's your solo album. Just do it.' Then the idea came up of getting a little label together. There was quite a ballsy young man I knew called Jamie Davis, who used to work in the Camden branch of Tower Records. Whenever I walked in there, he would approach me bearing cassettes of songs or demos by bands he knew, convinced of their greatness, telling me how badly they need a deal, and this, that and the other. 'What a confident bloke,' I thought.

So I went down to Tower Records and asked Jamie if he wanted to help me set up a label. 'Yeah, definitely!' Niamh put everything in place, and Transcopic Records heaved itself out into the world. ('Transcopic' is not a real word, by the way, just one that popped into my head.) Jamie came up with some nice groups on the A&R side, and it gave me a channel separate from Blur on which I could put my own stuff out. I'm not sure why I thought it was a good idea, as most of the releases ended up being licensed via EMI anyway. Perhaps the big label didn't want to be seen to be putting my solo stuff out, or maybe it was me wanting to look more independent. It's all lost in the mists of time now, but at least Transcopic gave me a chance to do other creative work. I enjoyed all the fun stuff that goes with it, like coming up with the logo, doing album covers and designing T-shirts and hats. Plus, of course, giving opportunities to other artists.

Transcopic releases had an aesthetic style of their own, with reverse-board artwork for the sleeves and CDs. It was a look I had seen on the American underground releases that I used to pick up in record stores in San Francisco or Chicago while on tour. I would rifle through the small-label punk stuff and pick up albums whose artwork was a long bit of cardboard folded in half, screen-printed and stuffed in a paper bag or transparent plastic sleeve. I liked the idea that it didn't have to be posh. You could sense the graft and the sweat that had gone into it, and it looked like it had been assembled in someone's front room rather than a factory – which was usually the truth. The reverse-board look of Transcopic was a reaction against the glossy box sets and digipacks of the late 1990s. Shabby chic was yet to arrive, and everything had to look clean, shiny and new.

I started to get a perspective on how the dynamics worked in other groups. Many of them became friends, but I could sometimes glimpse how fragile the relationships within bands were and how infuriating their stupid, petty arguments could be. There seemed to be a universal law that every group had to have one member who was a bit of a grumpy killjoy, far too precious about some musical rule, which basically prevented their band from progressing. Thankfully, Blur was never like that, although we had other problems, of course. But we never set ourselves any rules – anything was allowed, so long as it was true to the material.

———

If the Blur album was a successful reboot for the band, around us music was continually evolving and, like so much else as the millennium drew nearer, growing more intense. It was easy to forget that Britpop had been the centre of your universe, but the biggest developments in music during the 1990s were really taking place in a parallel electronic universe: dance music, techno, jungle and more experimental and abstract digital sounds. Occasionally these separate galaxies collided, in the form of the remix. William Orbit created probably the best remix of a Blur track ever, for 1997's 'Movin' On'. It was a fantastic eight minutes of complete disrespect for the original, and all four of us loved it the moment we heard it. After some discussion, William was mooted as a replacement producer for Stephen Street on our follow-up, *13*, which we started work on in June 1998 in Damon's scuzzy little studio in Ladbroke Grove. It was a far cry from the pristine, factory-like conditions William had established at his plush townhouse-studio in St John's Wood – like a musical Willy Wonka, with a gaggle of Oompa-Loompa-like assistants doing his bidding – but he accepted and bravely stuck it out.

At the same time, Blur was being asked to make remixes of other artists – it was all rather incestuous at that point. One of them was for Massive Attack's 'Angel', from their *Mezzanine* album, which involved me arriving at the studio to rubber-stamp a mix Damon had wrapped up the night before. 'Check this out,' he said, pressing the playback button. 'It's good, innit?' I listened and said, 'Er, yeah, I guess. If I could just suggest . . .' 'Great' he interrupted, 'so that's done then.'

I liked our version of Massive Attack, although it could have been a more collaborative effort. In the late 2000s I did a solo remix of the Beastie Boys' 'Double Trouble', on which I added some Hammond organ and extra samples. I also remixed a song by Lowgold – I found out that, by strange coincidence, me and

Lowgold's singer, Darren Ford, had lived on the same army estate in Colchester in 1976.

Stephen Street, who I know was a bit cut up about being replaced, even though he understood our reasons, was an old-school producer who believed in making a band feel good about themselves if they needed it, offering a sympathetic ear and good advice. William Orbit had those qualities too, but he had a more New Age aura about him – he was more cosmically and psychologically aware. It made his interpretation of sounds and songs intangibly different from Stephen's approach. When we were mixing '1992', I had a strong desire to push it in a particular direction and pointed out one little note in the guitar line. 'What if we tried to grab that note and put reverb on it?' 'We can try,' he said, and this small suggestion ended up with us sending every sound that was going through the mixing desk back through a plate reverb, and messing madly with the gain controls. It was just me and him in the studio, and he was wrenching these knobs around with wild eyes, pulling this mad noise straight down to tape, while I laughed my head off. On the finished track you can hear where that note kicks in; the reverb sounds like you're heading into a thunderstorm. That was magic to me. It was like he was conducting this huge tempest, this massive force.

William encouraged us to try out some pretty perverse sounds. He was quite comfortable when I upped the fuzz on songs like 'Bugman', as well as finding gentler textures for more trad songs like 'Coffee & TV' and 'Tender'. On 'Caramel' we explored realms we'd never ventured into before. We ended up hearing it on the radio of a taxi in Los Angeles, while sitting in the back with William and Beth Orton. I remember thinking, 'I can't believe this song's made it onto a Californian jazz station.'

He encouraged us to experiment and take risks, which was marvellous. We would spend most of the day jamming, and then he would take over, staying up all night, trying to piece together the bits we had left on tape. When we listened to the results the next morning, it transpired that he had transformed our fragmentary offcuts into fully fledged songs that seemed to spring directly from our creativity and subconscious. I don't know how he did it, but he had an amazing, alchemical way of structuring our raw material. He panned our scraps for musical gold dust, revealing in the process a Blur even we didn't know existed. The album ended up full of little masterpieces, and I still think it's a really lovely record.

———

One of those songs took my involvement to a new level. I was listening a good deal to a phenomenal album called *I Can Hear the Heart Beating as One* by the US band Yo La Tengo. I wanted us to have a song with a similar vibe to their 'Stockholm Syndrome', a cute, straightforward, poppy thing. At the same time, Damon had a vague idea for a song, but he still wasn't committed enough to try out a vocal melody and couldn't be bothered to come up with any lyrics for it, so I volunteered to write some. 'Go on then,' he agreed, 'but if you write the words, you have to sing them.'

That night I sat in my front room in Camden and scoured through my old notebooks and diaries for the seeds of lyrics, which I then developed and threw together to make the song 'Coffee & TV'. It had the 'Stockholm Syndrome' feeling I was after but reflected my anxiety and feelings of alienation – that the world is a scary place. It also coincided with me knocking alcohol on the head for a while, so my recreation consisted of drinking coffee and watching TV, which would take me away from this big bad world. A few different musical ideas fed into it: a 1970s middle-of-the-road, Eagles kind of vibe; a Velvet Underground 'Sister Ray' groove; plus bits of 'The Diamond Sea' by Sonic Youth. I came up with a run of slightly unexpected chord shapes, paring down the chords to two or three notes and accentuating the third note and the octave of each chord.

With William at the controls, I had a crack at the vocal myself. The first take was too jumpy and aggressive, and Damon made sceptical noises. I went in and did another one, softer and nicer this time, and it seemed fine. After that I jammed in a quick guitar solo as a placeholder. We got on with something else, but when we listened back to the track a week later, everyone said, 'Wow, that solo's good.' So we kept it.

'Coffee & TV' reached number eleven in the charts, which is probably the highest position a song of mine has ever achieved. The video – the brainchild of Garth Jennings from Hammer & Tongs – was declared best video at the MTV Awards. I usually found making videos an ordeal, but this was one of the few times I enjoyed it. It was about myself as a missing person, with my fictional 'family' – a mum and dad wearing Graham glasses, and a sweet little sister – mooning over my portrait in their suburban home. The idea of me going missing was a Blur in-joke, because I failed to turn up for things quite often. In the video my photo was also printed on a 'Have you seen this person?' ad on a cute animated milk carton, which goes wandering far from home. (The missing-person ad mentions that I had last been seen holding a baseball glove – a detail that was supposed to help the video get airplay in America.) We filmed it in an amazing show house somewhere in Middlesex that looked as if it hadn't been redecorated since the early 1960s. That's where I saw my first Eames lounge chair, with matching ottoman. I set my heart on one and eventually found a Herman Miller version in an antiques shop in Marylebone, which I still have. The video's innocent charm acted as a mild antidote to the leery laddishness of 'Country House'.

The album was called *13*, mainly because that was the number of tracks it contained. But '13' could also be drawn in such a way that it looked like 'B' for Blur. I wrote out the digits and our name on the front cover, which was the only time I drew the band's logo myself. Unfortunately I didn't get the 'r' right at all. It's much too curly, like old-fashioned handwriting, and I still curse myself for that. An oil painting of mine called *Apprentice* also appeared on the cover.

We had a meeting to discuss promoting the album, during which Damon gleefully conceded, '"Coffee & TV"'s going to have to be a single. Shit! I'm going to have to sing that for the rest of my bloody life!' In the event, I always took the vocal on that song, even though it was a scary moment, because the guitar part is bloody tricky in itself without worrying about singing in tune. But it was a nice moment too – fans treated it as if it was Graham having his little turn in the spotlight, and they would shout, 'Go, Graham!' I always felt they were rooting for me, and it's funny to see the way they nurtured these tiny loyalties and rivalries. 'Don't listen to Damon – he's a cunt! You're the best!'

———

There was a small bedroom at the top of my house in Camden where the window frame had rotted away – the perfect artist's garret. I occasionally painted up there, including the picture on the cover of *13* – for which I had in mind a figure resembling the young monk played by Christian Slater in *The Name of the Rose* – plus a few others that were used on our singles. I wasn't doing an awful lot of oil painting, though. I was starting to discover the possibilities of digital art, and the cover of the 'No Distance Left to Run' single – a black mountain with a sort of door at the top – is one of my earliest digital paintings. I preferred working that way because it is so simple to move the paint around and change your mind about details. With oil paint, one wrong move and you're spending the rest of the day trying to correct a blob that went astray. I never worked terribly carefully, so I could ruin a painting pretty quickly and never get it back to how I wanted it. So the idea of digital painting was an amazing liberation, at a time when things were also becoming freed up musically.

We were certainly getting the hang of crafting hit song material by that point. Damon had a talent for sussing out the limits of what the British listening public could deal with, and he could engineer a song that played to their intelligence without tipping too far over the edge: a nursery-rhyme lyric; a catchy chorus; hip-hop drums; a girl singing. The logical conclusion – the jackpot – was to engineer a cute band in cartoon form, like an update on the Banana Splits. By the end of the 1990s that's increasingly where his energies were being directed.

In around 1997 Jamie Hewlett began sharing Damon's flat in Westbourne Grove. I wasn't too pleased when, just after Damon had stopped seeing Justine Frischmann, Jamie took up with my ex-girlfriend Jane without informing me. It was there that he and Damon dreamt up the idea of Gorillaz. I thought it was rubbish. I might have been a bit jealous or treated it as a faddish obsession with hip hop on Damon's part. Gorillaz' music was cute and catchy but not particularly my thing. I liked 'Kids with Guns', especially live. I also liked the way Gorillaz became a sort of exhibition; that Damon became a curator of talents as they moved through the group. It takes guts to reach out to people like De La Soul and just say, 'Hey, d'you fancy appearing on this track?' He's got a lot of bottle, Damon, in that way. That was the best thing about Gorillaz, for me.

I don't know what Alex and Dave thought about it, as we didn't really discuss it together. For them, I think, it was just a side project that didn't threaten the future of Blur to any extent. I might have occasionally laughed it off as Damon trying to create a new version of the Monkees or the Banana Splits, but deep down, even though I acknowledged that he was working his butt off, I was bitter about Gorillaz doing so well. Success like that inevitably comes at a cost, which in this case was all the promotion and touring he had to do, instead of focusing on Blur. Although my *Sky Is Too High* album had come out that summer, for me it was always a side project. I didn't treat it as the launch of a solo career and didn't get a permanent band together or do many live shows around it. Damon, on the other hand, was cooking up a project that would go on to fill massive arenas and attract huge festival crowds.

———

Nineteen ninety-nine saw the publication of the first official biography of Blur, written by Stuart Maconie, and in the autumn our label put together a chunky box set of singles, *Blur:X*. Blur was starting to accumulate a history and an archive, including our enormous stage props: massive Ultranol pills, giant hamburgers and a micro-wave oven that Damon used to climb into and be 'cooked' with a frantic strobe light. Artists and music clubs were spearheading the gentrification of east London districts like Dalston and Shoreditch, and the Lux Gallery in Hoxton Square was one of the hip institutions leading the charge. They wanted to mount an exhibition of Blur-related artefacts. Given our arty aspirations, there was a lot to exhibit. We all donated personal stuff, as well as band memorabilia. Of course, eventually it became the gallery's project, which had its tedious and annoying aspects. The show was open for only one weekend in September 1999, and it seemed like a lot of work for a mere couple of days, but it was called 'Blur:X' to chime in with the release of the box set, and our trinkets, T-shirts, handwritten scrawls, paintings and drawings looked impressive when hung in the modern, minimalistic gallery space alongside the black-and-white op-art backdrop we used to hang at Seymour gigs. Plus, they threw a good opening-night party.

There were plenty of journalists around that night, and I was probably a bit short with some of their questions. It may have been part of the millennial rush – everything speeding up and getting out of control in the run-up to 2000 – but I felt as if I was being prodded for too many comments and surrounded by too much infrastructure, when what I really wanted was to talk to my friends and my mum, dad and sister, who had all turned up for the big occasion. I was still close to my family and was in the habit of visiting them at least three or four times a year, even when Blur was at its busiest. I had made enough money to buy each of them a car, and one Christmas in the mid-1990s I showed up in Colchester with masses of Christmas presents bought in London and five hundred quid's

Jupiter-style Monster (2001)
One of many from my Priory sketchbooks.

A Shadow Full of Faces (2001)

Elephant Dagger Boy (1993)

A painting inspired by Martin Carthy's 'Bill Norrie' (2015–17)

A painting inspired by Shirley Collins's 'The Cruel Mother' (2015–17)

Beaked Creature Ripping Some Stuff Out (2001)

The Old Gerbil Men in Jars (*c.*1993)
Enjoinment (*The Shitting Captain*) (1993)

*Pinstripe Monsters and Aloof Woman on
the London Underground* (1993)

worth of booze. They were excited by the presence of famous people at the launch party, though whenever they encountered them they rarely knew what to say. They were happy about the work I was doing, although they never asked me in any detail about the actual music. For them, I was still the youngest son/baby brother who needed worrying about.

I didn't get much time to hang out with them, though. As usual at fun events like this, Blur was the centre of attention, but that was precisely why we had a lot of obligations to fulfil. It was a battle to be able to relax and enjoy things. That reflected the wider reality of what Blur had become. The groups who had paved the way immediately before us, like the Jesus and Mary Chain and My Bloody Valentine, were no longer the 'alternatives' they had started out as but had moved from the periphery to become central to the musical history of their age. I felt that an era of amazing music – our era, even – was coming to an end. We had also tried to do something different, something alternative, when we started out, but it all got mulched into Britpop, the umbrella term for all that was good and bad about 1990s music. What the mainstream loved about Blur was our singles – the side of the group that I think of as 'the high-street Blur'. But if you took the trouble to explore our back streets and alleyways, there was more interesting material lingering around there. Perhaps it was only by operating as a solo artist that I would be able to keep on prowling around those darker districts.

JUST
FREAKED
OUT.
BACK
SOON

I n March 2000 I was overjoyed when me and Anna had a baby. I had been so excited when we went for the scan – it was the moment I realised this was something I had always wanted. We had planned everything all out and decided on a waterbirth at home in our basement. Typically, though, the best-laid pregnancy plans can easily become chaotic in real life. Anna's waters broke while we were out shopping in Tesco on the Camden Road. We rushed home, and I began filling the pool, trying to keep a constant temperature, as we had been instructed. We rang the midwife, who sounded disarmingly relaxed about the whole affair: 'I'll be there in a bit . . .' Eventually, at ten-thirty in the morning a female biker turned up at our door, who turned out to be the midwife. Five minutes later, she was down in the birthing room with Anna, and our little girl – Pepper – plopped to the surface. It was a life-changing moment.

Early that same year, I had begun recording my next solo album, *The Golden D*, with engineer Ben Hillier at Matrix and Mayfair Studios. With Damon involved with Gorillaz, I had found myself with more time on my hands to write new material of my own. This second album was quite different from my first. Ben was into extreme and perverse sounds, always willing to experiment and stretch the sonic envelope, which was why I liked him. He made recording seem easy. We filtered drums through synthesizers and sampled loops from LPs. I'd never seen anyone so fast on Pro Tools: he could keep up with the ideas as they were coming to me, which was pretty quick. No sooner had I played something than he would be frenziedly click-click-clicking on his mouse. I was impressed at how quick the workflow could be, how fast a track was finished.

While I was recording *The Golden D*, I skateboarded every day from my place on Camden Road to the studios we were recording in. I thought it would keep me fit, and it gave me a cardiac and adrenaline rush. A couple of times I descended into the dark, murky skater's underworld beneath the Southbank Centre. With its hardcore skate kids blasting metal and hip hop from beatboxes, and graffiti plastered on every available surface, it gave off a slightly menacing vibe. It was a different tribe from skaters in the US, where the board was more like a bicycle. In London, it was intimidating, especially in skate shops like Slam City Skates in Covent Garden, which had a branch of Rough Trade Records in the basement, whose staff could be equally intimidating if you didn't know what you were looking for.

A skateboard is a great alternative art canvas, and I have periodically drawn all kinds of ideas for images to be printed on boards. I like its very specific, limited shape and having to fit in graphically with that. My favourite skateboard was unusually wide, featuring an illustration of a First World War soldier in a gas mask, with trenches in the background. Above the door in my music room at home hangs a promotional skateboard, emblazoned with an image from the Beatles' *Yellow Submarine* cartoon. I was given that by Parlophone in the mid-1990s, around the time I was getting into skateboarding. I wasn't that brilliant. I managed to do a kick-flip once, and I used to ollie a little bit, but mainly I enjoyed using it to get about. I had a few pals who went skateboarding around London on Sundays, and they were extremely good – a couple were even professionals. That meant I lagged behind them in terms of skill, and more than once I found myself in mid-air, jumping down a flight of concrete steps, admonishing myself that I really shouldn't be doing this. I would drink too much, falling off the board and ending up in hedges on the way back from the pub.

With my interest in skateboarding it's perhaps not surprising that *The Golden D* starts off with a slamming skate-punk track called 'Jamie Thomas', which was a tribute to one of America's most daring 1990s skateboard dudes. I was watching a lot of skateboard videos at the time, especially promotional films by the skate brand Toy Machine. They featured Bam Margera, the prankster whose outrageous skating antics influenced later shows like *Jackass*. He and his mates were doing insane tricks to a soundtrack of hip hop, Santana and Iron Maiden. 'Dragonaut', by the stoner/drone-rock outfit Sleep, was another thing I really got into around then. Then the film *Gummo* came out, which had some crazy death metal on the soundtrack. I loved it. It might have been intended as dark and satanic, but I could also picture elves bouncing around to it. So I tried to do my own version of that – extremely fast, shouty metal.

The Golden D has a lot of holes. It's definitely not my best record. But it reflects the fact that I was trying out things I had never done before. There was 'Oochy Woochy', a weird hip-hoppy number that was almost Tribe Called Quest-like. Ben and I actually made the loops from proper vinyl, the old way. He brought in a couple of records, and we grabbed a sample and played some unison bass and guitar to make it sound old. It was a reaction to things like Guru's *Jazzmatazz* – the remixing and looping of 1950s and '60s jazz.

Most of the vocals were improvised over all that, as in 'Satan i Gatan', for example. I always thought it was funny whenever Swedes cursed, '*Aah, Satan i gatan!*', which means something like 'Satan's in the road!', spoken the way we would say, 'Bloody Nora!' That song was mostly chaotic, operatic nonsense. But it was a fun process – Ben and I were just mucking about, chucking drums through old Moogs and messing up the sounds. I also included cover versions of two tracks by the US alternative rock band Mission of Burma: 'Fame and Fortune' and 'That's When I Reach for My Revolver'.

I think I was first introduced to Mission of Burma by my girlfriend Jo in the mid-1990s. She was always trying to get me into different bands by playing me one song that could act as a gateway drug, the one that would suck you in. (She did that with Pavement too.) I liked Mission of Burma instantly. They didn't sound American; at first I thought they were some long-lost English band who might have supported Wire at some point. I'm a very rhythmic person; I like drums and choppy singing and guitar-playing. Mission of Burma had all of that, plus a punky, tribal quality. Some moments were quite chanty, some more aggressive, and some, like 'Einstein's Day' – one of my all-time favourite songs – were just desolate and poetic. But one thing that especially appealed to me was that they never sounded macho. You didn't feel these were people who were violent or had disrespect for anybody. Song titles like 'Max Ernst', 'Heart of Darkness' and 'This Is Not a Photograph' gave you clues that these people were coming from an art–poetry direction. That was good enough for me.

'That's When I Reach for My Revolver', from their 1981 album *Signals, Calls, and Marches*, is an anthem for the notion of 'better out than in'. It's an exercise in channelling frustration, meandering and simmering along for nearly the entire song, before suddenly exploding into enlightenment or pain. Clint Conley sings, 'They tell me . . . we're nothing . . . but slaves!' – there it is, it's out, he's finally said it. The best music can lock into your feelings at a particular moment in time, and you find your way through them along with the singer. That bit of 'That's When I Reach for My Revolver' brings tears to my eyes. Peter Hammill does something similar in Van der Graaf Generator's 'Lost', with a final ecstatic shout of 'I love you!' – a magical peak achieved after striving to get there for eight minutes.

Conley's delivery on 'That's When I Reach for My Revolver' is something the Americans do very well. They're not afraid to wear their hearts on their sleeves, and when he shouts the refrain, you hear all the onion-layers of a personality, from a six-year-old kid to an unstable adult. You wonder: why is he reaching for a revolver? What's he going to do to you? Is he shooting into the air? Is he off to murder someone, with the weapon concealed in his coat? Or is he going to use it on himself? He feels helpless and needs to regain a sense of power, and maybe the revolver offers that. But, in the end, all he really needs is just to shout those words out loud. It's a brilliant image that makes you imagine all sorts of possible scenarios.

I met Mission of Burma a couple of times and liked them as people. We did a photo session together for a French magazine; there were lots of daffodils and the photos came out extremely well. I had a good chat with Clint and the band's other guitarist, Roger Miller, over dinner at the ICA, and later, at their gig, Clint dedicated 'Einstein's Day' to me. American punk and post-punk musicians generally didn't work hard at constructing mad or eccentric personalities; their thoughts, words and music were enough. They didn't want to scare old ladies and wore pretty conventional clobber. It was a mindset that was political and not so much about destruction and vandalism.

The Golden D came out, warts and all, in June 2000. Around the same time, Damon was in Mali at a music festival in the desert, which led to him exploring all kinds of African grooves. I still hadn't fully developed as a guitar player and songwriter, and I hadn't yet grasped the idea of an album as a body of work, as a concept, even though I'd been weaned on *Sgt Pepper*, *Tommy* and the Pretty Things' *S. F. Sorrow*. My own stuff was still kind of scrapbook-y, and it would take some time – not until *The Spinning Top*, nine years later – before I was able to weave a coherent theme around the songs that I was putting together.

'The Golden D' refers to the chord of D, held on the fretboard but leaving out the middle finger. So it's a D with an open E on the end – a nice chord. Some people speculated that the album was about Damon, but they are always looking for an excuse to think that. I could slip over on some ice one morning and someone would say, 'Oh, it's because he was thinking about Damon.' In reality, I don't spend very much time thinking about him. We initially bonded through a mutual love of music, and what began as a creative friendship developed into a state of unspoken brotherhood. When we wrote music together, it was focused and intuitive. Outside of that we weren't great conversationalists, and it seemed selfish to expect emotional support from each other. Whatever other crappy burdens we were carrying around, they would normally get offloaded elsewhere, onto others. That's how it's always been between us. We still composed in much the same way as we always had. Damon would come up with a song idea and a demo tape, and I would listen and try to channel what he was getting at and sculpt it into a memorable song. It was a partnership of equals, in which each of us tried to please the other. Men's friendships, based largely around banter and mickey-taking, tend to be about keeping each other entertained.

———

At home, despite our relationship perking up in the early months of having a newborn, things were not going well with Anna. For various reasons, it was difficult for me to be apart from her and Pepper while on band business. Being a parent was certainly nothing like I ever imagined it would be. I was hopelessly romantic as a teenager, fondly imagining I would find a gorgeous partner, we'd have a beautiful baby and live happily ever after. I just thought that's what happens. But after various problematic relationships, I started to realise that family nirvana is actually a difficult thing to attain. By the time I had a baby of my own, a lot of tricky issues were overlapping. Most of all, I was depressed, and drinking again.

On 8 March 2001, the day after Pepper's first birthday, I checked myself into the Nightingale Hospital in Camden, a private institution specialising in addictions. I was prescribed the antidepressant Seroxat, which kept the worst of my anxieties at bay. I was there for twenty-eight days. It reminded me of my first visit to AA in 1996, when I was so nervous that I was sweating right down to my fingernails. At first I couldn't even pluck up the courage to go in; I sort of hovered near the door, and this woman who was taking the meeting motioned me in. I sat and chain-smoked at the side of the room, read the encouraging self-help slogans on the wall and listened to what people were saying. Afterwards, the woman who ushered me in had a little chat with me, which ended with her giving me a kiss on the top of my head and saying, 'You'll be all right.

Come back.' I thought, 'Wow, what a lovely woman.' Eventually I got to know people in there and kept on going – not for that long, but enough to know that the place wasn't really so scary.

The same month I went to the Nightingale, Damon, Jamie Hewlett and their friends finally released the first Gorillaz album. I wondered how this very zeitgeisty new project, which the critics and style magazines all seemed to adore, would affect our band's future. Damon also wanted Blur to work with Norman Cook, aka Fatboy Slim, which I wasn't too keen on, concerned, per-haps, that Blur would also become a kind of big beat conceit, à la Gorillaz. Meanwhile, in a music-press interview, Stephen Malkmus of Pavement accused us of ripping off his ideas and called Blur a second-rate Radiohead. (It didn't help that they had a song called 'Range Life' the same year we had 'Parklife' out.) It was pretty gall-ing to be slagged like that by one of your all-time musical heroes. The few times I met Stephen he was fairly aloof, and I was shy, so we didn't exchange many words. But he was always very pleas-ant and gracious. If we ever did sound similar, Pavement and Blur achieved that independently of each other. My guitar-playing was certainly influenced by Pavement, though: I loved the way their choppy chords also managed to sound smudged round the edges.

––––––

As the end of summer 2001 drew near, I was exhausted and didn't care about anything very much, least of all myself. I had nosedived into an extended drinking binge that was hard to pull out of. Cool opportunities were unfolding for us at the time that I barely remem-ber. We were booked to record a track with Marianne Faithfull for her new album, but I was in a bit of a strop when the day arrived and the whole thing seemed completely boring to me.

To all intents and purposes, I was still a member of Blur – but only just. Being in the studio with them was a welcome distraction from myself. Having conversations about music and working on tracks were a balm that could temporarily alleviate my looming sense of anxiety. I experienced panic attacks on the Tube a couple of times. There was a particularly bad one at Old Street, when the train made a piercing screaming sound and suddenly – in my imagination – seemed to be accelerating sharply downhill. The noise made by the friction on the rails reached a pitch that rose over me like a tidal wave, leaving me terrified and disorientated. I got off the train and had to curl up on the platform. I had occasionally had fainting fits in the past, and they had freaked people out. No one offered me any assistance or comfort on the platform – this was London, after all – and I eventually managed to calm down. A lot of my anxiety was based around the self-perpetuating fear of not wanting to draw attention to myself by having a fit in public.

At the beginning of August 2001 my next collection of solo material spread its wings and took flight. I had recorded, mixed and mastered *Crow Sit on Blood Tree* in a two-week stretch in May of that year, in a little studio called Zed One, behind the Unicorn pub on Camden Road, with Ben Hillier producing. It was a bit of a scrappy job, but it has a consistent sound – more acoustic and intimate than anything I had done before.

The songs had some humour in them, as well as certain lyrics that were rude and embarrassing, so I buried them low in the mix. There were songs about fatherhood in there; 'Tired', which was about being a knackered parent who's not getting enough kip, and

'Bonfires', which was a sweet lullaby about the darkness of the out-side world. 'Thank God for the Rain' was a little protest song with a chord sequence more juicy than anything I had written in Blur, and which I was proud of. Then there was 'Hurt Prone', which certainly described my self-image at the time. That one was a first take. It rocks out at the end, with nothing to anchor it down – no click tracks or anything, just totally free. It worked really well, despite its wilful amateurishness and deliberately bad singing (we messed around with the vocal afterwards to make it sound even worse!). There's an unhingedness to it that many might consider unprofessional. My drummer, Stuffy, once joked, 'It's almost as if you want to fail.' But, actually, he was kind of right. Perhaps I *was* sticking spanners in my own work because I didn't feel that I particularly deserved to be successful. Why not just make a mess instead?

In that way, the unvarnishedness of *Crow Sit on Blood Tree* said a lot more about me as a person than I realised at the time. I wasn't as convinced of my own worth as some people were, and self-deprecation had become my default setting. I tried to force myself to project more confidence, but once you start to interact with other human beings, it's extremely difficult to act the way you told yourself you would in front of the mirror! You leave the house and you find yourself among Them, out there, and you immediately revert back to the template – the person you have spent years and years learning to be. It's the same with my albums: as I've grown older I'm less in it for what people are going to think, but at the same time, I must be seeking some kind of affirmation, because I put myself through all the bother of putting music out. God knows why anyone does any creative work. Art's complicated.

I put albums out without bothering to promote them properly. I didn't do many gigs. I had some money and a young child, and I was concentrating on trying to be a decent dad and exploring normal life as a sober person – and trying out relationships as a sober person. This proved a lot more difficult than I thought it was going to be. I met some great people whom I possibly should have stuck around with, but didn't, because I was an amateur with an emotional age of six. Unfortunately for all concerned, they weren't the kind of people my dominant self found interesting at the time. The affairs I had were not emotional roller coasters – no disastrous downs and exhilarating ups – and I found it boring, not knowing that undramatic relationships were exactly what I needed. I was accustomed to a lot of drama, and – unfortunately – that's what I thought all 'normal' relationships were like.

By autumn 2001 I was aware of an increasing buzz of anxiety, which peaked every now and then. It wasn't anything extreme. Generally I've always been a pretty happy, cheerful person; I enjoy joking around and I've never had problems making friends. But the anxiety was a threatening presence. These panicky moments, my increasingly heavy drinking and the pressure of starting a new album with Blur all swirled up into a perfect storm. As we prepared to record the new album, Damon tried to reassure me, saying it would blow over soon, it was only a matter of time. But in the end I didn't turn up to the first sessions for *Think Tank* in November. I was in rehab.

———

In November 2001 I checked in for a twenty-eight-day stay at the Priory. That year had seen a slow ramping-up of issues and problems, with my personal relationships spinning out of control. In many respects, my world was smaller than it used to be. I was drinking, on and off, depending on whether I was looking after Pepper. The pain of my break-up with Anna had certainly been exacerbated by my drinking. I often sought refuge in pubs to escape the discomfort. When Blur started recording again, I was in the fast lane of a bender that had been juggernauting on for several months and I couldn't steer it over onto the hard shoulder. I had to crash the vehicle just to get my hands off the steering wheel.

I had never undergone any kind of psychotherapy before. The Priory offered personal, one-on-one consultations and group therapy, after which everybody gathered to eat together in this funny little dining room. I enjoyed the way each day was built around a structured routine. I think that is a really important thing for us humans. As a child you're surrounded by routine, but in later life, certainly in the creative industries, it's up to you to structure your time, and for long periods you might not have any structure at all. Gravity is turned off; you float up into the air and don't quite know how to return to an ordered life. No one teaches you this stuff, so it can be quite confusing.

I found group therapy incredibly helpful. Everywhere you turn there is either a professional or fellow patient willing to listen critically and sympathetically while you confess all your troubles, fears and insecurities. In return, you are witness to all of theirs. Taking part in it, for the first time in my life I realised that I had never properly had the chance to express how I felt without being ridiculed. They reckoned I was using alcohol because of my anxiety, but since alcohol is a depressant, it was having that effect on me and the anxiety was getting worse, so I was going round in circles. Just gaining this insight into my own condition was productive. Before I went in I assumed alcohol alone was responsible for my peace of mind. In reality, it was biting my arse and making my reasonably anxious self unreasonably so.

In the Priory, I encountered people who were much more messed up than I was, with a surprisingly wide range of lifestyles: everyone from drug-addicted lawyers and accountants to sports agents and DJs who had overdone things at raves. Very different upbringings and experiences had led us to this common point. We were all in this together, sequestered away in this privileged retreat, talking things through over a twenty-eight-day programme, all day, every day, with about an hour or two of communal telly-watching in the evening when everyone was absolutely knackered.

The therapy was of the supportive kind. You're coached by people who are themselves recovered addicts, so they know what they're on about. They help you to understand that you're not on your own and that everybody there is suffering from similar things, including a load of baggage they've been lugging around since childhood. It can be pretty brutal, and if someone in a therapy group isn't pulling their weight, they get a lot of crap from everybody else. But I learnt some great coping techniques, including cognitive behavioural therapy (CBT), which has almost become a natural way of thinking for me. CBT is a certain kind of dialogue in your head. You learn how to talk yourself out of anxiety or pull yourself away from fearing the worst. If I'm anxious about a forthcoming live show, for example (as I often am) – convinced I'm going to play the wrong chords and mess up every song because I haven't rehearsed enough – I can now reassure myself, 'Hey, you know what? It's not going to be the end of the world. The ceiling isn't going to fall on you and kill you if you make a mistake. It'll be all right.' The audience will see that you're a human being, which strengthens the connection.

I also use the Serenity Prayer, which I consider a work of genius: 'Grant me the serenity to accept the things I cannot change, the courage to change the things I can, and the wisdom to know the difference.' It's a very good piece of advice! Partly because it's so simple. For people who like to make everything as complicated as they possibly can, simple is good. Can you control a person or influence what they're saying? No. But can I control how I *receive* what they're saying? Yes. I can say, 'This guy is angry and calling me names, but I know I'm not whatever he's calling me, so let's forget it.'

The detox also involved working through the 12 Steps programme. Each step is a little exercise that you are supposed to practise every day until it becomes automatic. It's quite a long journey, with much to process. You need to come clean about a lot of stuff and apologise to anyone you have upset. That's where it gets tricky, but if you stick with it, you can sort out your history and give yourself a clean slate. From then on, you clean up your damage straight away. Instead of letting bad vibes fester unremarked upon for twenty years, you say sorry to your partner directly after you've snapped at him or her, and it's over. Most of all, the 12 Steps programme is really about keeping in good spiritual health and not being afraid to ask for help. That's the biggest one, and the most difficult.

I took some notebooks with me and kept myself entertained by reinterpreting the treatment in my own visual language. They are full of drawings of things that had been unleashed in therapy sessions – monsters and various dark imaginings. I tried to draw my interpretation of what that day's doctor or psychologist had been going on about. I didn't particularly welcome these dark visions, but they had a way of turning up uninvited, like dodgy guests at a party.

When you spend a lot of time around alcoholics, you're frequently confronted with thoughts of madness and death, since you're forced to ask yourself, 'Do I want to end up in prison, insane or in a coffin?' Because if you don't deal with your addiction, those are the only options going forward. Sometimes I would draw a hideous monster and show it to others in the Priory, and they'd say, 'Whoa! Graham's drawn another monster!' and we'd all have a good laugh. It's not like I was sitting there drawing hideous creatures in a tortured state of mind. Many of the pages in my notebooks are an absurd mix of the funny, puerile, moronic, traumatic and nightmarish. Most importantly, the act of drawing itself was a way of tricking my brain into not noticing my depression – let's call it 'sleight of mind'. For however long it takes me to make a drawing, I'm somewhere else, occupying a different area of my brain, instead of sitting in a bath full of fear.

On one of my drawings, I scribbled the words 'the pickle line'. That's addiction-speak. 'You've crossed the pickle line' means that you were once a cucumber, but after the cucumber crosses the pickle line, it becomes a gherkin. And once it's become a gherkin, it can't ever go back to being a cucumber. In other words, it's impossible for an alcoholic to revert to *not* being one. It's a hefty wake-up call. At the start of your treatment you assume that it will take you six months to knock your addiction on the head, and then you'll be 'back to normal'. But it doesn't work like that. Once alcoholism's activated in you, there's no getting away from it, no such thing as responsible drinking; full-blown abstinence is the only alternative. For some, it's difficult to accept. They don't want a doctor telling them they can never drink again. But that's the way it is. Calling it 'the pickle line' is a fun way of digesting a truth that's difficult to stomach.

After my first stay at the Priory, I tried to get as much support as I could. They continued the aftercare for another six months and assisted me in getting a sponsor for meetings and things like that. I received support from the Priory for another eight years, on and off. When you come off alcohol, you're throwing away the crutch that's propped you up in your anxiety, and it can leave you debilitated. But if you try to replace it with something else, that's just as bad.

Between 2009 and 2017 I thought I had the whole issue completely licked and under control. I truly believed that I could have a few drinks over a couple of days and then stop when I had to; I'd be fine, apart from the hangover and the odd nightmare. I finally understood that it wasn't the drinking itself that was at the root of the problem; it was what was happening between the relapses. In the months between each relapse – OK, let's call them 'binges' – I was anticipating and planning the next one. It's important to gain an insight into what was going on in your life when you picked up the bottle in the first place. Why did you pick it up? If what you're doing when you're not drinking is thinking about drinking, that's not living; it's being stuck in a trap.

After the last blowout (as late as July 2017), I immediately went to a meeting, got a sponsor and worked on getting through all twelve steps with enormous momentum. That made me realise that previously I had been half-hearted in my approach. I hadn't fully understood what I was saying or doing and spent too much time between steps. After all, there's no guarantee that you'll reach the end of all twelve steps and automatically feel great.

I am convinced, though, that the 12 Step programme is a work of genius. By the time you get to number four (making a searching moral inventory of yourself) or five (admitting, to yourself and others, the exact nature of all your wrongs), you feel like you've been shot from a catapult, propelling you onwards and upwards. Then it gets harder. Step nine was the first fence I fell at. It asks you to make clear and direct amends to those who have suffered because of your addiction. You look at that step and you feel the fear immediately. But I saw it through.

After completing the programme, to keep yourself in decent shape spiritually it's good to help other people, in the same way that others helped you. You can meditate or pray. Praying doesn't have to be to God; it can be to anything you want – a statue of Beethoven, for example, or an ash tree. It's mainly about externalising the stuff in your head. Speaking it out loud – giving yourself a pep talk – is incredibly helpful: it cuts out the cross-talk in your brain. It all boils down to being a decent human being: not lying or being horrible to people, and not believing you're the centre of the universe.

Ultimately, though, I have learnt that the best thing you can do if you think your drinking is out of control is not to worry about spending weeks in an institution such as the Priory; just get to a meeting as fast as you can. It's scary, but you must do it. You have to latch onto somebody there whom you think looks in good shape and start talking to them. At first you might be concerned that they'll say, 'Ugh, go away, you horrible drunk!' But people are actually very friendly. There's a lot of good humour in those rooms, a lot of happiness, laughter and mickey-taking. And if you are in a really bad place and need it to be serious, it can be that too. They call it the Gift of Desperation, because you're desperate enough to start doing something about your predicament. In those groups I learnt to recognise hope again.

Meanwhile, my relationship with Anna, Pepper's mother, had continued to deteriorate, and we separated in November 2001. I thought it was the best thing for both of us, given my levels of anxiety. I felt like I should be concentrating more on my own needs. I became increasingly aware of walking the tightrope every day, of the importance of balancing one's own needs with those of the people around us, especially our daughter. There was enough money coming in from the previous ten years of Blur, new publishing deals and royalties, which enabled me to live a happier, quieter, smaller life.

My acoustic guitar had been my only roommate during my first stay at the Priory. I even managed to write a few songs on it while I was inside. They were the starting point for my next album, *The Kiss of Morning*, which I began work on in April 2002, shortly after I had been discharged. It was a lovely feeling to wake up early for a change, sober and clear-headed. I hadn't got round yet to putting curtains up in my bedroom in my Camden house. That's why the album's called *The Kiss of Morning*, because I started waking up with the sunshine blasting through the windows, and I felt caressed by light.

FINGERPICKING GOOD

A t turning points in their creative lives, musicians often refresh themselves by looking to folk music, whether it's in terms of subject matter, instrumental technique or just a general sound and feel. Even though *The Freewheelin' Bob Dylan* is one of my favourite albums ever, I embraced folk relatively late in life. While hanging around the Camden record shop Rhythm Records in the late 1990s I had come across a British folk-rock compilation called *Rave On*, which had tracks by Maddy Prior and Tim Hart, Shirley Collins and the Albion Country Band, Martin Carthy and Shelagh McDonald. And back in the mid-1970s my dad always used to crank up the radio whenever Steeleye Span's folk-rock hit 'All Around My Hat' came on – he loved a bit of power-folk shuffle. It must have made an impression on me, because I thought it was really cool too. But I abandoned that kind of music during the Blur years.

Coming fresh from that first stay in the Priory, in my newly enlightened state folk started to make sense again. I listened with fresh ears to singers like Shirley Collins and tried my hand at finger-style guitar-playing. I studied recordings by master guitarists like Davey Graham and Bert Jansch and thought, 'Instead of sitting here moaning about not being able to play that way why don't I give it a go?' A huge part of the appeal of English folk was the voices, in particular Maddy Prior's and Martin Carthy's. They played together for a brief period in one of the early line-ups of Steeleye

Span, and I was wowed by the incredible harmonising textures they wove together. Their voices weren't flowery but nasal, straightforward, almost deadpan, coming from a completely different, more ancient origin from, say, Mariah Carey, Ray Davies or Otis Redding – or even Nick Drake. Unlike the Rolling Stones, who gathered no moss, this music had been sitting there gathering a hell of a lot of it.

The Kiss of Morning was more folk-influenced than anything I had done before. There were none of the metal or skate-punk-type elements I had used previously, and some moments even had shades of country blues. After I had written 'Song for the Sick', a rather angry song whose words were written at four in the morning because I couldn't sleep, I realised that the melody is a rip-off of the American folk song 'Which Side Are You On?', which dates back to the Depression and was made famous by Pete Seeger. Another song, 'Latte', has a Bert Jansch-style fingerpicking element.

I was determined that the album should be completely organic, so I recorded it with Mike Pelanconi at his Titanic Studios in Wood Green, which was full of lovely old analogue gear. I had some great musicians on *The Kiss of Morning*: Louis Vause played Fender Rhodes piano, and pedal-steel guitarist B. J. Cole came and played on a couple of tracks.

It was a pretty confessional album, and some songs were resentfully autobiographical. I regret giving so much away in 'Song for the Sick', because it was about a real person who was actually a great bloke. He had started seeing an ex of mine, which by that time wasn't strictly my business, and he was really only doing the same thing I had done myself: falling in love. After hearing that he had been teased for having a song written about his love life, I thought, 'Who am I to criticise somebody who only did what I did, who is human and has feelings that they acted on? Is it because I'm angry with myself? Why am I angry with him for not shying away from what he felt?' Eventually I apologised. 'It's all right,' he said, 'it didn't bother me.'

'Latte' was another song taken from my own life. I had stopped drinking and was fully comfortable in my own company, without getting bored out of my head. After pottering around Camden Town, watching people and picking up ideas for songs, I usually ended up at Henry J. Bean's pub on Camden High Street, drinking lattes by the pint. The food wasn't great, but there was a girl working there who was fascinating. Whenever she reached up for a glass, she threw a beautiful shape. We'd make some small talk, and at about two o'clock I'd saunter off home with way too much caffeine sloshing around. One day I said, 'Can I give you my number?' And she said, 'God, I was wondering when you were going to do that! It's been weeks!' I went out with her for a few months, and it was her that inspired the song 'Latte', because I remembered how she 'stretched into a form that would hurt your eyes to see'.

I often wonder if the artwork scared some people off. This one was the most expensive package I had made so far: a gatefold sleeve, printed twice on reverse board because the ink sank in, and with a silver coating on top. I drew the main image while sitting in Henry J. Bean's. It's small enough to keep in an envelope. I got quite exhausted by it, because I wanted a nice booklet inside the CD, which meant doing tons of drawing and painting for it – blue elf-women and borders and silver foil. I spent weeks trying to get this flipping artwork together, but I've never been one to have my own phizog on the front of an album cover. I knew the game I was supposed to play, but to me it was unattractive. You'd see these beautiful posters for George Michael's new album, with its flawless black-and-white photograph of the artist; even Damon's solo album *Everyday Robots* features a picture of him sitting on a stool in a cool coat. There's nothing wrong with that, but I thought it was much more arty and indie to have images on your cover that came from a weird, intuitive, arty direction.

What I think I finally began to understand, after finishing *The Kiss of Morning*, is the extent to which songwriting is a craft, just as much as it is an art. The secret is to do a little bit every day. Sit with your guitar and see if you can get a song together. It doesn't always work, and in that way it's no different from drawing, but after a couple of weeks you'll end up with a clutch of four or five songs that give you a buzz of satisfaction. It's rather like being a gold prospector: you need to be prepared to spend a long time in the wilderness before you finally hit a seam. When you strike it, you keep excavating, until suddenly four songs have become forty, of which fifteen are really good.

I also began to focus on keeping it simple. Country songs, I found, are fantastic teachers in this regard – they practically write themselves. (Although you have to be careful, because it's easy to write one that's been written already.) Three chords – C, G, F – a story, a pretty melody and an A minor chucked in to capsize the whole thing into sadness.

———

Folk as a genre tends to get a bit of a bad rap because of the 'hey nonny nonny' clichés and the skipping about, but that image is very misleading. A folk song really can be as serious as the news when it's sung in that deadpan, untrained way. It makes the songs all the more powerful. Anyway, morris dancers are as tough as old boots. I've heard plenty of stories about bikers turning up to country pubs and taking the mickey out of morris dancers, only to get themselves beaten up and chased off the premises. Morris dancers can drink tons more ale than bikers – and they've got sticks.

My first brief encounter with one of the most venerable figures of British folk – Bert Jansch, to be precise – was not terribly auspicious. I played on the same bill as him in 2003, at a festival called Down the Dustpipe at London's Royal Festival Hall, curated by Pavement's Stephen Malkmus. Not only did I appear with a new and rather hurriedly rehearsed band, but still being sober, I drank fifteen cups of coffee during Bert's set. Even back in the early 1960s Bert was known as the most formidable guitarist on the folk-club circuit, and as I watched him play, I began to have a very bad feeling about the whole evening. I was due to start my own set directly after his, playing two or three acoustic songs all on my own. Once on stage I played standing up, with my guitar strapped around me. This was something I soon learnt to avoid when performing acoustically, because as I started the first song, I felt my knees turn to rubber, and my already weak voice took on an involuntary and very embarrassing vibrato. I was shaking and sweating, and as if that wasn't bad enough, I was struggling with my old, clapped-out Harmony Sovereign guitar. It was absolutely horrific. I've never known a feeling like it.

Until the mid-2000s I associated the acoustic guitar with pain and difficulty. Whenever Blur needed an acoustic part, I just grabbed whichever acoustic guitar lay close to hand. It put me off the instrument, because they were so horrible to play. When I decided to have a proper go at finger-style guitar and learn a bit more about it, I took myself down to Denmark Street and went into the back room at Hanks. I was interested in smaller-bodied guitars that had more space between the strings, and came away with a Martin OM28V (OM refers to the body shape, 28 means rosewood, and V means vintage neck profile). It was a couple of grand – a lot of money. I'd never spent so much on a guitar before, but the difference was amazing. I chucked my plectrums away, attempted to grow my nails and knuckled down to try and learn it. I spent hours playing it every day.

The day I bought that guitar, in 2005, Davey Graham and Bert Jansch were playing at Oxford's beautiful Holywell Music Room. It was built way back in Joseph Haydn's day and functions mostly as a classical concert hall. There's no PA, just an organ at one end and spartan wooden seating. Davey, who was one of the great folk geniuses of the 1960s, had been away from the music scene for a long time, but a fan of his, Mark Pavel, had started to manage him and was trying to reactivate his music career and make him some money. Despite Davey's status as the granddaddy of English country blues/jazz/folk – he made an incredible album with Shirley Collins in 1965, *Folk Roots, New Routes* – he was living in straitened circumstances just round the corner from me in Camden.

I phoned Mark and said, 'I'm coming to the show tonight and I've just bought this guitar.' He said, 'Bring it with you!' So I drove to Oxford, went into the dressing room, and there was Bert, on the sofa, playing some blues to warm up. Davey was walking up and down with a drink in one hand and a set of Tibetan finger cymbals in the other at one moment, then clipping his nails and muttering to himself the next. Bert was just sort of nodding and smiling at him.

Bert took a look at the spanking new guitar I was carrying and said, 'I used to have one of these – let's have a look!' He ran through a few licks and then exclaimed, 'Cor, these strings are like tree trunks, aren't they?' I found it rather devastating that Bert Jansch thought my strings were too thick. Then he kindly explained that using thinner strings made it much easier to perform the kind of bends that you need for his style of playing. So it ended up being an educational evening.

Bert and Davey each did their allotted fifteen minutes on stage, then came backstage. I was showering them with fanboy compliments when Mark asked me if I would like to take a turn and play a few songs. 'Shit, really?' 'Yeah,' he said, 'just do a couple of songs in the break.' So that led to me trying to tune this new guitar. Tuning a guitar in front of guitarists you admire is thoroughly humiliating at the best of times, and I couldn't get the B string – always a difficult one on the acoustic – in tune at all. I asked Bert, 'How do you tune a B string?' He replied, 'You can't.' I looked up at him, expecting to see a sympathetic smile, but he was poker-faced. Was it true or was he ribbing me? I didn't have a clue and cackled nervously, my cool well and truly lost. It calmed my nerves a little, though, to think that maybe even Bert Jansch might struggle to tune up sometimes.

I went on and did a couple of songs, panicking because my nails weren't right, but I got a good clap and escaped as fast as I could. In the end, though, it was a lovely experience, and I have grown to adore Bert's voice and guitar-playing more and more. I've struggled to learn some of his songs and those of his former group, Pentangle – one of my favourite bands ever. For me, Bert's records have proved to be an education and a well of inspiration. I sit and play a song or two of his every day as part of my practice and for the sheer enjoyment of playing them. I like how the songs make my fingers move and am always surprised at the sound coming from my guitar. I will never stop learning from Bert.

The next day Davey happened to be doing a similar double-header gig with Martin Carthy, so I went to that one as well, and that's when I really started to get to know Martin better. I loved his tunings; he spent a lot of time on them and thinking about how he should voice the chords and how they should back up these old folk melody lines. I love him. He was quite paternal and taught me all sorts of small but necessary tricks, such as how to grow your nails ('Rub a bit of Vaseline on them every day, then just leave them alone and *don't bite them*'). I asked him about his Fishman Blend pickup system, which allowed him to blend the microphone with the under-saddle pickup. He always kept up a really good, thumping bottom end, where he'd be damping and clonking the fat string. I was experimenting with thumb picks and noticed that he had this quite sharp, pointy zither pick, made of brass or copper. He gave one to me, which is now in my spares tin, and I absolutely treasure it. But when you've got a really good pickup system on your acoustic guitar, with the tunings dropped down so your bottom E is as low as a C, and thump that through a PA, the pick makes a hell of a noise.

———

Martin Carthy once said folk songs are full of people who are all trying to do the right thing, but it always ends in tragedy. There's one song in his repertoire, 'Bill Norrie', in which a man thinks his wife is having an affair; he disguises himself as her, heads off down to the greenwood, meets his young rival and lops his head off. 'Husband he had a long knife, it hung down his knee / He took the head of young Billy and off his fair body.' As if that wasn't enough, the lady then reveals her murdered lover was actually her son, born from an incestuous liaison with her own father. It just goes from bad to worse, like some appalling horror movie.

Electric folk – Steeleye Span and Fairport Convention, for instance – sometimes had that shuffling pub-rock beat, but there was always something otherworldly and magical about the voices of folk and the lessons in life they were handing down. They're cautionary tales, mysteries, edge-of-your-seat stuff. I've seen Martin Carthy playing in the back rooms of pubs. He stands right in front of you, singing, with people sitting around him on rickety chairs. A strange lyric might crop up that makes a couple of girls in the crowd burst out laughing. People wander in and out of the pub; some walk past Martin carrying beer, while he moves his headstock out of the way. The informal setting really appeals to me. It's not high art, it's folk – by and for the people.

There's also a wonderful continuity. Martin's way of working has hardly changed since the 1960s. He still gets on the train to go to a gig and kips in someone's house rather than a hotel. I'm sure he must love it. His brain is crammed full of so many incredible tunes, like 'Bill Norrie' – a great song whose chords he once taught me. I've also played 'The Grass Grows High', which was one that Martin made popular, at the Roundhouse.

There's something I find very romantic about that generation of peacenik folkies, with their acoustic guitars and duffel coats, and who all met each other on CND marches. Jacqui McShee, the singer with Pentangle, is more jazzy, and a lovely, welcoming person as well. Because I am much younger and come from the Britpop world, that generation of musicians could easily have treated me as a pretender, but none of them have ever had a weird word to say to me about anything. I think they've always felt chuffed that anyone is still interested in that music and wants to celebrate it and play it. Martin once told me, 'Sod all those people saying you can't do this and you can't do that. The only disservice you can do to folk music is not to play it at all.' That makes sense, and the folk community believe the music and the tradition are too important to worry about whether or not it's being done 'right'. Well, most of them . . .

I've always liked carols and the older hymns which have their roots in folk songs, in the same way that Christianity built its churches on pagan sites to whitewash the old religion. Even while I was at school I could recognise that the 'Coventry Carol', which is rather bleak, was medieval in origin. I just find it beautiful. I do love the really old folk songs, the ones that seem to be about magic and witchcraft, like 'Alison Gross', which Steeleye Span did a great version of: 'She must be the ugliest witch in the North Country.' I was also struck by a Shirley Collins compilation, *Fountain of Snow*, which featured her singing and playing the banjo, while her sister Dolly accompanied her on the portative organ. I loved the repetition and droney quality of her version of 'The Cruel Mother'. It's a mysterious murder ballad, and it makes you wonder what would drive a woman to do something so extreme as murder her two children shortly after they were born. But the song contains just enough information about her situation: she may have been a noblewoman, and the children were born out of wedlock, so the shame caused her to commit this outrageous act.

I did a series of paintings about many of these songs. They're pretty hair-raising, those stories, and yet their language can be as dispassionate as a news bulletin. 'Lucy Wan' is another pretty heavy song, about incest and death. Lucy's pregnancy is described as: 'There's a baby growing between her two sides.' Her brother runs her through with his sword because she's carrying his baby, and then the mother comes along and says, 'Why is there blood on your sword?' At first he lies: 'Well, I killed the horse because it wouldn't do what I said,' and 'I killed the greyhound because it wouldn't catch a rabbit.' The mother's having none of it. 'That's not the blood of your greyhound.' Finally he drops the bombshell: 'No, it's the blood of my sister, Lucy Wan, she was pregnant with my baby.' It's an object lesson in how a song can turn dramatic events into an almost iconic moment – rather like a painting, in fact.

BEETLE
UNDER
A
ROCK

While I was sorting myself out in the Priory, the rest of Blur got well under way with work on *Think Tank*. A few months after I came out, in May 2002, I rejoined them in the studio – Ben Hillier was producing – and put guitars on about four songs, including the long track 'Battery in Your Leg', which I was pretty pleased with. In an effort to be open and honest about myself and what I was capable of, I concluded that it would be risky for me to engage in the promotion and touring for this album, although I made it clear that I was there if they needed me. There were still plenty of counsellors around me advising, 'Be careful what you get yourself involved with. Don't plunge straight into work, don't put yourself in any danger. People, places and things: be aware of those three when you go back out there.'

I didn't feel like I was being taken very seriously by the band and had a meeting with our manager, Chris Morrison, who advised me to take time off from the studio sessions. In fact, to all intents and purposes I quit Blur after recording those four tracks. It took the rest of 2002 for them to finish making the record, in a process that included creating a makeshift studio in Morocco for six weeks and trying out different producer–collaborators, such as Norman Cook. I had said earlier that the idea of working with Norman didn't appeal to me, but that was based on instinct rather than any actual impression of him; in fact, we had never actually met.

Alex got married bang in the middle of all this. Dave noticed me at the wedding and said, 'God, well done for having the guts to turn up – good on you, mate.' I had a bit of a laugh that day with Damon and the others, and Alex placed me next to him at the wedding breakfast, which was a nice gesture. I was surprised to see him devouring huge pieces of lamb, as previously he'd been a staunch vegetarian who used to throw fish out of the window if he ever found them on his plate. At some point I went to the bar for a coke, where I found myself standing next to Norman. There had been an awful lot of fuss made in the press about the two of us having a problem with each other. He asked me awkwardly if we were OK. 'Everyone seems to think we hate each other,' he said. Did they? I didn't really know anything about it, so we had a big cuddle. I liked him; we were cool.

I was absent when *Think Tank* came out in the middle of 2003 and Blur went on tour. Secretly I was happy to observe that they needed five extra musicians to fill my shoes. Poor Simon Tong, the former Verve guitarist, was drafted in and had the thankless task of working out all my ridiculously stupid guitar parts. It was a confusing time for the band – and probably for the fans too. The tour was demoralising for Blur, and the group was effectively laid to rest after that. The break was something we really needed, regardless of how it came about. Damon had stuff going on: not only Gorillaz, but he was also becoming much more involved with African music via his Mali Music project. Alex was tied up in a project with Sophie Ellis-Bextor. I was getting my fingers and mind around writing more songs, putting the next solo album together, bringing my daughter up, keeping away from alcohol and staying at home a lot. Just that was enough.

I refer to these years, roughly 2002–6, as my beetle-under-a-rock phase. My energies were focused on living a quieter, more sober life. I was co-parenting a little girl and wanted to give most of my attention to her. I was content with scuttling out to buy food for that night's dinner, picking up Pepper from school, cooking meals. Once, standing in line with Pepper on the way in to London Zoo, I caught sight of Damon and Jamie Hewlett ahead of me in the queue. When we got in, I saw them heading off in the direction of the gorillas – the ones after whom I believe their band was named. I felt far too awkward to say hello and spent most of the afternoon steering Pepper away from the monkey house towards the opposite end of the zoo. Thankfully our paths didn't cross, as I don't think I would have known what to say to them.

Privately I was quite wrapped up in my own world, developing my skills as a guitarist and finding myself as a songwriter. When I wrote the material for my next album, *Happiness in Magazines*, in late 2003, I felt like I'd turned a corner. I'd love to tell you that waiting for a good song to strike is like waiting for a bus to come along, but it takes practice and persistence. I'd always instinctively known how songs should be constructed, and I was constantly involved in structuring and arranging them in Blur. I had a feel for the little devices and details that a song needed in order to catapult the Blur audience into a rousing, memorable chorus, but I hadn't quite managed to go as widescreen as that with my own material. 'Freakin' Out' and 'Bittersweet Bundle of Misery' were the first of my solo pieces that I felt matched the dynamics and structure of Blur, rather than providing wilfully apologetic indie introspection.

I felt like my songwriting was expanding. It was no longer so self-denying or miserable, or just noisy for the sake of it. Now I was making properly structured pop songs like the Kinks and the Beatles used to make, with proper intros and short guitar solos. At the same time, I was learning how to be a bit more mischievous lyrically and to express myself less clumsily. I was able to write in a more cheeky and sarcastic vein, rather than it being heavy and heart-on-sleeve. That lightness had something to do with me reaching my mid-thirties and mellowing out a little, my music tastes changing. All that rubbed off on the album.

Lyrics are a lovely struggle, as you work out what kind of emotional drive or direction a song needs. A song has to have a concept or a subject; once I crack that, I see the lyrics arriving in a rush. Sometimes it's tricky to open up the box of words that are going to be available for you for a particular song, and you need to find the key, which could be as little as half a sentence. Normally I try to trigger that association by singing vowel sounds or phrases that don't quite make sense; in among the music, the strange poetry of lyrics starts to subconsciously suggest itself.

Sometime in 2003 I went to a show by the Californian indie group Grandaddy, and at one point in the set the singer, Jason Lytle, kept repeating this phrase which sounded to me like, 'There's happiness in magazines . . .' I don't know for sure if that's what he *was* saying, but the phrase stuck in my head. I don't believe there is much happiness in magazines, although many of them try to convince readers otherwise by encouraging them to consume the products they promote and advertise.

The song everyone remembers from *Happiness in Magazines* is 'Freakin' Out', released in March 2004, which was my first solo Top

40 hit (in with a squeak at number thirty-seven). The *NME* called it 'maybe just the best flaming rock 'n' roll record of the week, the month and almost certainly the year'. It was one of the first songs to give me the confidence that I could make it as a solo artist, to make me feel OK about searching out Stephen Street as the producer who might give it the welly it needed. It was the first time I consciously tried not to do myself down or act like a control freak and got other people involved.

I remember Steve Lamacq playing the single on his BBC Radio 1 show and saying, 'Phone in if you think you know who this is – I bet you can't guess.' People came up with some extraordinary suggestions – one even thought it was John Lydon – and I felt gratified that I was capable of making records Steve Lamacq could get behind. They weren't noisy, resentful rants any more but proper songs with some of the angry energy of the old punk songs, a bit like Buzzcocks.

When 'Bittersweet Bundle of Misery' came into my brain, I was sprawled on the sofa in front of the news, twiddling around on a guitar. The three chords at the beginning of the chorus formed a nice little sequence, and it gave me the momentum to relax into it. It's about my weird resignation to the fact that my significant other is a five-year-old; the loving realisation that my main relationship is with my daughter – my bittersweet bundle of misery. It's wonderful, and mildly depressing at the same time. Unless you're a parent, you'll never quite understand why that is. I was trying to have other relationships, and having a daughter would sometimes make that complicated . . . Although 'love' – a much-overused word in pop – is nowhere near adequate in describing the emotion you feel for your kids.

'Bottom Bunk' is about going on a crappy holiday where you are forced to share a sleeping area with someone who winds you up. One of my favourites is 'No Good Time', which was about New Year's Eve back in 2001, when I went to one of Danny Goffey and Pearl Lowe's New Year's Eve parties. I had just come out of the Priory, and the Libertines and all sorts of people were DJing, while I was hiding, petrified, in the corner. I met a mouthy and extremely confident kid called Mairead Nash there. I was stunned by her amazing self-assurance and thought she would go far. Not long after, she was DJing on the BBC as part of the duo Queens of Noize. I also met Liv Tyler that night, who was absolutely lovely and favoured me with the warmest smile I had ever seen. Still, being at a celebrity party was uncomfortable because I was trying to stay sober and there was a lot of drinking going on. Hence, 'No Good Time'.

'All Over Me', from *Happiness in Magazines*, and 'Just a State of Mind', which appeared on the next album, were dredged up from a well of typically British melancholia. For an English songwriter of a certain age, that world view, laced with self-deprecating wit, seems to be the default setting. I've never come across bands from any other nation that do it quite so well. The Swedish band Bob Hund managed something close to it, and Anna Waronker's splendid group That Dog touched on it, but the English are world-beaters at romantic, honey-dripping melancholia, which I believe comes from an academic or classical mindset. If you think about early, psychedelic Pink Floyd, and the songs Rick Wright used to compose – 'Remember a Day', 'Cirrus Minor' and 'Seesaw' – they're almost churchy. That's what I've always loved about Pink Floyd: those elongated outros with an organ circling round and round;

you can almost hear the ghost of a choir and the babble of a brook, and birdsong trailing on for ever. That, for me, is bliss in musical form. I have known that shivery feeling in Grantchester Meadows, on the edge of Cambridge, where you can walk around and look at cows and the ancient church, and sit in the garden of the Orchard Tea Room and enjoy a view that hasn't changed for several hundred years. The countryside pokes right into the city. I love that.

My nationality is important to me. That's not the same as being nationalistic. I've never felt hugely defensive about England, Great Britain or the United Kingdom. I'm not an imperialistic sort; I don't feel the urge to conquer foreign lands or wage war. So much of the country we are supposed to be proud of is under private ownership. When it comes to ancestral land, much of it was effectively stolen in the eighteenth century. So it's a bit rich when toffs chase you off with a shotgun or whip you out of the coppice if you trespass on their estate. I am very fond of the land and the people: I think that's where the real English are to be found. I'm probably as English as you can get – which means I am likely to be descended from ancient Norwegians or other invaders.

England hits the sweet spot for me, in so many ways. It has a decent climate, doesn't get too hot or cold, and none of its insects are likely to kill you. I did see an adder once, curled up in my outside drain, but when I came back hoping to move it along with a forked stick, it had cleared off. Most of the dangerous beasts of Britain tend to make themselves scarce before they can do much damage.

Occasionally, when life gets too complicated, I remember that it is technically possible to go and live in the middle of Yorkshire, forget about everything and live like it's 1890. No internet and minimal possessions – it sounds attractive sometimes. You could be in your own world, regurgitating your own thoughts, no longer drawing on anything but yourself creatively. In the end, though, I don't know whether that's particularly healthy. Most of my art and music is based on what I see in the streets or hear on the news and my reaction to it. If I lived in the country on my own for too long, I know I'd get bored, and that would signal danger. A hermit's life is not for me; I would eventually need human contact. I like affection, even if it's just a kind word or two.

———

During this period of self-care and renewal, I resolved to start following the advice of my record label a bit more, instead of being a bloody-minded hermit and refusing to promote any albums or go on tour. After the success of 'Freakin' Out', I was enjoying playing punky songs again. I got my little band together, and we all determined to have nothing but fun on stage – to give it a good old blast and then clear off sharpish. I dressed them up in an indie uniform. We bought jeans and took them in at the bottom, adding nice shoes and boating blazers. We revived stripy T-shirts, at a time when there were hardly any in the shops. Whenever we were in Paris, we'd go to the Saint James clothing store and buy stuff up, or else find a funny, stripy T-shirt from the 1960s or '70s in Camden Market. We all ended up looking like a cross between Dennis the Menace and a French onion seller. It was our look, like a badge, and it helped me break the ice at the start of a gig: 'Cor, there's a lot of stripy T-shirts in the audience tonight.'

We listened to loads of old psychedelia and garage punk, Scott Walker, Wire and Sham 69. We really liked that energy and a hooligan-ish type of vocal delivery. It was fantastic material to play live, even though it left us knackered. I gave everything to those shows and wouldn't be able to talk for the whole of the next day. My voice would be shot until half an hour before the next gig, when it would suddenly come back after a Red Bull and a painkiller.

We drew great, enthusiastic crowds, but I didn't feel that many of the Blur audience had come with me. I suppose a lot of them preferred Damon's Gorillaz project, and admittedly my stuff was a pretty acquired taste – a bit like the Ruts paired with whiny vocals. Many of the reference points might have been lost on people, which I can totally understand. Within the band, though, we understood intuitively what we were trying to do. The others would familiarise themselves with the songs as I had recorded them on my albums, then we'd rehearse them together. Technically I was a bandleader, but I didn't act like one. It was more like playing with a bunch of mates, especially when Lucy Parnell and Jen Macro came on board later on. That beefed things up considerably, with four guitars going at times, making a big old row. But it was really all about playing with people I was comfortable with. Me and Owen Thomas, my guitarist, went back a long way – we're exactly the same age, love a lot of the same music and have a similar sense of humour. We're almost like brothers. I had known Toby MacFarlaine, the bass player, for a long time too, having spent many hours chatting about all sorts of nonsense in pubs. The drummer, Stephen Gilchrist – or Stuffy, as he's better known – was the only member who got in after an audition. I liked him straight away, and he was a good drummer. Eventually Lucy and Jen came in via him, and we became an extended indie family.

I liked it because there was no pressure. The others didn't have to go through any of the usual crap that bands are presented with. If there were any interviews to be done, it would be just me, so they could go off, have a few pints and grab something to eat. Unlike Blur's later days, it didn't feel like a career. For them it was a great life, watching *Old Grey Whistle Test* DVDs on the tour bus and checking out the Clarks shoe shop in whatever town we were playing in that night. We usually played at fairly small venues, and it was almost what you imagined being in a band would be like when you were a teenager. The audiences had fun, we had fun, and that was it. Although occasionally our exuberance meant that it hurt, because we certainly thrashed those guitars. There was blood everywhere most nights. Blood, sweat and giggles. The whole experience reminded me what a blast it was, being in a band. And not only did I have that, but I also had the time and space to take to the road and go exploring.

ROUNDING
BENDS
AT
ILLEGAL
SPEEDS

One day in the early 2000s I was flipping through a copy of *Positively 4th Street*, David Hajdu's book about Joan Baez, Bob Dylan and Richard and Mimi Fariña in the 1960s, when the pages fell open at a photo of Dylan in Woodstock, sitting astride a gleaming Triumph Tiger motorbike. Not only did it strike me as the most romantic snapshot of two-wheeled freedom I'd ever seen, but the bike was the most beautiful work of industrial art. As soon as I caught sight of that photo of Dylan on his Triumph, I realised I needed some of that. So I went up to Edgware and did my compulsory basic training for motorbike riders, followed by a five-day all-access course, then took my test (a couple of times) – and that was that. I bought an old 1957 Tiger Cub, which is only about 200cc, and at first didn't really know what to do with it – compared to the modern Honda I had been learning on, it was completely upside down and the wrong way round.

That one photo sent me on an unexpected journey that had me leaning into curves at an exhilarating seventy miles per hour and spending many happy lost afternoons with a spanner in my hand, overalls splattered with petrol and my nose stuck in sputtering carburettors. There are few things more exhilarating than rounding a big wide bend on a motorbike. I can totally relate to Steppenwolf's 'Born to Be Wild': money can't buy that sensation of freedom and the breeze stealing underneath your jacket, nor the sound and responsiveness of the engine as you accelerate out of a corner.

There's something beautiful about how a bike responds when you twist the throttle and feel the progressive power or snatchy tug of the motor.

When it comes to motorbikes, speed isn't the main attraction for me. It's more the way they look. For a while I owned a beautiful old Triumph Trophy from 1968. Old bikes have personalities. All of a sudden they can start behaving in weird ways and be as dangerous as horses. But I really like modern ones too. I have a Triumph Street Twin that looks a bit like an old 1960s model, but the brakes are bloody good, and you can feel confident that it's not going to suddenly fall to bits, leaving you sitting on a seat that's flying through the air. It certainly feels like that could happen when my 1962 BSA Shooting Star is shaking about underneath me.

I had finally got my own genuine rock 'n' roll obsession: building up a collection of motorbikes. Around the early-to-mid-2000s I would zoom around the Peak District, with my girlfriend sat on the back. Eventually we went on longer trips to France and Spain. There were a few hairy incidents, such as stray dogs running out in front of us on a motorway or run-ins with drunken Spanish lorry drivers (I have seen a number of them topping up their water bottle with booze at a service station, just before climbing back into the cab). One of the most spectacular routes was crossing the Pyrenees into France. We sped along a deserted road through northern Spain, then suddenly crested a mountaintop and found ourselves looking down on a fairy-tale valley that was like the kind of lush landscape you'd find on a box of Swiss chocolates: green meadows, cows and waterfalls. It was unbelievable. We ended that trip with a couple of days at Lourdes, giving our backsides some much needed rest among its healing waters and grottos.

I went through a period of getting creative with bikes, sticking a tractor seat on an old Harley or removing the tinware – the tank and mudguards – on a Sportster and replacing them with some battered parts that I'd covered in blackboard paint. I chugged around on the Sportster for a while, with a little bag of chalk hanging off the handlebar. I'd draw things on it and write 'Honda' or 'This way up' (with an arrow on the side of the tank) – stupid stuff like that. That scruffy bike was what's known as a 'rat' – one that's been left to fall apart. I just wanted a moving canvas to scribble on.

I have owned modern bikes, but I scared myself by driving much too fast up the M1 on a Suzuki GSX-R. After that I steered clear of sports bikes and got into more vintage hogs. Eventually I had eight of the things, but I didn't know what to do with them all, so I auctioned off my whole fleet at Bonham's and donated the proceeds to the NSPCC. Nowadays I just own one bike, a lovely green BSA Shooting Star from 1962.

Owning a motorbike gave me a much-needed feeling of freedom and possibility, and also opened up England for me in new ways. Despite having seen a good deal of it from the Blur tour bus, there's a totally different England to be found once you leave the motorways and main roads and steer away from the towns and cities. I would get on the saddle, throttle back and buzz around the rural C-roads. From London it was easy enough to zoom down to Kent, have a snoop around and then zip back again in a single day. A tax adviser had recommended that I invest in some more property, and on one of these trips, sometime in the middle of 2002, I found an old converted barn in Barham, in the eastern part of the county, which I bought and lived in for about a year. As soon as I moved in, this lad from the neighbourhood came round and started talking to me, and then he turned up again, and suddenly there were reporters from the local newspapers at my gate and it was time to leave. But I had fallen in love with Kent by then, so I hired a property expert to find me a place.

My pastoral rocker's retreat turned up the following year in the hamlet of Stodmarsh, deep in Kentish farmland, a few miles east of Canterbury. The property was in the middle of a field, so there were no roads near the house. The only human being who was even remotely nearby was John, the woodsman, who lived in a smaller house next door. He drove off every morning on his ancient tractor to work in the woods. He would come round to fill his water containers from my outside tap, but apart from that, there was no one there. I could wake up, wander down the stairs and have a walk round the garden in just my underpants if I wanted to, without causing any offence. I liked beating the bounds of my Kentish fiefdom in my undies, feeling the grass and flowers and soaking up the immense horizon of fields and sky. Like many other artistic forebears who have enjoyed a spell in the countryside, being there gave me a psychic recharge.

I had some good times out in the country, living like a hillbilly. I kept a rattly old Harley-Davidson Wide Glide there, and whenever I trundled into Canterbury, decked out in my German military jackboots, army trousers and shitty leather jacket, all the sportsbike lads would laugh their heads off. There was lots of innocent fun with girlfriends who came down to visit, mucking about in the garden on motorbikes. There was a big sit-on lawnmower in the barn, with a trailer that Pepper used to love riding in.

An annual highlight was the War and Peace Revival Show at The Hop Farm, just outside Tunbridge Wells. It's like a massive outdoor army surplus jumble sale, where you can buy original 1940s clothes, demob suits and overcoats. I have spent a fortune there over the years. It lasts four or five days and includes battle re-enactments, so the fields are full of armoured cars, motorbikes and sidecars, and other full-size versions of the accessories I used to have for my Action Man, as well as people standing around in historically accurate Nazi uniforms, smoking fags. Then along come some American GIs, and they all head over to one of the fields and start throwing grenades at each other, with hundreds of mega-geekoids watching. At the end of the night the bars fill up with SS men, Panzer commanders, Tommies and marines. It's bizarre, but also interesting.

Back in Stodmarsh you could get a good meal at the local pub, the Red Lion, where I often used to sit – after slipping off the wagon a little bit – with Robert, the landlord. He actually allowed people to smoke cigarettes inside, so we'd sit there drinking IPAs and having a smokeroo, occasionally interrupted by a customer, to whom he was more often than not hilariously rude. If you asked for chips, he'd throw you out – 'Wrong pub – on your way!' Like a cross between Basil Fawlty and Uncle Monty from *Withnail & I*, he was a lovable bastard with a big moustache and a red face who hated mayonnaise.

He knew I was a musician, and one New Year's Eve he invited me to bring my guitar to the pub. I taught myself a few covers, like the Box Tops' 'The Letter', and installed myself at the end of the bar with the guitar and a couple of beers. People came up to me all evening, asking, 'All right, mate? Do you know whatchamacallit by Eric Clapton?' And I'd say, 'Yeah, I do actually, do you want to hear it?' And they'd go, 'Yeah!' and I'd just play it. I was a human jukebox, and most people were surprised that I could respond to

their suggestions so quickly. In the gaps I strummed some instru-
mentals I'd learnt from Davey Graham's records, like the Henry
Purcell-inspired 'Hornpipe for Harpsichord Played Upon Guitar'
and other early-music pieces. People seemed to dig them.

———

During this period in the mid-2000s I dabbled with a few diverting
side projects and wrote the songs that ended up on my 2006 album
Love Travels at Illegal Speeds. Just before that, we folded Transcopic
Records away. I wasn't in the business to be a label boss, and in the
end I told Jamie Davis it was costing too much money to run.

I recorded the album in early 2005, with Stephen Street producing, and that same year I was named best solo artist at the *NME*
Awards. There are so many directions a song can go in, so many
purposes it can have. Some tell a story, and there's a good deal of
that in the folk tradition, of course. Others, especially in pop music,
are more focused on describing and holding on to a particular emotional state. But I do like the way a song can set up a scenario,
narrate a short interaction or articulate a feeling. There were plenty
of tales to chronicle when I lived in Camden Town. I made up 'You
& I' while Pepper was in the bath once. I was singing 'It's going to
be a while till I get to see you smile' to her because I was just about
to go away on tour. Even as I was singing it to her I was thinking
about how the chords would work on the guitar. So really it's about
having to go on tour and leave your five-year-old daughter behind.
'What's He Got?' was the product of me doing lots of hipster-
watching on the streets and thinking, 'If women like you like men
like him, why don't women like me?' I suppose I was a kind of indie

George Formby for a while there. 'He's got the same boots as me, he's got nice jeans on – how come he's got this incredible creature on his arm?' I could always answer my own question: because he's probably confident, he gets out there and he asked her straight out, 'Hey, fancy going out on a date?' I could never seem to do that. But it was fun to whine and whinge about it and ignore the fact that I could probably have managed had I been bothered.

That frustration with myself and self-deprecating humour permeated so much of my earlier songwriting, plus just feeling miserable, sad, lovelorn, isolated, alienated, different and strange. The whole punk-rock curriculum, in fact. I can be extremely despondent, usually between half past ten and midnight. Depending on what sort of day I've had, I sometimes sit there, thinking, 'Oh, blow all you fuckers. That's it, I'm going to move to the Dales, where no one will ever find me. Screw you all!' But I've always been extremely romantic, so underneath it all lies a strong sense of idealism.

The LP signed off with one of my sickly-sweet outpouring-of-devotion-type songs, 'See a Better Day'. It talks about 'the sunlight in your eye . . . your miracle smile . . . I'm so in love with you' – it's just a huge, throbbing outpouring of love. Even though I do like story songs, sometimes stories are tricky. I was looking for a new way of telling them – and, in fact, a fresh approach to melody and playing the guitar.

My painting for the cover was a great, lumbering comet that didn't look like it would move very fast at all. I was interested in how comets and celestial bodies were rendered in medieval paintings and folk art such as the Bayeux Tapestry: hovering above the Earth with ribbons of fire streaming out the back. Inspired by those, my comet looked like a big flying tent trailing a strip of bunting.

While I was recording the songs for *Love Travels* I met the folk singer Kate Rusby and made an image for the cover of her album *The Girl Who Couldn't Fly*. I wanted it to have a swirly, handmade woodcut vibe to it, like Egon Schiele or Edvard Munch. It featured a topless, Kate-like female torso, seen from behind, with two scars on the shoulder blades, and was meant to be an innocent vision of an angel who'd had her wings removed. Kate wanted a butterfly hovering over her head, and I took that image from a huge CD-ROM of natural history library images that I kept at home. She was in a relationship with Johnny McCusker at the time, and he was very mischievous about the picture: 'Can't we have a full-frontal, Graham?'

———

As I have said, I had some relationships during that period which were perfectly pleasant, with some of what I thought were the most together and emotionally stable women I'd ever met. But there was something going on with me that found 'together' and 'emotionally stable' a bit boring. Unfortunately my emotionally hungry core seemed to crave drama-laden, bonded-by-trauma types of relationships. That's when I started to think that something wasn't quite right, and it took me a long time – nearly twenty years, in fact – to do anything about it. In 2006, however, I embarked on what became a fourteen-year relationship. I was introduced to Soraya by mutual friends. Initially we met online and exchanged messages for about a month on the then cutting-edge social media platform MySpace. It was a beautiful summer that occasionally chucked down sudden torrents of rain. Our early meetings involved basking in the sunshine and then getting instantly soaked. Love travelled at breakneck, if not actually illegal, speed. Should I have been suspicious of a relationship that moved so fast? I'm more wary now, but when that sort of love starts to bubble up, it's so powerful that we ignore our gut feelings and just go for it. It was intense, seductive, a sweeping-off-the-feet sort of relationship. After several years as a beetle under a rock, I thought my prayers had been answered.

I was still intensely involved with folk music. In London, and especially down in my Kentish retreat, I was practising for eight hours a day, going deep into scales and extended techniques. I've become a lot more comfortable as a finger-style guitar player, and by now I've done enough gigs that way for people to accept it as part of my repertoire. In some ways, I'm almost better in that mode than on the electric guitar. I've reached a level of ability that I'm satisfied with, so I don't pressure myself to improve as much as I used to. I could probably get even better, but then I wouldn't have much of a life! I like the sound of a guitar straining and creaking under the treatment meted out by a pair of hands, when the wood seems to be in a certain amount of pain. In the end, of course, you want the guitar to do the job of accompanying the songs. They are the important thing, the end product, and getting too flowery and crazy does them a disservice. So I always remind myself to keep things simple.

Traditionally, the standard tuning of an acoustic guitar is like orchestral tuning, as it's designed to be part of a bigger ensemble. But when it's used as a solo instrument, this method is less logical. Innovators like Davey Graham invented open tuning systems, such as DADGAD, which was partly inspired by the sound of North African and Middle Eastern scales, and which gives the instrument an entirely different flavour. It makes the tone of the acoustic guitar bigger, wider and better for accompanying yourself alone. A whole generation of folkies – Martin Carthy being one of them – tweaked the DADGAD tuning for their own use. Following these threads led to my interest in the world of English luthiers. I bought a guitar and a ten-stringed cittern from the amazing Fylde Guitars in the Lake District, and another guitar from Ralph Bown in York, who made guitars for John Renbourn. You can get fantastic guitars for not an awful lot of money – a lot better than a Martin at the equivalent price. I started exploring the best ways to amplify acoustic guitars and got pretty geeky about it. In the end you go with what's simple and works best. I've had bad experiences using pre-amps for acoustic guitars, with stereo cables coming out and both an internal microphone and an under-saddle pickup. I've taken all that on stage and the damn thing has refused to work, leaving me sitting there in front of an audience, staring at it like an idiot.

Playing these guitars in open tunings give you an almost sitar-like sound – you can strum a chord and put a melody line over the top. It helps me get out of habitual, clichéd chord changes. Davey Graham's 'Jubilation' was one of the first things I decided to teach myself, as well as a hornpipe tune he sometimes played and some Renaissance lute music from Spain, Portugal and England that I found so lovely to listen to.

———

This period was really one of discovery for me, and it included a few scattered opportunities to express myself in other areas and reconnect with my interests in literature and art. I may not be a voracious reader, but every now and then I latch on to an author and blaze through their books like wildfire. Soon after I got to know Damon at school, I saw him reading *Steppenwolf* by Hermann Hesse, so of course I had to read it too, and it made quite an impression on me. I went and read all of Hesse's work – *Siddhartha, Knulp, Demian*, everything I could find – and at last came round to *Narcissus and Goldmund*, Hesse's novel from 1930. That was a pretty thick volume, but I made myself jump in and ended up really adoring it. So it was a nice surprise when someone from Peter Owen, a small independent publishing house, approached me in 2006 and asked if I fancied writing the foreword to a new edition of the book. I installed myself at Quinn's in Kentish Town, sat at the bar and wrote it over two or three days. It was lovely because it took me back to being in art school, where the book helped to inform me and a few of my chums about which side of the fence we were on, not just as artists who wanted to draw, but as people: how free we wanted to be (or thought we were); how willing we were to meet a challenge or try something that would normally make us uncomfortable. The book is about a wanderer trying to find himself, and is full of oppositions and polarities – masculine/feminine, conscious/unconscious, Apollonian (rationalism)/Dionysian (party animalism).

In my foreword I explained how I first came across the book via the recommendation of an art teacher I had when I was seventeen called Helen Napper. She was a wonderful teacher (and is still actively making art), with wild black hair and incredible crazy-green eyes, and usually dressed in a little suede skirt. She often did outlandish things that pissed off the more uptight graphic artists in the class, like hanging Sellotape from the ceiling with a long piece of string, attaching a weight to the end and whirling it around so that it swung in huge circles. Then she'd say, 'Draw it! Draw it!'

Filthy students like me and my friends Deb Sippings and Rosalind Bird were very impressed and inspired by this, and we'd take out our lumps of charcoal and smudge away on the paper, while the graphics people stared at their precision pens, wondering what to do. It was an interesting exercise that taught us who was in which gang. It would have been good if a sponge had been on the end of that string, like the lyric in Captain Beefheart's 'Dirty Blue Gene'.

One day Helen told me I should read *Narcissus and Goldmund*. A cool teacher had singled me out for recommendations – I felt sort of chosen. When I reread it for the new edition, I was reminded how much I loved the simple adventures of Goldmund. One day he's a monk gathering herbs outside his monastery, and when he spies this beautiful peasant girl out doing her thing, they have a chat and that's it, he decides to run away with her and embarks on a series of merry adventures through plague-ravaged Europe. Meanwhile, his best friend, Narcissus, stays behind and develops self-knowledge via a different path. What Oscar Wilde said about all sinners having a future and all saints having a past – that's what the book is all about, really. It's also about creativity, patience and dedication to a craft. It's two different journeys to the same destination.

———

In the middle of 2006 the artist Julie Verhoeven asked me to make some music for *Ver-boten, Ver-Saatchi, Ver-heaven*, an installation she was creating at the Riflemaker Gallery in Soho. She's a brilliant artist whose work playfully riffs off the fashion industry, and I love the self-deprecating eccentricity of it. My home recording set-up was pretty limited. I called my contribution 'english shoes squeek', and it was a creepy ambient piece made by placing a couple of mics near the floor to pick up the little sounds made by the floorboards and a pair of my leather-soled shoes. I added mellow feedback through a bass amp, played a sound-effects album that had only the noise of steam locomotives, and then coughed and blew raspberries into the mics. I wanted something that didn't have a beginning or an end – just a strange, atmospheric amplification of what I thought would be going on in the gallery. The end result was an hour long, playing on a repeat loop.

These activities were all interesting in their own right, but I was always aware that my association with Blur was a significant factor in being asked to do them. Conversely, Blur felt to me like one of my ratty motorbikes, left to rust away in a forgotten garage. The history of music is littered with unresolved feuds. All sorts of petty dynamics are in play that can drive a wedge between members of bands. Things like being relegated to the back of the picture, while Damon is photographed up front. With us, these sorts of things weren't a lasting problem, thankfully, but I'm convinced that Blur needed those years of inactivity in order to survive. There might have been some residual anger with each other simmering away, but deep down we knew we were still brothers who just needed to follow separate paths for a while. No one wanted it to end with an irretrievable split, like Pink Floyd. Some bands separate temporarily and leave it too long before getting back together, and before they know it a key member has passed away. I have never been a fan of lasting resentments. When you do a programme like the 12 Steps, you realise that those kinds of emotional blockages are your enemy. You have to resolve things and not carry resentments with you, because they're the most damaging things to lug around.

Low-level rumours about a Blur reunion popped up frequently in the late 2000s. Damon, Alex and Dave were considering going back into the studio, and we had a lunch together in 2007, at which no plans were made. About a year after that, Damon's band Africa Express were playing in London, and I went backstage afterwards to reconnect. We arranged to meet up straight away and bonded over an Eccles cake. Everything was fine. Remind us, what was the problem again?

CONSIDER
THIS
A
SPELL

My work on new, complex guitar techniques continued, undisturbed, for hours and days on end in my house at Stodmarsh. I worked my way through a pile of guitar instruction DVDs by the great master John Renbourn, paying particular attention to a series called *The Jazz Tinge*. I had all sorts of folk instruments lying around the place: flutes, tin whistles and a banjo on which I attempted to perfect the technique known as frailing, or clawhammer, where you strike the strings downwards instead of up. There was one session that lasted about two days straight, during which I wrote a lot of new material with these folky textures. 'In the Morning' was one of the best tracks that came out of that marathon session out in the countryside, sitting at my old, beaten-up pine table.

That marked the moment when I finally felt confident enough playing in that folk idiom to write songs in that style. In the first decade of the 2000s bands like the White Stripes and the Hives had steered alternative rock back towards a primitive, stompy garage approach. In a funny way that suited me too. I was being influenced by things like Billy Childish and the Kinks, and I found it easy to get a two-chord riff together and then sing something mardy over it about some weirdos I had spotted in Camden.

I took on the inevitable guitar player's challenge of learning Davey Graham's 'Anji', playing the fiendish tune over and over, trying to coordinate its different rhythms between finger and thumb, until eventually I could perform it on automatic pilot. Gradually I developed my own touch and my own patterns, and like Martin Carthy and Big Bill Broonzy, I liked to dampen the bass notes and give them a really good *thunk*. As a result of all this study, in around 2007–8 I wrote the whole of *The Spinning Top* using alternative tunings inspired by listening to Bert Jansch and Davey Graham, and songs like Pentangle's 'Train Song' – it's rattly, all the instruments are played as if they were percussion, plus of course you have the incredible Danny Thompson on bass, who gives the whole thing the swing of a jazz rhythm section. *The Spinning Top* was the culmination of those years of hunkering down and worming my way into fingerstyle, sitting at the kitchen table in Stodmarsh with a big pot of tea and just hammering away, day and night, and recording chunks of it as I went along.

As songs emerged, various stories started to appear, and I ended up presenting the LP as a 'concept album', tracing the symbolic life of an individual from birth to death. It was a process of joining the dots rather than having too much freedom, and I found that having a set of parameters, or boundaries, helped me to shape the overall piece. For example, 'Caspian Sea' is a weird story about a soldier having a supernatural experience with a feminine water spirit. I've always thought the outline of the Caspian Sea resembles the shape of a woman, which led me to think, 'Maybe it actually *is* a woman' – like a siren or kelpie. As a Piscean, I tend to believe in these seductive archetypes. Her part was sung by Natasha Marsh, a classical singer with an incredibly high voice – I wanted that kind of supernaturally high singing that you hear on some of Michael Nyman's or Ennio Morricone's vocal works, and she delivered precisely what I'd imagined. At the end, a chord is left hanging there, and I bend the notes around it in an effort to make it feel unbalanced. I was into the twelve-tone music of the Second Viennese School of composers around that time, and that track has tone-clusters and *Sprechstimme*, whereby you glean what you're going to sing from a set of symbols. These are distant echoes of things I learnt as a thirteen-year-old in Mr Hildreth's music class.

I played many of the instruments myself, but Graham Fox, a fantastic jazz drummer, came in to play, and would perform with me when I toured *The Spinning Top* later. Three of the tracks feature the guitar of Robyn Hitchcock. I also managed to get the one and only Danny Thompson on board to play the double bass. He really is the peg that holds the entire folk revival in Britain together, from playing in Pentangle and with Nick Drake, Richard Thompson and John Martyn in the 1960s and '70s to guesting on records by every-one from Tim Buckley to Marianne Faithfull, Kate Bush, David Sylvian and Talk Talk. He immediately said yes and joined us for a day-long session. I had set everything up beforehand, so he had only to slot himself in. At one point engineer Mike Pelanconi was fiddling about with the positioning of a microphone while Danny was standing there playing, and he casually said, 'Great-sounding bass, Danny.' Danny stopped at once and said, 'Oh yeah? How does it fucking sound now?' Danny knew how to play that bass, and it was only sounding bloody good because of his way of playing it. Mike crawled back to the control room, mortified.

Danny was the man who, as he told us, used to hand two hun-dred quid to pub landlords before embarking on a night of boozing with John Martyn, 'to cover the damage'. He still used the same acoustic bass that he'd found in a junk shop in Victoria in the 1960s. It might not have been a particularly good example, but he always stuck with it. I asked him what the action was like, and he let me have a go. Honestly, trying to press the strings down, it seemed like they were an inch and a half away from the fretboard. To press one down with your left hand took stupendous effort. Danny was a proper man. I remember Alex mucking about with double basses in Blur a few times, and it seemed easy enough to get a simple sound out of them. They were nothing like Danny's bass, though: it would kill you, and that's how he liked it set up. Then again, his hands were like huge bunches of bananas.

Danny worked his bloody arse off for ten straight hours, until he was knackered, and then he packed up and left. 'That's it. I'm tired, man, I'm tired.' He was all over that album, and he did a brilliant job.

'In the Morning' turned into a super-long song thanks to me trying out lots of different riffs, based around an open G tuning. I wanted to record it totally analogue, and Mike Pelanconi helped with that, along with Stephen Street. Some excellent Indian musicians – Jas Singh, Gurjit Sembhi and Jaskase Singh – added dilruba, jori, taus and esraj to that track, which gave it that eastern-tinged folk crossover feel I loved from the Davey Graham, Incredible String Band and Pentangle records of the 1960s. 'Sorrow's Army' reflected my lifelong obsession – due to being an army kid, no doubt – with battlefields, dead soldiers and bloody uniforms.

I included a great many guest musicians as a way of not being too in control. The Indian musicians worked around and against what they saw as the scale and the limitations of my music. Jas, the dilruba player, found it tricky as he didn't want to break any of the rules that exist around Indian classical music – it's a spiritual discipline, and there are certain scales you can play only at certain times. When he came on tour with me, his teacher, Ranbir, accompanied him. He said, 'Oh, Jas should have just done what you told him to do, silly bloke!' But it ended up well, and I loved the dilruba – it added some drama to the arrangement.

The album was recorded in late 2008 in Studio 2 at Olympic Studios and downstairs in Stephen Street and Cenzo Townshend's space, which is known as The Bunker. Pillars run all the way through the building, and when you put your ear to one of them, you can hear music being channelled from the main room upstairs. Eric Clapton was recording there at the same time, and once while I was doing a vocal the pillars were vibrating like a thundering amplifier, so loud that Eric's soundwaves were picked up by my mic. It's an unplanned guest appearance.

I began to feel more at home in the folk community. At the BBC Radio 2 Folk Awards in 2008, I was honoured to be invited to present the 'Good Tradition' Award to Shirley Collins. In my handing-over speech I called her even more British than Ray Davies, which was a deliberately self-ironising joke, implying that a mere pop star like me thought Ray Davies was absolutely as British as it gets. There is a deadpan, almost newsreader-like quality to the way she delivers the lyrics of those old English songs. Which is appropriate, because folk songs *were* the newspapers of the day, in a way: it's how people passed stories along – 'You won't believe what happened in Bruton Town the other day' – and because they rhymed and had simple melodies and chords, they were easy to remember. The thing about singing a folk song is that it's a lot easier to remember because it's telling a story, and as you progress through it hints to you what lyric is coming next.

I was scared stiff at being this pretender from a Britpop band popping up at a folk awards ceremony, handing a gong to someone as venerable as Shirley. But all the folk people were absolutely lovely to me. They acted as if they were glad that younger people like me could act as advocates for the music, in order to keep it alive. Shirley herself was amazing; it was like talking to the Queen. We stayed in touch, and I did a couple of gigs with her, in which she told her stories of travelling through the American South with Alan Lomax in the late 1950s. At the time she still preferred to speak rather than sing, as she had long suffered from dysphonia, which left her unable to use her singing voice in a concert situation. Eventually she conquered that syndrome, and in 2016 released the album *Lodestar*, which had a lovely darkness to it compared with the more skippy pastoral folk she was doing in the 1950s and '60s. There was supernatural stuff going on in the lyrics, and her interest in the number three was also quite telling.

At around the same time I met and supported singer-songwriter and guitarist Beverley Thompson (formerly Beverley Martyn, when she was married to John). Like Shirley, she had spent many years being unable to sing in public, but now she was back performing again, with so much more experience infusing the music.

Once, on Shirley's birthday, I went down to Lewes, where she lives, and watched her favourite morris side do some dancing. It's flipping tiring. I liked the Englishness of the local folk tradition, the unpretentiousness and the non-rock 'n' roll character of it. Like the dance, the body of English folk songs has been passed on by generations of people who have never felt the need to sing them in any other way. Maybe a verse gets lost down the line and another added, and some of the words change, but I really love that. It's a shame the English don't celebrate and value their own roots to the same extent as the Scots, Welsh and Irish. Historically there's a sense of shame and embarrassment surrounding English indigenous folk traditions, which is ridiculous as some of the English folk songs are so beautiful and sad. The decline of the folk tradition is definitely a loss for this country. Obviously the telly has replaced a lot of that, and it would be weird if a family decided to sit together in their front room and start singing from the floor.

———

In January 2009 Olympic Studios closed down, making *The Spinning Top* one of the last albums to have been recorded there. Cenzo Townshend called me in a panic. 'Graham, they're chucking everything into skips, and your flipping Farfisa's here. What are we going to do? They're going to chuck it in a skip!' I had no idea some of my stuff was still in storage there. Workmen were ripping out all the wooden acoustic cladding and chucking it away, along with old Rolling Stones master tapes. That stuff is full of magic, and it kills me to even think about it. They took one look at my Farfisa organ and probably thought, 'What's this piece of shit? Bet it doesn't even work,' and out it went. Luckily I raced over there in time to rescue it.

It wasn't only my keyboard being rescued from oblivion in 2009. The main event of that summer, the result of our reunion a couple of years earlier, was a Blur tour – the first time the four of us had performed together since 2001. At our initial rehearsal, on a beautiful summer's day, following a sticky start we ran through 'She's So High' a couple of times, and suddenly everything kicked in and felt excellent. After another few songs I started thinking how nice it would be to wind down later with a nice big glass of red wine. I went to the off-licence on the way home and bought a packet of cigarettes and a bottle. As I was in the middle of a huge Kevin Ayers phase at the time, I put one of his albums on. On the track 'Whatevershebringswesing', Ayers exhorts us to drink wine and enjoy a good time. 'OK, Kevin,' I said. 'Let's.' I poured myself a nice big glass of red and lit up a cigarette – my first in six months. What a feeling. After eight years of sobriety, it was quite a rush.

The next day, and after every subsequent rehearsal, I went to the pub and had a couple of drinks and a cigarette, and slowly, furtively let alcohol trickle into my life again. I wasn't open about it and didn't tell anyone in the band. I was keeping an eye on it, as much as possible. There were a few times when I got pretty drunk, but mostly I wouldn't allow myself more than five or six pints. I wanted to avoid hangovers, because if I woke up with one I would definitely want a curative drink. I worked out that five or six pints of IPA didn't give me a hangover, just a welcome feeling of weightlessness and peace.

There were some big shows on the itinerary, such as the O2 Academy in Newcastle, Glastonbury Festival and two days in Hyde Park. For me, the prospect seemed nerve-wracking, but we began with a couple of warm-up gigs at the East Anglian Railway Museum in Colchester and a tiny in-store gig at Rough Trade East in London. The fifth show on the bill found Damon, Alex and I returning to our old haunt, a packed-out Goldsmiths College, on 22 June. We emerged onto a stage that I had once invaded as a student member of the audience, buzzing on one of those Traffic Light cocktails. Now it was us up there in this dangerously hot auditorium, hopping about under its precariously low, sweating ceiling. Sitting backstage in bathrobes afterwards, we were disappointed to learn that the actor Jude Law had tried to visit us in our dressing room with his kids, but had been turned away. I was feeling so sick with heat exhaustion, I would probably have thrown up on his shoes anyway.

Being on tour with Blur in 2009 was a vastly different experience from what it had been in 1991, or even 1996 for that matter. It was as though the band was enjoying a second life. There was a positive energy around us, as if audiences and others we met along the way were still pleased to see us after all this time. After spending most of the 2000s worrying whether I had taken the right decision by walking away from the group, it was a relief to find out how quickly Blur could be restored. The intra-band problems of the past had melted away, and relations between us were markedly improved. We had less to prove – both to the audiences and to each other. That meant we could get on with the job of entertaining and giving everything to the music. The days of rolling between venues in a bumpy van were also over. We flew between shows, usually first class, and stayed in nicer, posher hotels than before. The technology had altered too. The live PA systems we played through were ten times louder, while also being a hundred times smaller. Speakers were no longer set up in stacks that Damon could clamber over as if they were a rectangular mountain range; now they hung in clusters above the stage. The only black cloud was my secret drinking. I would usually sneak a bottle of backstage lager into my bag and slink off for a little private time in one of the Portaloos. Glamorous stuff. This continued for a couple of years, and I thought I had it under control, until I realised that what I was doing wasn't healthy and went for a top-up session in the Priory.

There was a record-breaking crowd of around eighty thousand sweaty, shirtless folks at the June 2009 Glastonbury Festival

– probably the largest assembly that's ever been seen at a Blur gig. The level of sheer noise coming off that seething mass of humanity was just extraordinary. With all the flags and pennants waving as the sun sank behind the Somerset hills, we launched into the slow, heavy riff of 'Beetlebum'. It was like facing an army in *Game of Thrones*, but instead of going into battle, we were entering a magical, emotionally charged atmosphere. Damon broke down in tears during 'To the End', a reaction to all the tangible euphoria in the air.

Our tour management had worked out an exit strategy for after the show which involved effectively leaping offstage and straight into a bus that would speed us away from the site in order to avoid the worst of the evening traffic. Enthusiastic comments and raves rang in our ears as we raced to our vehicle and abandoned the scene of our triumph. I felt fantastically uplifted as I left and thought it was a shame we couldn't stick around to bask in the post-gig afterglow.

The tour wound up in Scotland a couple of weeks later, on 12 July. By that time we had made it through two days at Hyde Park, as well as large outdoor festivals in Ireland and France. Before heading to the T in the Park festival at Kinross, in south-eastern Scotland, we were installed at a hotel in Edinburgh, about thirty miles away. A seafood platter of smoked mackerel and oysters was on the lunch menu, but something didn't feel right when it was time for the Blur team to board the bus heading for the festival site. As I walked down the grand staircase to the lobby, I was assaulted by waves of heat and dizziness, and the world started spinning around me. 'I don't feel so well,' I muttered, before my legs buckled under me and I rolled down the flight of stairs. Amid the grogginess, I heard

Damon saying, 'Graham's having one of his things,' and a nurse who appeared out of nowhere pronounced I had a case of food poisoning. That was my cue to evacuate from both ends.

By now it was about five o'clock, at which time we were supposed to be sallying forth in a luxury coach to enjoy what we hoped would be a victorious appearance at T in the Park. Instead, an ambulance was screaming towards us, while Alex chose that moment to light a consolatory cigarette, which promptly and predictably triggered the hotel fire alarm. Everyone in the building was ordered out, which meant there was an impromptu audience of annoyed and inconvenienced guests and staff to watch me being wheeled into the waiting ambulance.

At the local hospital, while our tour manager asked every passing doctor and orderly whether they thought I would be able to play the show, I was hooked up to a saline drip, which worked miracles. My digestive system is always quick to process food in any case, and now I rose from my sick bed like Lazarus – that rogue oyster had been expelled just as quickly as it went in – and we jumped into a van and screeched away in the direction of T in the Park. The band Snow Patrol, playing before Blur, had been frantically induced to extend their set. I leapt out of the van and grabbed a bottle of beer, just in time to bound onto the stage with Damon, Alex and Dave, several hours after our scheduled start time. Thankfully it was worth the wait: all of us locked together to play a blinding, energetic set, with Damon especially throwing himself around just like the old days. It was an excellent climax to one of the maddest days I've ever experienced with Blur. Nevertheless, we parted company in typically low-key fashion, with a simple 'See you, then . . .' At this point the tour seemed like it had been a consolidation and celebration of everything we had already achieved, and there were no managers or executives pressuring us for a new album or any more live dates. In any case, we all had our own projects and activities to get back to.

———

My next job was to promote *The Spinning Top*. We had played a few dates around the album's release in May that year, and more shows were lined up for November. My regular band expanded into the thirteen-piece Power Acoustic Ensemble. At first it had been me, Graham Fox and bassist Gareth Huw Davies, a jazzy line-up that included me on sax now and again. By now I was on texting terms with Martin Carthy, and I invited him into the big band for a major concert at the Barbican, in London, in November. I even persuaded him to play a Fender Telecaster again, just like he did in the early days of Steeleye Span. There was also Robyn Hitchcock (I had guested in his band Heavy Friends during a 2007 tribute to Pink Floyd's 1967 Games for May concert at London's Queen Elizabeth Hall), my friend Owen Thomas, Lucy Parnell and Jen Macro on vocals, and some of the Indian percussionists. Louis Vause, who played piano on *The Kiss of Morning*, came along too, adding a very wheezy organ on 'November', which is full of pseudo-medieval harmonies. It was a good time.

2009 also saw the release of Pete Doherty's first solo album, *Grace/ Wastelands*, on which I played most of the guitars. It was Stephen Street who initially got in touch with me about it – I think the producer just wanted someone like me there for support. I knew Pete a little and was a massive fan of *Up the Bracket*, the first album by his band, the Libertines. The spirit of that record was incredible, and I considered it one of the best things I'd heard in twenty years, mainly because of its anarchy and chaos, as well as the great songs. He was ten years younger than me, but in some ways my spiritual brother. He was a Piscean who actually shared my birthday – 12 March – and his dad, like mine, was a military man, albeit the RAF rather than the regular army. All these similarities meant I felt a camaraderie and a connection with him. Despite having a pretty tarnished image as a bad boy and drug-abuser whose life had spun out of control, both with the Libertines and his later band Babyshambles, in private he struck me as being impressionable and vulnerable, rather too trusting – which unfortunately made him a bit of a magnet for scumbags. It was too easy to cast Pete as a wastrel. Sure, he had pissed a lot of his talent up the wall several times, but when he managed to see through the murk and spot the opportunities that were there for him, he really came up with the goods. The songs he had written for *Grace/Wastelands* touched me deeply. I found myself really caring about him, and I wanted to be there to help him if he needed it.

Not that he did. We ended up sitting in the live room and playing a few tunes together, showing each other a couple of chords. After recording one or two takes we went back to the control room to find Stephen holding his head in despair, because Pete had about eleven chains and crucifixes hanging around his neck, which were rattling against the guitar. Right through that album, all you can hear is the jingling of his necklaces! It drove Stephen – who likes things neat and tidy – crazy. Me, I never even wear a watch in the studio. I keep my noisy trinkets well away. That's not to say I don't possess them, although unlike Pete I prefer pagan symbols over Christian ones.

Around this time I developed a new hobby: exploring car-boot sales in forgotten corners of England, such as Thanet, in east Kent. These are the sort of places where old witches get rid of their shit: symbolic objects, cauldrons, incense burners and tripods with three (the magic number) feet. It gets you outdoors, and you taste a flicker of the old religion. It helps you understand psychedelia better too. Witches didn't literally fly on broomsticks, but they did take hallucinogenic journeys using all the correctly harvested herbs and mushrooms.

As I discovered, magic is out there to be found, if only you tune in to the right station. I began dropping into esoteric bookshops – Treadwell's in Bloomsbury, in particular – and asking the warlocks behind the counter for some recommended reading. They pressed volumes by the likes of Vivianne Crowley, Robert Cochrane, Evan John Jones and Doreen Valiente into my hand, and I became aware of weird happenings in sylvan haunts such as the Queen's Wood in north London, inside a ring of thirteen ancient oaks, a classic clearing for black and white magic under a full moon – workshops, solstice celebrations, Wiccan rituals, lunar worship and the veneration of various pagan gods and goddesses.

In fact, ever since I bought my house in Camden, I had spiritualists living next door. The end wall of my garden was part of an amazing building called the Rochester Square Spiritualist Temple. Every summer until around 2014 they had an open day. You paid a fiver, and that allowed you to go in, wander round and have a few readings: tea leaves, palmistry or the odd clairvoyant who could divine everything about you just by looking you up and down. The temple drew people with all sorts of mystical gifts, who had different methods of telling you about yourself.

Bored one day, I went in and handed over my fiver, and met a man who told me he was talking to my grandad. I was sceptical and only answered 'yes' or 'no' to his questions, deliberately not giving away any telling details. Still, I admit it was disconcerting when he described a sweaty, worn-out T-shirt of mine that I often used to wear. Burgundy, with a thin blue stripe through it, it had been washed so often that the armpits had basically disappeared. This gentleman said, 'Well, your grandad's saying you're doing really, really well these days, but isn't it about time you threw that burgundy T-shirt away?' I was nonplussed, unsure what to believe. There are probably loads of early live pictures of Blur showing me wearing it, because it was one of my favourites. Then again, how would this guy know about that T-shirt and what it actually meant to me? In the end, whether he really was speaking to my grandad, or whether he had just seen me in the street wearing the T-shirt and thought to himself, 'God, that looks a bit of a mess,' I understood why these communications from beyond this realm could be a comfort to people. Whether or not the contact was genuine didn't matter; the fact was, I felt really good afterwards. I felt watched over and looked after, and that was enough.

Years later, the centre was threatened with demolition, with luxury flats to be built in its place, and I lent my name to the protest against the redevelopment. There was an amazing mural inside the building and a beautiful altar with star-shaped light fittings. Once I received some drum treatments in there, where you lie down on a blanket and close your eyes, and they beat drums over you. You feel the air moving and the drum shifting around; it's quite a nice sensation. A large part of what makes it beneficial is the feeling that someone is caring for you; you just have to lie down and let it happen. Beyond that, I don't know whether there's any genuine shamanic stuff going down, or whether it's simply a break from the norm for fifteen minutes. But it does verge on the magical. People think magic is a lot more than it is, that magic is waving a wand and changing something into something else. I looked into it further and found that there are different types of magic, each with its own purpose: low magic, which could be charging up some stones or a staff at full moon and using them to project energy; high or ceremonial magic; or just the beating of a drum near you when you're relaxing. I think people expect too much of magic, and it's been misrepresented for a long time. Which doesn't mean it's not useful.

Of course, magicians are nothing without their inventory of magical instruments. My own witch doctor's staff was, of course, the guitar, and as I continued to refine my technique and expand my instrument collection, I found myself being asked more often about my secrets.

THICK-SKINNED WORKHORSES

I n 2011 I was honoured when Fender released their Graham Coxon signature Telecaster, based on my 1968 Telecaster, which I had named 'the Shed'. This was because mine was particularly beaten-up. It looked as if someone had sanded it down, knocked it about with a hammer and sploshed creosote all over it – the drip marks had visibly congealed on the back. In other words, it looked as if a rookie handyman had been practising their DIY skills on it in the garden shed.

In the early days of Blur I played a butterscotch '52 reissue Telecaster with an Air India sticker on it. After being allowed early retirement, it now resides in a display case of Britpop memorabilia at the Hard Rock Café in London, along with Noel Gallagher's Union Jack Epiphone. Fender guitars have a longer scale length than Gibsons, which puts more tension on the strings, making them harder to bend. The '52 version had a wider neck than the skinnier 1960s models. I wrestled with that beast throughout the 1990s, assuming that was just what Telecasters were like – trying to ride a bull. Because I thrashed it so much, I needed to have thick strings on it, and that made it even more difficult. As the sweaty fingertips of my left hand slid up and down the neck, the strings would slice lines into the pads of my fingers, and before I knew it the fretboard was awash with blood. I used to superglue bits of my fingers back together so I could get through gigs. Halfway through the set, my hands would soften up once more because of the sweat, and it would happen all over again. It was pretty painful. Some guitarists take a big glass of brandy on stage and dip their fingers into it every few minutes to numb the pain. I didn't go that far, but I was definitely a very physical player, so perhaps it would have helped.

Even though it had caused me a lot of agony, I was happy to put my name on a Telecaster. They are great. You can chuck one across the room to your roadie, and if he misses it, it's like, 'Fine, that'll be OK tomorrow.' In the middle of a particularly hectic song, I've chucked it up in the air as far as the lead will allow, right up into the lighting rig, and watched it fall to the ground. It crashes down on stage and makes an infernal racket, but it's absolutely fine – and usually stays in tune. They are workhorses with very thick skins.

Some guitarists get associated with certain instruments – like Pete Townshend and Paul Weller with the Rickenbacker, or Jimi Hendrix with the Strat. With me it was the Telecaster and the Gibson SG. I used a Fender Jaguar on tracks like Blur's 'He Thought of Cars' (on *The Great Escape*). The Jaguar was interesting because it had a shorter neck, but I got one mainly because certain guitar heroes of mine, like J Mascis and Thurston Moore, used to use them – although you can even see them turning up in old footage of the Jackson Five and the Beach Boys. It was a surf guitar that ended up perfect for a more grungy sound – an interesting alternative to the Stratocaster. They were originally designed as jazz guitars, with a woody, bassy tone. It was a long time before I got my own Fender Jazzmaster, which I used on *The Magic Whip*.

But I loved my Jaguar. I found mine, dated 1966, in a shop on Denmark Street, and I still own it. For me, it has that beautiful spy movie/spaghetti western sound that instantly conjures up the music of Ennio Morricone or John Barry with a single strum. It was a machine of wood and wires that summoned up images of *The Ipcress File*, James Bond and John le Carré.

Back at school, whenever I drew a guitar it was usually a Fender Telecaster. It's incredible that it was Leo Fender's first design, and it's still one of the most sought-after guitars. To my eye, though, the Telecaster's shape looked awkward. I thought the headstock looked malformed compared to the Stratocaster, particularly the big headstock of the 1970s versions. I also used to draw the extremely cool-looking Rickenbackers, but when I eventually got my hands on one, I found it a pig to play. It was very planky and un-ergonomic.

I've been told I play the guitar like a drummer, which makes me think, 'Well, I am probably originally a drummer.' If my sister hadn't had a guitar knocking about, perhaps I would have chosen the drums instead. The thing is, these guitars weren't really designed to play the kind of music I was into. They weren't even designed to be played by people like Pete Townshend. For me, the Strat is the most awkward instrument. There's knobs and all kinds of stuff that get in the way. If you're playing properly, like a grown-up, that would be fine, but if you're swinging your arms about and being less physically restrained, they're awful. Pete Townshend found that out the hard way, by stabbing his hand with his tremolo arm on a couple of occasions.

The Telecaster was like a hot rod: stripped down to the essentials. I probably completely overplayed mine in my manic, anxious way: over-squeezing the neck, bending chords out of tune because I was holding the neck too tightly. I played guitar the same way I painted; in fact, I've often referred to the instrument as a sort of sonic paintbrush. I'm much more interested in what the guitar can do for me, rather than what I can do for the guitar. Sticking a load of echo on it and plugging it into a bunch of distortion units, then manhandling the guitar, twisting it about or grabbing the neck – like automatic drawing or action painting – will produce sounds and shapes which inspire me in both my songwriting and the way I perform.

Guitars eventually lost their mystery for me. I do know people who go weak at the knees when they look at my collection, but over time I have come to think of them simply as tools of the trade. A guitar can look amazing, but ultimately it comes down to playability and the job it's capable of doing.

In 2020 I had a guitar made for me by the English company Manson, and I absolutely refer to it as a tool. It's matt black and has several features I requested. I told them, 'I want these knobs here, out of the bloody way; I want tremolo; and I want a sustain switch that will make a note go on for ever. Plus I want the controls to be as simple as possible, well out of harm's way, and no sharp edges.' It's about making a guitar that would be safe enough for a kindergarten! The result looks cool, and it does the job perfectly. I also commissioned a guitar from Friedman, with one of my paintings on it. That's a stripped-down rock 'n' roll machine, and probably the most comfortable guitar I've ever played on.

I've always loved – and been extremely nerdy about – effects. The tremolo, for its classic sci-fi atmosphere. The wah-wah – not in a Hendrix way, but just to push the guitar into its most trebly range. Echo, or anything redolent of psychedelia. Vibrato and reverb to create big sounds. My collection of FX pedals only grew over the years. I'd create a sound at my leisure in the studio, but then I would have to recreate it live, so my pedal board got bigger and bigger, until eventually it had evolved into an integrated spaceship-like console with lights blinking all over it. There weren't many to choose from in the 1990s, but now there are so many companies manufacturing incredible guitar pedals.

I didn't follow through on the folk influences that were all over *The Spinning Top*. That album was conceived in a countryside setting, at a very specific moment in my life. By the time I came to make the next album, *A+E*, I was in a totally different mood. My inspiration tends to go through cycles. I had played and listened to so much folk music that eventually I had to cleanse my palate with more minimal punky stuff, like Wire, and even jazz musicians such as Jackie McLean. In 2012 the cycle was in a new rotation, and I wanted to keep things electric and simple.

Most of *A+E* wasn't written on a guitar at all. Instead, I made some home demos by picking up a bass and getting a fat riff going, then adding a drum machine. They were all jams, made up from start to finish. The guitar parts were fitted around them, as I figured out the chords over the bassline, and those parts in turn triggered ideas for words and sentences.

When I took the material to the Pool, at Miloco Studios in Bermondsey, in 2011, with Ben Hillier producing, we worked quickly, replicating the demos in as few takes as possible. I was living in my house in Kent at the time, so I rode my motorbike to the studio and back every day. I liked the way Ben worked. There was no control room in the Pool; we were all in the same space, with several mics lying around, all of which were live, meaning lots of random stuff was sucked into the mix. Occasionally, listening back to the tapes, you'd hear a strange noise and wonder what it was. I was using crummy old solid-state amplifiers, plus some synthesizers – it was all fairly anarchic and excellent fun, like working in a big playground.

'Advice' was improvised from start to end. I put a guitar line down randomly, followed it with the bassline, put some drums on and then sang over it all. It was based on a memory from the 1980s, when me and a couple of mates went to a teenage party in Brentwood, yanked out the tape that was playing and replaced it with a Smiths album. Then we danced about in a way that most of the lads at the party considered 'faggy', resulting in a beating. Having expected a night of getting off with our mates' cousins, instead it ended with us roaming around the desolate suburban streets of Brentwood, wondering how we were going to get home.

'Seven Naked Valleys' was a darker, more psychedelic take on 'Yellow Submarine'. The picture in my head was of travelling in a submarine close to the bottom of the ocean, admiring the way the undercurrents create rounded ridges of sand and smooth rocks. All these marine curves are echoed in the female body, and I have always been interested in the visual similarity of those forms.

'Running for Your Life' was based around something that was shouted out at a very early Blur gig in the north of England some-where. We went on stage, and Damon bellowed, 'Hello, we're Blur, we're from London!' in his chipper way, and someone shouted back, 'Well, fuck off back down the M1, you cunt!' Loud and proud. I remembered that when I wrote the song and made up this silly fighting chant about southerners, northerners and all that. As a Midlander, I'm allowed to do that.

The album had some morose moments, but I don't think they came from any real place of darkness. 'Knife in the Cast' is a bit of a broody number, a surreal track that doesn't mean an awful lot.

That's about as despondent as it gets, but basically it's quite a cheerful little record in the end.

We completed about twenty tracks in those sessions, and ten of them ended up on *A+E*. The rest were quite different – more retro-influenced, 1980s indie in style – and I compiled them into a separate album called *Castle Park*, which has never been released. I don't know if it ever will be, but there's some nice stuff on it, and I've played a lot of it live. At first I was going to put everything on one massive album, but it would have been too much, and *A+E* in the form it was released felt like the right direction for me at the time. It was aggressive, wild, funny and perverse – a lot more fun.

By the time the album came out in April 2012, we had entered the age of streaming, and the whole presentation aspect of albums, artwork included, was being downgraded. Marketing people would insist, 'Your artwork isn't going to end up much bigger than a postage stamp, next to the list of songs.' It annoyed me that I wasn't allowed to have an arty cover because of people on computers. I got narky about it with the people at Parlophone, and in the end I snapped a picture of my girlfriend's bloody knee with my Ericsson phone and put text on it: 'There you go.' Perversely, the label loved it.

I launched the album at the Cockpit in Leeds, which was one of my favourite small clubs. I had the place in mind while making the whole album, in fact. Years before, my band had played a show elsewhere in Leeds, and we went out afterwards. We ended up at the Cockpit, and I've never seen so many cool-looking kids in my life – the haircuts and shoes were all immaculate. It was an indie night and a couple of bands were playing, and something in me must have clicked: 'I want to write an album that would be perfect if you heard it at the Cockpit in Leeds.' That's what *A+E* is. The club was in a building with a long arched tunnel where the sound bounces off every surface, and I imagined the record blasting away in there.

There's no mystery about the album title: it does just refer to Accident and Emergency. I should have written it with an '&' instead of a '+', because I often get asked if it is some kind of algebraic puzzle or whether the letters refer to chords, as in *The Golden D*. I messed that up. It's none of those things; the album is simply a collection of accidents and emergencies.

———

Blur reconvened in the summer of 2012 for a handful of live dates in the UK and Europe, played in front of big, appreciative audiences. They were mostly lovely shows that took us from Wolverhampton Civic Hall, an old favourite of ours, to outdoor festivals in Scandinavia. The tour's climax came with a huge event in London's Hyde Park marking the end of the 2012 Olympic Games. It was a really enjoyable show that took place in a pre-'broken Britain', pre-Brexit London – a city that already seems to have vanished. Soraya was pregnant that summer and was just entering her third trimester in the month I was away on tour. In October our daughter, Dorelia (Dore for short), was born at the Portland Hospital.

Towards the end of the year Paul Weller invited me and Damon to his Black Barn studio to improvise with the poet Michael Horovitz, who was one of the leading lights of the British counter-cultural underground. His International Poetry Incarnation event at the Albert Hall in 1965, featuring Allen Ginsberg, William S. Burroughs, Adrian Mitchell and loads of other luminaries, was the first major event of the psychedelic era. I had my saxophone with me, as well as the guitar, as Paul wanted us to be a free-jazz trio backing Michael's live beat poetry. We set up our instruments and tinkled along, making a fair amount of skronk and noise, reacting in real time to Michael's recitations. The liberated positivity of the 1960s survived in Michael's personality, and I find his poetry very amusing, naughty and mischievous. He was a lovely, emotional man, and his poetry is raw and open and full of insights. The whole messy jumble eventually came out in spring 2013, on a twelve-inch called *Bankbusted Nuclear Detergent Blues*.

Paul was good friends with Noel Gallagher, and at some point he must have mentioned this crazy session. Damon's and Noel's paths had also crossed a few times recently – they had enjoyed a bonding drink and had put all the 1990s Blur–Oasis rivalry nonsense behind them. Noel was putting together a charity event in March 2013 for the Teenage Cancer Trust at the Royal Albert Hall – which Michael described as his favourite pub – and invited us to join him. It was a groovy night. Me and Damon, with Paul on drums, played Blur's 'Tender'. Noel joined us on stage, and we harmonised on the 'Oh, my baby' lines. My parents were in the audience, although my dad wasn't too impressed by my sax skills.

Previously I had played a benefit concert in Brixton in aid of the Japan Disaster Fund, which was put on by Noel's brother Liam. He was charming that night, so all these extracurricular experiences meant that the hatchet was well and truly buried.

———

Blur, by this time, was an open-ended concept, a wayward beast that we eventually managed to keep on a leash. After the re-formation tour of 2009, we were relatively comfortable in each other's company again, both socially and out on the road. We never got together just for the sake of it, though – we needed a reason, or the prospect of new recordings, to inspire us to go out and play. When in 2013 we embarked on a variety of live dates in different parts of the world – Mexico, California's Coachella Festival, Hong Kong, Indonesia, Europe, Russia, South America – we were older and more accepting of each other. The insecurity of our twenties was gone. Blur was less of a life-and-death situation; none of us were particularly skint; our careers and reputation were established – in fact, we were now part of the 'old guard'. Playing live with Blur gradually turned into a celebration of what we had achieved, a chance to get away from home and have some good times, to turn up the amps in front of thousands of smiling faces and get off on it, with no strings attached. We got to see our crew, we got to see our backing singers, we got to hang out with the brass section. By now all of them were like old friends.

During some of those shows I would look across at Damon jumping around on the stage and think, 'God, does he really need to try so hard? He's going to do himself an injury . . .' Even I lit up the fireworks now and again, with the occasional backwards roll or bit of guitar abuse (Damon has admitted to writing certain fast, punky songs especially for me, merely so I can jump about like an idiot), but usually I just concentrated on playing as well as I could and looking out at the big audience. 'You don't have to kill yourself entertaining these bastards!' I told Damon, and eventually he saw it my way . . . Well, maybe just for one gig.

I can't deny that when you have trotted out your hits over and over again for so many years, you do start going through the motions. I don't know how many times I had to play 'Country House' in 1996, but because it made the fans so happy, I just gritted my teeth and gave them a bit of a dirty look, and they knew what I meant and found it funny. They knew I wasn't a big fan of the song, but I was playing it for them, and that's what mattered. (It's like a plumber coming round and saying, 'I'll unblock your loo, but I'm not going to fix your blooming kitchen tap.' He'll only do it, begrudgingly, if you stand there cheering him on: 'Yay, the kitchen tap, I love it!' Once he starts, he really enjoys the job, but first he needs to be coaxed.)

During this second reunion tour I saw our hits as the fun, daft songs that they always were. But when I experienced the audience's reaction, it reminded me that there's more to a Blur concert than whether I enjoyed myself or not. Seeing other people getting into it is so much more fulfilling than anything I personally might get out of playing. We all need our dollop of jam on the porridge, but ultimately it's the fans that need to be served.

————

In early May 2013 we arrived a day or two early in Hong Kong to play a show at the AsiaWorld Arena. Our next stop after HK was supposed to be a festival in Japan, but the news came through that the event had been cancelled at short notice. I was delighted to hear it, because we were staying at the Four Seasons, which was the nicest hotel I'd ever been in. I was in a suite with a big, round jacuzzi, cool sliding doors, a private sitting room and a gigantic bed. I looked forward to the prospect of some rock 'n' roll R&R for a few days, having a swim, steaming away in the jacuzzi, getting a massage and reading a book. But no. Damon suddenly announced that he had booked us into a local studio to jam some new ideas and see what came out. He also announced it to the thousands of folks in the audience at our show, who screamed with ecstasy at the thought that we had chosen their city to make a new Blur album.

So, instead of luxuriating and being fussed over in one of the world's top hotels, it was back to the day job. The next morning I got on the underground and headed for Avon Studios, a tiny, boiling box on the mainland side of Hong Kong. We got some good ideas going over the two or three days we spent there. Damon had prepared some chord sequences, and we took Dave out of the live room and put him on a rudimentary drum kit, with us in the control room. We left Hong Kong with forty hours of melodic jams and half-baked ideas on a hard disk, finished the tour and went back into our separate hidey-holes.

Blur in hibernation doesn't mean that the members are asleep; everyone is busy doing other projects. But that jam session had stuck in the back of all our minds. We needed to turn it into something usable, and to do that we needed a trusted third party, because there was bound to be a lot of crap to cut out. Eventually I hit on the idea of hiring Stephen Street to sift through the material. Jams can be a useful tool, but you need to be mindful of the moments when the energy cranks up or someone hits on a crucial chord change. I met up with Damon and suggested giving Stephen that chore, and he was relieved that somebody else might want to take the reins. He had often complained about other people relying on him to take the initiative, which may or may not have been true. As a workaholic and visible front person, he brings it on himself to a certain extent.

I did a month's work on the tapes with Stephen, and it was a rewarding process. 'Go Out' is a classic example of a track that originally had hardly any chords, but I retrospectively overdubbed some new ones to create a different tension in the melody. I was back doing my favourite job: basic structuring. By the end, there were some songs that had two choruses, because I didn't know which part Damon thought of as the verse and which was the refrain. There was one song where we had both separately written chorus lines. We had put them down at the same time, and it was funny how similar they were. Our respective vocal parts started and ended on the same note, and took different twists and turns in between.

I injected increased dynamics into 'Thought I Was a Spaceman', giving it these huge surges with ascending guitar parts in the middle. We got Alex in to tidy up the bass here and there. I am competent enough on the instrument, but Alex has a gift for getting the gist and then flying off with little gestural flicks of his hands. That is what makes it an Alex James bassline rather than a boring Graham Coxon one. There really isn't a bass player like Alex. He has always tried understanding the theory of bass-playing. Normally I start to panic when bassists do that, because it means they're going to drift away from the root. This isn't bloody jazz! A good bass-player can keep that root note while suggesting other interesting ones, without knocking you in a split second into chaos. Alex's way of playing the bass is informed by a mixture of Joy Division/New Order and ABBA, so he's a little hyperactive. Like me with the guitar, I guess.

Stephen and I reached a point where we had done all we could with the material, and it was complete apart from the vocals. It was time to play it to Damon. We arrived at his studio in a state of trepidation, but when we played him 'Go Out', with its big, aggressive gestures, he started jumping around and dancing. 'Yeah, we've got him!' I thought. 'He's fallen for it.' He said, 'Oh, shit, this is good. Now I'll have to write some lyrics.' He was kind of pleased that we'd pulled it off, but he saw a lot of work ahead.

The Magic Whip came out in 2015, and it sent Blur out on another round of gigs and interviews. We toured the UK, appeared at festivals on the Isle of Wight and in Hyde Park, and ended our burst of activity in November with a show right after the Abu Dhabi Grand Prix.

It was a long way from the Camden Falcon in 1991. There was a fair amount of paranoia about the engagement in Abu Dhabi. The management warned us to keep a tighter lid than usual on our behaviour, and I was convinced I was going to end up in prison on account of my vaping equipment. At the airport we went through a special gate and into a palatial receiving room. Women served us cakes and tea, and no one checked our baggage. The hotel and the racetrack reminded me of the American desert. But it wasn't often that Blur played to an audience of people who looked like warlords, weapons salesmen, dictators and playboys, with white shirts unbuttoned to the navel, slicked-back hair and expensive shoes and trousers.

In the bar I felt out of place as a scruffy musician, but at least there was another guy puffing enormous clouds of smoke from a vape, so I felt a bit more relaxed. From the balcony I watched the cars speeding past, listening to the mad noise the revving engines made. It was quite disturbing after a while, like the whine of a Stuka dive-bomber. Afterwards there was a flypast by some jets trailing green and red smoke, which hung in the air for a while before dissipating into the dusky Arabian night. It left a stunningly cinematic image in my mind's eye – appropriately, perhaps, as my musical career was on the brink of diverting towards the arenas of film and television.

MOVING PICTURES, JADED HEARTS

My work with film had begun in around 2010, when I was involved with the soundtrack for a supernatural thriller called *Curio*. The movie had a consistently malignant atmosphere, and most of the music was noisy and unpleasant. I used a big pipe organ and made a few arrangements of 'Underneath the Spreading Chestnut Tree'. It's one of my favourite songs, probably because it was included in *The Black Windmill*, a 1974 film starring Michael Caine. I saw it when I was far too young really, but it made an impression on me.

Since my earliest dabblings in bands, there have been huge changes to the way music is recorded. By 2015 there seemed to be less need to book studio time, even though I loved working in that environment. When I was asked to provide a song for Lone Scherfig's film *The Riot Club*, I realised that I could do it from home. So I started looking into the best gear to buy. I can be very OCD about purchases. I'll sit down for several days reading consumer reviews before buying a toaster. The same goes for recording gear and software. I was flapping around, thinking, 'God, I'd better get Logic or something, and an interface for the instruments . . .' But I got a cheap mic and did that one song, and realised how easy it could be. Gradually I accumulated more and more home-recording equipment, until suddenly I had a studio in my spare room. For me, that really is where the magic happens.

The song was called 'We're Out There Somewhere', and it

appeared over the closing credits of *The Riot Club*, which was adapted from the play by Laura Wade and based on the antics of Oxford University's Bullingdon Club, whose members have included many Conservative politicians over the years. It was a bit of a stodgy song; I could have done better. But it was a useful introduction to the sometimes confusing world of writing music for films. It's a world where you work to a set of instructions, and the next day someone has changed their mind, so you have to chuck a load of stuff out and start again. The day after that they get in touch and say, 'Oh, actually, that thing from two days ago – we rather like that.' By the end, you're left with ten bits and bobs of half-formed ideas. I've got a folder of over a hundred songs on my computer that haven't been used. They all started life as music for films.

The music supervisor who got me involved with *The Riot Club* was called Matt Biffa. He had worked on music consultancy for an impressive range of movies and TV productions, from the first *Harry Potter* to *Carol*, *Paddington*, *Sex Education* and *I May Destroy You*. Not long after *Riot Club* was broadcast, in around mid-2017, Matt contacted me again and mentioned a British-made series he was working on for Channel 4 called *The End of the F***ing World*. It was based on a graphic novel by Charles Forsman and sounded intriguing, so I said yes and began working on it from home, to a brief. Soon my inbox was filling up with edited film sequences sent by the production company, which contained sample pieces of music – the Beach Boys, Beck or Scott Walker – laid on top as a rough guide. They are placeholder sounds to help you understand what the scene is about and offer clues about the characters. You take all that in, then try to compose a song that the Beach Boys, Beck or Scott Walker never quite wrote. There was one song – 'A Better

Beginning' – where I felt I approximated the Scott Walker sound pretty well, getting in character and accessing my inner crooner. What I liked about the whole process was the genre-hopping and time-travelling – sliding between 'early Beck' to 'Devo' to 'out-and-out Buzzcocks' to 'Bob Dylan'. I found that I was good at it and that it was excellent fun.

I also got a kick out of the fast turnarounds. These songs had to be polished off in three hours, which left no real time to waste on details, such as whether to add a tambourine here or a maraca there. If a fantastic harmony line occurred to me a week later, there was nothing I could do. It was simply 'Track done – tick!', send it off, and on to the next cue. When I needed inspiration, I hopped into the bath with my iPhone. That always oiled the machinery. Sinking down into the bubbles, an idea would come up and I'd sing it into the phone, then get dressed and go and record it. I'd give it a quick mix for balance and then send it. Once I got going, three or four songs a day would zoom off. I probably gave the producers far too much, but for the first time ever I was writing songs that weren't such a big deal – not intended to be released as singles or on an album, with all due pomp and ceremony – and having fun. They had a specific purpose that was different to that of the songs I wrote for myself. At the same time, it loosened me up, and my recording technique improved enormously. I developed a workflow whereby I had a mic set up to sing into; I then grabbed my acoustic guitar and just sat there, or else took out my little mini-keyboard or organ. And very quickly I'd have a hundred songs.

Everything in the first series of *The End of the F***ing World* had already been filmed by the time I came to write the music. I came up with an instrumental theme for the character of Alyssa, a self-confident and painfully honest teenager played by Jessica Barden. The melody was a tool for representing this character: it could be pushed and pulled or stripped down and mined in order to provide the emotional drive required by a scene. When it was time to work on the second series, I wanted to get a head start, so I began writing as soon as I received the scripts. Much of it wasn't usable, apart from the song 'She Knows', which I completed pretty early, on the strength of the script. Lucy Forbes, the director of the first four episodes of season two, heard the song before she began shooting and told me she loved it. To get them in the right frame of mind, she played it to the actors while they were shooting a scene in which the character Bonnie kills a man in a hotel room by accident.

Writing very quickly, then forgetting what you've done, is quite a salutary experience. When I come back to it, I hear a lot of energy and excitement in the recordings. There's an element of play-acting too, which I really enjoyed. One of my favourite songs, 'Angry Me', is a sloppy, Beck-type number. It includes an organ solo, obviously played by me, but because I'm not very good, as the singer I take the piss out of the organist. I took my lead here from songs which have an audible interaction or conversation between the band members, like on the Velvet Underground's 'Temptation Inside Your Heart', for example. I did that a couple of times, and I enjoyed the fact that it would sound authentically like a band, even though it was all just me. It created a sense of tension, as if this argumentative group wasn't going to last long.

Composing music for TV series in my home studio has made me more hands-on about everything, more self-sufficient. I found out an awful lot more about what I could do with sound and took my time. The circumstances of writing music to order, for a specific function and to a deadline, meant that the songs didn't have much time to ferment. I had to keep pushing on to the next cue, without dwelling on the material too much.

———

With *The End of the F***ing World* streaming worldwide on Netflix, it was time to take my songs in front of new audiences. Working on the soundtracks had made me prolific by this point: as well as coming up with roughly two hundred songs for the series, I had written around a hundred of my own, including a couple that ended up on my *Superstate* LP. In September 2018 I embarked on a two-week tour of selected cities in the US, just me, my guitar and a looper pedal, a roadie and a van.

The shows were small and intimate, and I liked that. It was an artistic challenge as well: two hours is a long time to hold people's attention with finger-style acoustic guitar. At most venues the audience was sat close enough that I could reach out and pat them on the head if I wanted to. I dealt with that by not putting pressure on myself from the moment I walked on stage. Before the first song I pointed out that this was a very intimate setting and asked the audience to join me in treating this as an informal gathering. 'I'm not really a professional. I'm just playing a few songs and having a good time – what do you reckon?' That generally evoked a positive response. There's a game I like to play with the audience: they have to guess which songs are autobiographical. After each one I'd say, 'Well, what about that?' and they'd shout out their ideas. If indeed it *was* autobiographical (and let's face it, most of them are, to a greater or lesser extent), I might reveal a bit more of the song's backstory to them.

That kind of trick would never work at a Blur appearance at something like a massive festival in Jakarta. But in little clubs and bars across America, where the crowd are leaning on the edge of the stage or draped across your monitor, watching you from three feet away, maybe even trying to engage you in conversation as you're playing, that kind of personal approach works beautifully. If you're a bit bashful, it can get kind of intense. That's when my self-effacing Englishness pays dividends.

My fans (of course I know they're fans of other artists as well, but while they're watching me, they're *my* fans) are generally pretty amiable, and we have a good dialogue. I can be cheeky with them and tell them off: 'Don't do that, put your phone away . . .' I'm not a particularly grumpy person; I'm usually quite a positive, buoyant sort, and it goes against my grain to be grumpy for very long. So I feel in my element at shows like that.

This more low-key kind of touring was a pleasant change. Touring with my band earlier in the decade was good, but it knackered us out. I gave everything to those shows. The bigger, rockier gigs were very similar to Blur's concerts. I'm still blown away by the audiences that came to see us, because they were big, and the folks at the front still looked about seventeen! Young people are far more sussed now than they used to be. They're more intelligent, they care more and they look cooler. If you play at a destination away from the typical rock circuit, like Uruguay, they're extremely happy that you've bothered. 'Everyone goes to bloody Argentina, so thanks so much for coming here,' they'll say, and take you off to a shop to buy you some weird tea. You sign their stuff and pose for a few photos, then go back to your room feeling like you've made someone happy. The whole touring malarkey is fun but it's expensive: you need to rehearse, there's travel and hotels, tour support and plenty more that you only get to know about once you run your own show. I'd love to go out on the road with my band again – one day.

———

Around the time I was getting more into TV soundtrack work, another interesting project came up. Back in 2017 Jamie Davis, who had run Transcopic Records with me, moved to the States. For his fortieth birthday bash he decided he had to have a Beatles cover band. When he looked at what was available, he realised they were all crap, as well as absurdly overpriced. Then a flashbulb went off: he remembered that loads of his mates were amazing musicians, like Miles Kane, Sean Payne from the Zutons, Matt Bellamy from Muse and the Cester brothers – Nic and Chris – from Jet. He invited them to the party, threw them all on stage and commanded them to perform his own private Beatles gig, under the name Dr Pepper's Jaded Hearts Club Band.

I wasn't a stranger to the idea of crafting pristine reproductions of classic pop. Back in 2013 EMI Records had the idea of re-recording the Beatles' debut album, *Please Please Me*, at Abbey Road, on its fiftieth anniversary. The gimmick was to allocate exactly the same amount of time in the studio that the Beatles were allowed in 1963. A different artist was invited to cover each song, including Mick Hucknall, Beverley Knight, I Am Kloot, Glenn Tilbrook from Squeeze, Gabrielle Aplin, Stereophonics – and me. It ended up being quite a big production. Still, there I was, given the task of singing what I thought was one of the hardest tunes, Bacharach/ David's 'Baby It's You'. It's effectively a soul number, and with my apologetic little indie voice I wasn't confident I would have the tubes to pull it off. You really have to commit to the song, give it all you can muster – just like John Lennon did. The backing singers were incredibly encouraging and lovely, so I did my best and wasn't unhappy with what came out.

The impromptu tribute band went down a storm at Jamie's party, and a couple of guests asked them to play at theirs too. Stella McCartney begged them to play at one of her fashion shows, and that ended up being pretty special: her father Paul stood up from his seat in the audience and sang along on a couple of songs.

I first joined the Dr Pepper's Jaded Hearts Club Band line-up at a Teenage Cancer Trust concert at the Royal Albert Hall in 2018. Since then the personnel had been tweaked a bit, and the band now mainly consisted of me, Matt, Jamie and Sean, with Miles and Nic taking turns on vocals, depending on the song. It really began as a bit of fun, but we played a couple of gigs in LA where we went beyond the Beatles and played harder material by the Stooges, MC5, the Who and Cream. I loved having to learn Eric Clapton's bits and bobs, and I got the chance to do my Pete Townshend freak-out, which was a good laugh. We dressed in a rock 'n' roll uniform of leather jackets, black jeans and winklepickers – any excuse to get into that sort of clobber.

Then, of course, the idea of making an album was floated, so we tracked down some lesser-known soul and northern soul classics and attacked them with the same sort of early-Beatles, punk-rock attitude. Matt was usually in the producer's seat, trying to replicate the sound of early Beatles, but also diverting into Marc

Bolan-in-a-spaceship-buzzing-round-the-solar-system style and filling the bottom end with loads of fat, fuzzy bass. What's interesting about a lot of those old soul recordings is that they're skinny-sounding things, with a lot of instruments being lost because of how limited the studio dynamics were in those days. So we took the opportunity to redress the balance. We tried to keep it swinging and improve or expand on the groove – this is meant to be danceable stuff, after all – but also to fatten it up with the deeper low end that it's possible to engineer these days.

Matt's quite forensic about getting things right, while I'm a bit scruffy. This project forced me to smarten up. We recorded most of it in Santa Monica – Matt had access to one room of a studio on Main Street. Sean would pop over from the UK or send us drum tracks from home. Nic lives in Italy, so he'd come over and do some vocals and try to ramp himself up to match the sheer energy of Marvin Gaye. It's amazing how much power there is in Marvin's vocals, but when you listen to them they seem really relaxed. When Nic tried to rise to that level, we realised what amazing skill must have been needed to belt them out while barely breaking a sweat.

It's very difficult playing other people's music. 'I Put a Spell on You' was one of the tracks we decided to include on the album. I knew only Screamin' Jay Hawkins's version, because I used to spin it fifty times a day on the Good Mixer's jukebox. I don't like Creedence Clearwater Revival's cover, although we borrowed from it a little bit. But we mainly based it around Nina Simone's version, so as the lead guitarist I had to try and evoke a brass section and strings, which I did with a bloody great fuzz pedal. Hearing Nic's blood-curdling scream as it goes into the guitar solo, with everything distorting through the fuzz pedal, is exciting. We also did a song by Shocking Blue, the Dutch band who had a 1970s hit with 'Venus'. Jamie's a huge fan.

There's a macho side to the Jaded Hearts Club that's exemplified by Nic's style of big-chested singing. In reality, he's not an overly masculine sort of chap – none of us are. But there's something about making those girthy noises and a big, sexy row that helps all of us get a bit more in touch with our masculinity. In a fun way, rather than in a *Fight Club* kind of way.

———

That experience chimed with something wider going on in my life at the time, which was about becoming more conscious of how I express myself. Who is really the 'I' of Graham Coxon the solo artist? I'd be the first to admit that on my early albums I used to sing in a fairly childlike manner. Even at the time it got on my nerves, and I would ask myself why I didn't seem to have the confidence just to sing out. I became more aware of a reticence in the way I projected myself – as if I wasn't sure that I was meant to be singing at all. When I was making songs for the soundtracks, which were meant to be from different eras and by various types of bands, I tried to change my voice all the time, like an actor inhabiting the persona of the singer in this imaginary group. It could have been anything from a Devo-like robotic character to an early-Beck-type slacker, a Burl Ives or Roger Miller folkie, or even a crooner à la Scott Walker. It wasn't impersonation; more just seeing what my vocal range was capable of. I found that helped me to do the song justice.

My involvement with *The End of the F***ing World* led directly to me doing the music for another Netflix series, *I Am Not Okay* *with This*, which I worked on during 2019. I picked up on the idea of fictional band members arguing with each other, kicked it up a notch and invented a pastiche mid-1980s group called Bloodwitch. In the series, two of the characters bond over the group. The production company ended up using only a couple of the songs, but I thought, 'Why don't I just write a whole Bloodwitch album?' So I created an entire eleven-track LP, influenced by 1980s indie bands like Talulah Gosh, My Bloody Valentine, the Jesus and Mary Chain and some of the riot grrrl groups. Like a 'Best of', it's meant to tell the evolving story of this non-existent group, so over the course of the record it transforms from a cute indie sound into choral 'folk–horror-core'. I really enjoyed taking it in that direction, as well as getting the arrangements together.

For *I Am Not Okay with This*, I wrote a very American cowboy/Roger Miller-type song, 'There's a World Outside My Door'. I had to Americanise my voice convincingly to sing it or it wouldn't have worked. Otherwise, I generally sing in my English voice. I've never had a problem with it. Sometimes when vowels are heavily anglicised it sounds slightly awkward, but I have found a way of solving that by twisting them into northern English – words like 'can't', for example, which is always difficult to sing in British English. Another option, of course, is to change the word altogether!

———

During this period my friend Erol Alkan was asked to do some production work with Duran Duran. I had crossed paths with Duran founder and keyboard player Nick Rhodes at a panel discussion hosted by Miranda Sawyer in December 2017, where both of us and the singer Peaches talked about David Bowie, who had recently passed away. After the panel, Nick leaned over and murmured, 'Do you know, Graham, that Duran are going to be in the studio soon? I think it would be rather fun to have you along.' It turned out he was very familiar with my work with Blur. It was flattering, and I was taken aback, but it sounded like it could be good fun. When they finally got it together, a couple of years later, it was the original Duran Duran line-up, minus their former guitarist, Andy Taylor. Erol came back from a band meeting and told me that my name had come up as a replacement. So for most of 2019 I was popping in and out of the studio to work on their *Future Past* album. I was sitting in, jamming and helping them to write and get the songs together. I was even going to play live with them at various festival dates in 2020, until the Covid pandemic put a stop to all that.

Strangely enough, being in the studio with Duran Duran wasn't a million miles away from my experience with Blur. Musicians, I realised, are distinct breeds. As bass players, Alex James and John Taylor shared similar traits – although John was a lot more upfront and involved with shaping the songs. As drummers, Roger Taylor and Dave Rowntree were both pretty quiet and just got on with it. Simon Le Bon's an incredibly positive, energetic guy, like Damon in a way. Similar to me, Nick is very involved with shaping the chord sequences. While we were jamming and finalising these, I was fascinated by the way the band explored every nuance of a chord, chasing them down every avenue until their possibilities were totally exhausted. Just when things already sounded great, they found a new place to go with it, with even more amazing results. Simon would sit with it for a while, then suddenly start singing something, and just like that it turned into a brand-new Duran song – with me on guitar.

I thought it would be awesome for them to be weirder than before, to go back to an earlier fork in the road and make a kind of dark yet danceable disco. I started mucking about with guitar effects, creating more modulated sounds, fiddling about with them and getting some decent parts together. Like me, Nick also had a well-documented interest in fine art, and by this stage in his life seemed to be floating through a culturally luxurious existence. Those suave 1980s videos, like Roxy Music's 'Avalon' or Duran Duran's own 'Rio'? Deep in his heart, Nick is still grooving at that party.

ESCAPE
FROM
LA

n the period immediately following the Brexit referendum, Soraya and I began wondering what life in Britain would be like in the years to come, and whether it would be the best place for our daughter Dorelia to grow up in. By now I was in possession of a much-sought-after O1 visa for the US, and we were married. Worries about the UK's bleak prospects, coupled with our privileged freedom of movement in America, sparked the idea of trying to make a new life somewhere different. We picked Los Angeles because it sounded like a fun place to be, plus I had Jamie Davis and my Jaded Hearts Club buddies out there already to prepare the ground. Of course, moving to another country isn't a walk in the park, and the whole thing turned out to be a huge project in terms of logistics.

We moved over in January 2019, having found a house to rent in Sunset Park, near the coast in Santa Monica. After a year or so we graduated inland to Altadena, near Pasadena. I was working all the time just so we were able to afford to live, mainly doing soundtracks. Dore got a place at a school in Pacific Palisades, so a typical morning routine involved getting up at six, answering emails from England, putting breakfast on the table for Dore, doing the school run, coming back, working until picking-up time, fetching Dore and then playing with her until dinner. By ten o'clock I was ready for bed.

There were some good times out there. Dhani Harrison, the son of George, got in touch; he has offices and a clubhouse in

Santa Monica, where I took part in the Whammys (the alternative Grammys) a couple of times. I met a strange jumble of cool people there, like Elliot Easton from the Cars, Susanna Hoffs, Jakob Dylan, Beck and 'Weird Al' Yankovic. There was a perverse rule at the Whammys that you had to play either a Traveling Wilburys track or a song by any of the band's members. There were quite a lot to choose from – Tom Petty, Bob Dylan, Roy Orbison, Jeff Lynne or George Harrison himself – and it was pretty riotous fun.

In America, I was less likely to be recognised on the street. It's nice that people appreciate what you do, but one of the biggest untold stories in pop is the difficulty of being an object of fandom. When Blur started getting fan mail, I was usually the one who received the weirdest and most disturbing messages, the cries for help. The wisest course of action, I have learnt, is to make yourself less available. I admit I enjoy the affirmation and attention you receive through being a public figure, but being increasingly accessible in the digital world can leave you very exposed. Over the years I have tried to wean myself off being so available.

———

I do miss England when I'm away, and after spending most of 2019 in Los Angeles I felt there was something lacking for me there. Even its gridded street layout freaked me out after a while, because everywhere looked like everywhere else. Most of it resembled Jakarta. The city had its mega-scruffy neighbourhoods, which you never would have thought existed in California, whereas when I came back to England, and particularly north London, with all its wiggly walls, roses and musty, mossy smells, I felt like kissing the ground. I even loved the familiar little spiders that, unlike Santa Monican black widows, won't actually kill you. Nowhere else in the world can you encounter the peculiar eccentricities of English front gardens, the care people take of their little castles. You can feel the pride bulging out of every flower bed.

I returned to Britain in April 2020. When I say 'returned', I really mean fled. Sadly, my relationship with Soraya broke down irreparably during our stay in LA, and eventually I felt I had no option but to walk away and fly back home.

Leaving LA for London on my own was traumatic in itself. There was the awful guilt of having to leave my seven-year-old behind, packing my bags even while I was trying to tell her as gently and nicely as possible that Daddy had to go to London and work for a while. As I was saying goodbye, all the trauma and guilt came to a head. Because it was during the early days of the pandemic, I had to spend several nights in lockdown in a hotel in Santa Monica and wait till I was sure this was the right idea.

Eventually I boarded my flight, knowing that I had nowhere to go when I landed. My management found me temporary places in a block in Camden and in Tetherdown, in Muswell Hill, for a couple of weeks at a time. I was in therapy every day, because emotionally I was all over the place, tearful and confused. The therapy helped me to understand the reasons why I ended up in those kinds of relationships and why I viewed them as love, while believing that perfectly healthy, nice, well-balanced, caring relationships were tedious.

———

Therapy has given me so much more insight into my low self-esteem and anxiety, and the fact that my default setting is to feel like the lowest in the pack. I can go into the gubbins in my head and flick the personality switch from its default setting to 'Graham 2.0'. But as soon as I reach the checkout woman at Sainsbury's, it's clicked back to default again: 'You are a lower species than this person.' It's very difficult to keep the confidence levels up.

I think low self-esteem has a lot to do with suffering emotional neglect as a kid. Growing up when I did, before the age of the TV remote, I had to sit on the floor so that I could change the channel for my dad. I still feel uneasy sitting on sofas – I can't do it for very long, especially when others are around. It's very dog-like: I need to get myself lower than them. It's an odd default setting. So it was sort of inbuilt in me from childhood that I have the same rank as a dog, and my place is the floor. This is through no fault of my parents: they came from big families and had to grow up pretty fast themselves, and it's only these days that people are taking more care about being emotionally available for their children and listening to what they have to say and not taking the mickey out of them when they show emotion. Children need to be reassured that however angry or upset they're feeling, there's no shame in having strong emotions. If you shut them down or talk over and interrupt them all the time, they get the idea that their feelings are not import-ant. So they just close themselves off, the feelings are internalised and bottled-up anger turns into a strange humiliation, because they don't want to admit to it (they've just learnt that no one wants to hear about it). I've always had shame, I suppose – about nudity, about actually being a man – and doubts over what I can do that is appropriate as a man.

The feelings you can have as an adult, as a result of childhood emotional neglect, are very similar to those of an alcoholic – disconnection, inferiority, low self-esteem, feeling like you're living behind glass. It's a specific bunch of known traits. We shouldn't be disparaging about alcoholics or other addicts. They are medicating pain, and all you're doing by demonising them is racking up the pain and making the problem worse.

If I look back down the road of my life, I eventually alight on a vignette from when I was ten and accidentally shot my dad in the face with a spud gun. I received a kick in the arse that nearly made me do a somersault, a punishment that was totally unremarkable in the 1970s. I said, 'Ow, sorry, Dad,' and that was the end of the matter. But when something *isn't* there, it's very difficult to see it when you look back down that road. You can't see an absence of emotional availability, because by definition it's not there. It's a dip in the road rather than a signpost that sticks up.

All of that has informed my subsequent relationships. I tended to find it perfectly normal – a natural part of love – to be with someone who showed very little interest in my feelings or emotions. I have been working hard on reversing that. I probably should have started in 2005. But sometimes you need things to get so bad that the spell gets broken, and you wake up from being held in suspension and emerge into a moment of clarity. It's only when stuff reaches such a pitch, like a mental equivalent of the whining buzz Formula One cars make, that the self-preservation kicks in. Things had to get pretty bad for me to remove myself. You can put up with all sorts of shit if you believe you're doing it for the kids, but I realised that removing myself was probably better, in the long run, for Dore as well.

A
TICKET
TO
HEAVEN

have no idea what heaven is, but recently I've been trying to imagine my own version of it. *Superstate*, which was released in 2021, encompasses a comic book and an album, and took shape gradually over a four-year period. In *Superstate*, heaven is a planet, and alien beings from there visit Earth to choose a few people to take back with them. That's the simplest way of putting it. I don't dwell too much on the nature of heaven. If, like me, you prefer not to believe there's a hell, then there's no reason for a heaven to exist either. I'm not at all religious. I hear plenty of people saying they're not religious but spiritual, which seems like a cop-out.

Psychologically, *Superstate* was a game-changer for me. It had its origins in around 2015–16, in a TV series that was never made. Matt Biffa, the music supervisor who got me involved with Netflix, had an idea for a comedy about a fictional band who start out as a Simple Minds-style arty post-punk outfit and gradually get more posh and commercial over the course of the 1980s. They are under growing pressure to make their sound more commercial – that was my whole take on it. The idea of a series fizzled out, but not before I had begun working on some pieces of music for it, so I was left with these songs, none of which were particularly suitable for a standard Graham Coxon album.

Right at that moment, in January 2016, came the terrible news that David Bowie had died. The same day, as a tribute, I wrote the song 'We Remain', which eventually appeared on *Superstate*. The rest of *Superstate* followed over the next few years. It's faintly Bowie-ish, but there are also traces of Peter Hammill and Steely Dan, and it has a general 1970s vibe. Some of it is quite self-reflective, but I was in better shape and increasingly felt its value in helping me to break self-imposed taboos and express myself in a more varied and confident tone. While I was writing these songs, a concept started to emerge about an oppressive future society even more polarised than ours. There is less equality; the rich are a tiny minority, and the rest live in hovels, with unwanted children hanging around. You can listen to the album like a TV series, where one episode is about a particular scenario, then the next moves to another situation, and as the series unfolds you realise the characters are living on opposite sides of the same town, until eventually their lives intertwine.

Bowie's spirit loomed behind this project in other ways too – mainly in the way he created many different characters through-out his career. I found it liberating to act out songs while inhabiting another persona. It was as if I'd been handed a set of keys to unlock unused rooms in my voice. I was thinking of bands like Magazine – some of their lyrics are quite shocking, extreme and perverse. I thought, 'Well, maybe these characters can come from that direc-tion. Not gothic, but a darker sort of art punk, with synths, grooves and a bit of funk going on.' In some respects I'm acting every day. I drop into various characters to break the ice; once it's broken, I'm fine. I attack a lyric in the guise of one character, and either leave it like that if it works or go back to my own voice – with the character having helped me to find the right melody and words.

That opened me up and gave me a lot of freedom, and it was fun. In fact, it almost felt like this was my destiny. I don't believe in God, but in the last few years I have felt tested: forced down a channel that's painful but good for me in the long term. There must be some sort of divine purpose to being put through such a hard time. I started to think, 'Well, what *is* heaven?' It could be a planet, sending beings down to Earth, causing the sightings of angels that you read about in the books of the biblical prophets. My idea was that they were almost like original Old Testament angels – like two Möbius strips spinning around, covered in flames and eyes. Pretty scary.

'Yoga Town' could have been an intro theme for a TV series, and in fact it started life as an unused song for *The End of the F***ing World*. It's about a drunk mother in the garden – clearly a single mum – swinging a bottle around and effing and blinding at the sky, not knowing where her kids are (their whereabouts will be revealed in a later song). I like that kind of kitchen-sink drama, with rumblings of something heavy and interesting simmering away, before the dramatic pot reaches a rolling boil and overflows. I also realised it was about escape – escape from the human situation, and from a narcissistic society doing whatever it wants, with no accountability. In *Superstate*, the authorities keep the population down through compulsory sterilisation, and there are robot girlfriends and boyfriends to have relationships with. After all, we don't want the youth cavorting with each other and procreating, leaving us with all these new mouths to feed. The robot girlfriends are called L.I.L.Ys, which stands for 'Lady I Love You'; the males are M.I.L.Ys. There is also this idea that, one day, hunting down celebrities and people like me – middle-aged, white, liberal blokes – would provide great sport. North London would be a prime hunting ground, and red-carpet events a duck shoot.

Some of my vocals were altered to sound female. Having the technology at home meant it was easier for me to have an idea and slap it down there and then, without having to travel to the other side of London. You can work fast, get ideas down or reject them very quickly, moving on to the next thing. It's a lot like the instantaneity of painting: you put a figure in there, dislike it, scratch it out and do something else. Guitars will always be at the centre, but with a MIDI keyboard you can convert any source into any instrument you like, as well as creating moments of real fragility.

While I was recording the vocals to 'Tommy Gun', I involuntarily started crying. The subject matter was so close and pertinent at the time – not being around for your kids and needing to get them to a place of safety, but feeling doomed at the same time. The act of singing it makes it even more emotional, tapping into the deep subconscious, and I found myself struggling with certain lines.

In the middle of 'Heaven (Buy a Ticket)', there was an instrumental break, and I thought, 'Why don't we make this an ad break?' So I wrote a jingle advertising tickets to 'heaven'. A slimy announcer's voice interrupts the song: 'Hi! You know, a lot of people are asking themselves, "What is my life like right now?" . . .' I wrote it really quickly and placed it in the space in the song, and it fitted so well. It was one of my rare attempts at doing an American accent, so we had to tweak it to make it sound more relaxed. Afterwards, I was struck by the text I had written because it seemed to be a subconscious statement about how I was feeling myself. 'Am I truly happy? Do I love my spouse, my kids, my house? Am I fulfilled, sexually and creatively?'

Different types of angels, characters, voices both angelic and human: all these elements come into this collection of fifteen songs/episodes. People being visited by angels and not knowing why; the kids all doing their own thing, taking their own weird drugs and hanging/hiding out; and several groups of people, or tribes – the Astral Light people, who are religious maniacs, along with extremists and all these other groups. It accumulated in my head into this huge bloody thing.

I didn't produce any of the comic-book drawings that accompany *Superstate*, but I made plenty of art in tandem with the music – pretty crazy shit, including the cover, which has a tower of crowns with a spaceship above it – to try and put across my vision of this world. But I also wanted to see how other artists could interpret the story, so I invited writers Helen Mullane and Alex Paknadel on board, along with fifteen artists, each of whom would tackle a different episode. That way, if someone wanted to make a TV series out of it one day, then the storyboarding would already have been done.

In the end, *Superstate* has a happy ending. The human beings in this world have been longing to escape from Earth, and the song 'Butterfly' describes the moment they do. They contort themselves into shapes that create a strange energy, based around those Old Testament angels, and travel to heaven – which is in fact Earth itself – ingest enormous seeds and die. From the husks and out of their bodies a new, lush wilderness regenerates itself. It's the idea that somewhere lodged within you there's always the germ of new life and fresh beginnings.

———

During the period in which I have been writing down this odyssey, my life has been reordering itself and gearing up for a new start. I have been sober for over six years. The isolation that Covid brought has done funny things to the passage of time; for me, it's slowed everything down and enabled me to adjust to new circumstances in slow motion. For the first time in many years I have had the chance to step outside the tornado and observe everything that has been whirling around in the twister.

It's amazing what the mind will furnish you with if you let a song percolate for a bit. For that to happen properly, I find I'm taking more time over things and becoming even more obsessive about the process than ever. I spend most of my waking hours in my music room, and I can't think of anything more enjoyable than faffing about with songs, guitars and computers, trying out one idea after another, pressing a few buttons to find out what your chorus line would sound like if it was sung by a massive female choir in the Albert Hall.

I am working especially hard on finding – or reinventing – my voice; trying to accept that I'm not a seven-year-old in a man's body and to realise my full potential as a singer and musician; to either embrace it to its fullest extent or jack it all in. I haven't always received the right kind of emotional support and encouragement to be able to do that, but things are changing.

I'm in my early fifties now, but in terms of my development as a musician and artist I feel more like thirty. I don't feel burnt out. I am still discovering music that's new to me: the other night it was Roy Ayers, and I've gone through huge phases of getting hooked on Steely Dan and John Martyn. I listen to music with much more of a home recordist's ear these days, even enjoying things like Gerry Rafferty because of how smooth and beautiful they sound.

I've always liked writing poems, but writing lyrics for songs enriches my everyday vocabulary. I'm petrified of talking in clichés, repeating stock phrases off the TV. Language can be immense fun, and if a cliché pops into my mind, I tend to examine it from all angles and find my own route around it. You have to get your machete out and chop through the buzzwords, but it's worth it. I have occasionally sung 'I love you' straight up in a song, although it made my skin crawl. But what about some other way? How do you say 'I love you' in sixteen syllables, so it scans well and bobs nicely along the melody line? That remains the eternal challenge of the pop song, and I'll remain happily in pursuit of it for as long as I can.

I've lost many people along the way, although I've never felt like they've really left me. One tragic loss was Leo Finlay, the first journalist to write about Seymour and Blur back in the early 1990s. Others took themselves away on purpose: Graham Fox, Chris, Mathew, my lovely friend Christine, from my teenage years . . . They all decided for one reason or another that they could no longer stay with us in the realm of the living. One person who didn't mean to go was my mum. She really didn't want to. She had a lot more life to live, a lot more love to give. She went in March 2021, right at the point when I resolved to make a renewed effort to prove to myself that this life was worth living – that I had a duty to myself and my kids to forge ever onwards. I decided to live at the same time as my mum was taken from me . . .

Music has redemptive powers. It's been the only real constant in my life, and the one thing I have never grown bored of. It heals and it challenges. In December 2020 I was invited to play a short acoustic set at the Jazz Café in Camden, in aid of the Lebanese Red Cross. Eighty per cent of me didn't want to do it. It was bound to be uncomfortable; I hadn't so much as attempted to write a song during most of that year and was undergoing some pretty hefty therapy in order to get over my traumatic separation from Soraya and Dore. I was at a strange juncture. I could either decide that it was time to get on with the rest of my life or scuttle away to live like a beetle under a stone, just as I had in the early 2000s. Meanwhile, here was a chance to face humiliation, the delirium of stage fright, the nervousness and anxiety of soundchecks, all just to make a fool of myself in front of a few hundred people. But I have always perversely enjoyed these challenges. They are the hurdles I simply have to stumble over whenever I perform an acoustic set. It's the rawest, most naked kind of performance someone like me ever has to do, and the nerves lead to silly mistakes and make my voice trembly. On this occasion, the 20 per cent won out, and I agreed to do the show.

I didn't realise that this decision would change just about everything for me. On the bill were the Mystery Jets, Bessie Turner and the English singer-songwriter Rose Elinor Dougall. Rose and I had met a couple of times over the years but had never really talked that much. As a former member of the Pipettes and a solo artist, she had been circling around the musical universe just out of my line of sight, swinging past like a comet every now and then, releasing music that I felt was from another world, but one that I recognised. That night after we played, we snatched a conversation in the smoking area and decided that we should have a go at writing together. We left it pretty vague – would it be one song, two or something else? I didn't know, but we swapped numbers. We wrote to each other nearly every day over that Christmas, sending each other songs we liked. Then, one day in very early January we found ourselves slipping and sliding around Hampstead Heath in the mud, with the low-lying sun blinding us as we talked about ourselves and our lives. Something about Rose's good humour and bright mischief made me feel a certain kinship towards her.

Within a week we were recording. Our work was exploratory. Two people asked questions of each other, and as a consequence the void became less yawning. Music was created, and these two voices in the songs became two people: Rose and I.

In many ways my life at that time had never been such a wreck. There were so many struggles to overcome, but their significance started to pale – pushed to my mind's peripheral vision by my therapy and the music-making with Rose, which went more easily than expected. Before we knew it, our initial sessions progressed from awkward and hesitant to more comfortable and flowing, and we ended up with well over a dozen surprisingly varied and emotionally expansive songs. It was as if we had realised that this partnership was a gift, and we dared ourselves to be as honest and open as possible. It turned out to be a rare opportunity, both musically and personally. We grew closer than we could have imagined, and life became better than we had ever dreamed it could be.

This change of fortune seemed to me nothing short of miraculous. It never ceases to amaze me how consistently music looks after me if I really choose to look after it and brave the discomfort and frustrations it so often involves. It's an elusive beast that forces you to pursue it no matter how low you may fall, because when you have caught its wriggling tail and mustered the strength to hold on, there is no better feeling than experiencing the rewards it gives you.

Thanks to Rose's recommendation, I recently discovered the writings of Richard Brautigan, so if I end the day at a particularly low ebb, reading a couple of his little stories just before I go to bed usually helps me fall asleep with a smile on my face. Normally I feel optimistic, full of stupid energy; I love mischief, having a giggle and making fun of myself and everything else. My morose spells don't last for long, and that's what I try to tell anybody who's feeling godawful and sad: 'Don't worry, it'll pass. Just sit tight.' It usually does.

————

I have complained about the negative, destructive aspects of the music business, but I still have no regrets about choosing that path instead of art. My relationship with form, and art in general, is highly personal and I don't get much of a kick out of the way modern art has become so clinical, conceptual and monetised since I was at Goldsmiths. My work still revolves around exploring how I feel, so it's figurative, often depicting contorted human (often female) forms. I don't see it as vulgar in any way, more an expression of what I find beautiful or even sacred.

Painting in oils was so time-consuming that I didn't keep it up while Blur was having its success. I always kept a notebook with me, filled with pencil drawings. I planned to turn some of the sketches into full-size paintings one day, but didn't really get around to it. I never allowed myself the space to paint. Now that I have settled back in London again, I intend to change that – to create a room of my own to paint in. It has to be separate from the music room. In one former house, I tried to do both in the same space, but I could never deal with the mess. Tubes of paint, expensive guitars and recording equipment don't mix.

I still use digital imaging tools. The Wacom tablet, the Cintiq Pro, and various painting applications have become so much better in recent years, and I can now scan my drawings and colour them in. For the cover image of *The Spinning Top*, I scanned a pencil drawing I had done into Painter software and manipulated it a bit. I like the idea that you can take risks, and if it doesn't work, you can easily undo what you've just done. The freedom actually allows you to take more risks. With real paint, it's a much trickier proposition, and you have to get it right from the first stroke.

Maybe I care too much about visual art, but to have made it into a career would have felt like doing it a disservice. When the ICA, in London, hosted a small exhibition of my paintings and drawings in 2004, I looked at the works on the wall and saw their creator as a confused, inconsistent hobbyist or, at worst, a painter and decorator who owned a few art books. I was never going to be able to compete with the artists I loved as a teenager: Munch, Chagall, Picasso, Modigliani, Chaïm Soutine, the German expressionists and the American abstract expressionists.

The British artists of the generation I studied with made work that was either too clean or packed with too many in-jokes for my taste. I never particularly got on with it. When I look at the role drawing has played throughout my life so far, I can see that it is more like art therapy than the kind of art that makes a career nowadays. Music, and especially the guitar, was where felt I could actually take on my heroes at the same game.

I was always a lot more confident as a musician and located my identity in that. Music was my first love; it's the world where I exist. Art gives me a space for meditation and to exorcise my monsters. Just as some of my songs are quite openly about alcoholism, depression or anxiety, I sometimes wonder whether, if a psychologist looked at my drawings, I'd be locked up. But it's a safe way to express how you're feeling without being judged, and we should all be allowed to do that.

And all those monsters and grotesque creatures that kept popping onto the pages of my notebooks or canvases? I think I'm finally leaving them behind. For most of my life they have been exploiting my worries, my unease and vulnerability, which opened up a channel for them to emerge into the world. Those drawings, I can see now, reinforced what other people used to tell me about myself: that I was 'weird'. Actually, I'm not – not any more. I don't need to perpetuate that image. When I was starting out, I didn't have the confidence to challenge it. Now, I feel strong enough to confront the monsters head-on – to deny them the right to life. I realise they used to come from an external perception of who I was – they don't live in my head. These days when I make a picture, the motifs are much more about evoking physical closeness, my love of the female form, and a kind of magical sense of positivity. I have elbowed the monsters off the pillion and ditched them by the side of the road.

As I said, I have stayed sober for six years now. Although I'm very aware that temptation can always strike, so far I have resisted the impulse. In any case, the drinks I have refused have tended to be celebratory ones. Something there has definitely changed for the better. The darkest days of Blur are now long gone, and our professional lives are less under the microscope than they used to be, which means less pressure. It's fun catching up with Damon from time to time, and I remain supremely grateful for our friendship.

In my latest lyrics, I'm trying to break the laws I made for myself over the years, the ones that dictate what I can and cannot do. I'm beginning to figure out that there have been far too many artificial regulations. Singing them out loud to another person feels like putting my neck on the chopping block, closing my eyes and opening them again, wondering whether my head's tumbled into in the basket or is still attached to my neck.

We should be able to say, draw or sing exactly what we want, without being judged. Ultimately, everything I write, compose and make is aimed at the people out there who need to know they're not alone. If I can help them, even in a small way, then I would rather do it through my fingers on some sweaty frets, a hollow soundboard or a buzzing amp, singing the words that steal into my head in the night. It's hard, though. Sometimes I completely forget my strengths and become overwhelmed by my weaknesses, suddenly finding myself at a loss over what to do, say or play. I have to dig deep, find the inner resources, the resilience I have so often needed to rely on. Even Odysseus, after his twenty-year voyage back from Troy, arrived home unrecognised, in rags, having to prove to everyone who he was. It's a familiar feeling for an artist, but to be humbled like that is also valuable, as it teaches you to recognise who you really are. Alternatively, I could simply stop overthinking it so much and, as Rose might say in one of her more impatient moments:

'Do something that Graham Coxon would fucking do!'